GETTING
STARTED
IN PRIVATE
PRACTICE

D0951389

GETTING STARTED IN PRIVATE PRACTICE

The Complete Guide to Building Your Mental Health Practice

Chris E. Stout
Laurie Cope Grand

WILEY

John Wiley & Sons, Inc.

This book is printed on acid-free paper. ∞

Published by John Wiley & Sons, Inc., Hoboken, New Jersey.
Published simultaneously in Canada.

For general information on our other products and services please contact our Customer Care Department within the U.S. at (800) 762-2974, outside the United States at (317) 572-3993 or fax (317) 572-4002.

Wiley also publishes its books in a variety of electronic formats. Some content that appears in print may not be available in electronic books. For more information about Wiley products, visit our website at www.wiley.com.

0471-42623-7

Printed in the United States of America

10 9 8 7 6 5 4 3 2

To my students, who teach me what's important to know.

Chris E. Stout

Thanks to Diane Spiegel, Lisa Flesher, Barb Westfield, and Anthony Koch for being my allies and comrades. I am also grateful to Cristina Wojdylo and Peggy Alexander at John Wiley & Sons, Inc., for inviting me to contribute to this project.

Laurie Cope Grand

Contents

Series Preface

Getting Started

As the behavioral health care marketplace grows more challenging, providers are finding it necessary to develop smarter business tactics in order to be successful. We are faced with shifting payment structures, increasing competition, complex funding mechanisms, the bankruptcy of many managed care agencies, and growing malpractice liability risks, all against a backdrop of layoffs and dwindling economic resources. It is times like these that make Wiley's *Getting Started* series of books all the more important.

Many individuals studying in the mental health professions graduate with no idea how to go about starting their own mental health practice. Alternatively, there are many mental health practitioners who wish to shift the focus of their current practice into other areas. The *Getting Started* series of books provides the information, ideas, tools and strategies providers need to enable their practices to evolve and thrive in any circumstance. This series works to break down the ingredients of a successful mental health practice into more manageable components, and thus more achievable components. It is my goal to bring readers the best of the best in the *Getting Started* series in an effort to help them start, maintain, and expand their successful mental health practice.

The *Getting Started* series is not discipline specific. It is meant for all levels of behavioral healthcare students, as well as providers—undergraduate students, graduate students, and professionals in all the fields of behavioral health care. Current books include, *Getting Started in Personal and Executive Coaching* and *Getting Started in Private Practice*. Other titles will focus on various mental health disciplines including forensic practice, group practice, marriage and family practice, as well as topics such as integrating technology with your mental health services.

Successful practice in whatever area or specialty takes work; there are no overnight successes. But being successful is quite doable. This series provides the organizing methods most of us never learned in graduate or medical school training, or were only available by hiring one's own consultant. You will learn what works and what doesn't work without having to make costly missteps first.

Is establishing or growing your practice going to be difficult? To a degree, the likely answer is yes. Of course, it will take some work, but it will likely be well worth the effort. I hope you find the *Getting Started* series to be a helpful set of tools in achieving your professional goals.

Chris E. Stout
Series Editor

Introduction

Building a mental health practice is a challenge made even greater as managed care transforms our healthcare system. This book is a new practice-building tool that will make this endeavor more achievable for therapists in private practices of all kinds, including those who work alone or in groups. We will deconstruct the process of building a practice into manageable components so that you may focus on what is relevant for you and apply it to your business.

It is unfortunate that most graduate and medical school training programs lack even basic training on the business of private practice. As a result, many newly licensed clinicians are clueless about how to start and run an office. If you learn and apply the information in these chapters, you will begin to feel much more competent and confident.

This book is written for all levels and disciplines of mental health professionals, including the following:

- Psychologists (clinical, counseling, school, forensic, industrial/organizational, etc.)
- Marriage and family therapists
- Social workers

- Psychiatrists
- Professional counselors
- Pastoral counselors
- Addictions counselors
- Psychiatric nurses
- Psychiatric residents
- Graduate students
- Undergraduate students

When you began your graduate studies you probably focused on learning clinical skills and gave very little thought to learning the skills of running a small business. This is true of most therapists in training. The result is that after completing several years of education, training, internships, and written and oral exams, most newly licensed therapists have strong clinical skills but lack business skills. Those who hope to build a private practice find it rough going.

Several years ago, I (CES) decided to do something about this. As a clinical psychologist, I developed a seminar on practice issues and taught it to students at several universities, colleges, and professional schools in the Chicago area. I also developed the Morning Mentor Program™ and Best Practice, which provided similar content, but in a non-credit academic format. Today I work as a consultant, helping clinicians establish and build their private practices. Over the years I have found a variety of books on this subject, many by friends and colleagues. However, none really address the issues that I focus on in my teaching and consulting. As a result, I have created this book (along with coauthor Laurie Grand) and the *Getting Started* series.

Our goals are to speak to you as colleagues, providing many examples with realistic, actionable models as well as the forms that you can customize and use. We have avoided the fuzzy realm of "Is private practice right for you?" self-quizzes and other fluff. We keep the focus on showing you how to examine facts and numbers to help you realistically address the viability of your business.

Even if you have excellent clinical skills, fine ethics, strong motivation, and a personality suited for independent practice, you will not succeed without the business skills provided in this book. In addition to being a competent clinician, you must also be able to properly build, operate, and grow your practice.

This book and series seek to provide you with these skills. You will not find a chapter on whether you are suited for private practice, because we assume that you have already chosen that path. We intend to focus on business-related facts, skills, and practical application issues.

We have developed the following set of tools to help you understand the ideas presented in the book:

- Management Metrics™ identifies various ways to measure and track what's important in your practice.
- Do the Math™ indicates practical (and simple) formulas into which you can plug your numbers and run various scenarios and what-ifs.
- Stories from the Real World are vignettes provided by a variety of therapists who have faced the challenge of building a private practice. They share both successes and failures, and we hope you will learn from their stories.

These are all hands-on activities that help guide you in building your knowledge base and in tailoring your specific circumstances into a viable practice model.

We cannot promise that the information in this book will transform your practice overnight. As you probably realize, there is no magic when it comes to achieving success. It will require a lot of hard work, creativity, and persistence. We hope you find this book (and others in the series) to be helpful tools in achieving your professional goals.

We appreciate your feedback, suggestions, and success stories. You can send e-mail to Chris at cstout@ix.netcom.com or to Laurie at lauriegrand @comcast.net.

Discover Your Ideal Practice

WHAT YOU WILL LEARN:

Practice by Design: Go Solo or Join a Group?
> Independent Solo Practice
> Group Practices without Walls (GPWWs): One-Stop Contracting
> Network or Anchor Groups
> Caveats When Joining a Group Practice
> Independent Practice Associations (IPAs)
> Hybrids and Mutations

Practice by Design: Maximizing Your Appeal to a Group Practice
> Tips for Successful Interviewing
> What Employers Look For
> Questions to Ask Potential Employers

Practice by Design: Your Employment Status and the IRS

Practice by Design: Types of Business Entities

How to Decide What Type of Practice Is Best for You
> What It Takes to Work Independently

PRACTICE BY DESIGN: GO SOLO OR JOIN A GROUP?

Today's behavioral healthcare marketplace has created new challenges for mental health professionals in every type of practice setting. In the past, therapists with offices in one or two locations could make an adequate living and enjoy the benefits of working independently. Today, however, it is difficult to thrive or even survive in independent practice, especially in areas where managed care has become a major force. There are new challenges for every type of practice, including medium and large groups.

There are a variety of models for you to consider when you prepare to set out on your own. Let's begin by looking at the most common types of private practices.

INDEPENDENT SOLO PRACTICE

In this type of practice, the therapist works on his or her own. This means that you:

- Rent and furnish your own office space
- Work mostly on your own
- Do your own marketing
- Decide on the fee structure
- Find your own clients
- Do your own treatment
- Find your own supervision
- Get on managed care panels and lists
- Pay the cost of association memberships, subscriptions, publications, and so forth
- Pay the cost of continuing education units
- Pay for your own health and life insurance
- Design your own forms, stationery, handouts, and so on
- Pay all of the expenses associated with the practice
- Process the insurance reimbursement paperwork

In the past, solo practitioners answered only to themselves (while following the legal and ethical guidelines of the profession). Today, with

STATE LICENSING REQUIREMENTS

Most states and provinces require clinicians to be licensed in order to practice. This was not always the case, and many people are still practicing illegally by providing therapy services without a license. Other states have laws that regulate the terms of use of specific words (*psychotherapy, psychology,* etc.) rather than the practice of these disciplines. This means that a person without a degree, a license, or credentials of any type could legally practice psychotherapy as long as he or she does not call it *psychotherapy.*

We know of no third-party payor (insurance company, managed care organization, Medicare, etc.) who will pay for services provided by someone who is not licensed or registered in his or her state of practice. To learn whether your state has a licensure or registration act and what it may require, check with your state's department of professional regulation. Most of these departments have a website that you can easily find with a search engine such as Google (www.google.com) or Yahoo (www.yahoo.com).

WHERE DO PSYCHOLOGISTS WORK?

The American Psychological Association (APA) conducts an annual survey of its members to learn about salaries and sources of income. The work settings of the 9,116 respondents in 2001 were as follows:

- 65 percent were employed in independent practices
- 46 percent in individual private practices
- 19 percent in group private practices
- 14 percent in hospitals and clinics
- 3 percent in schools
- 2 percent in other settings

Source: Darnell Singleton, Antoinette Tate, and Garrett Randall, *Salaries in Psychology 2001: Report of the 2001 APA Salary Survey.* APA Research Office, January 2003.

the advent of managed care, solo practitioners may work alone but must fulfill the requirements of managed care organizations in order to obtain reimbursement for their services.

Many therapists look forward to the challenge of handling the many aspects of building a private practice. Others find the responsibility overwhelming, especially when they are just starting out. There are many ways to join forces with other therapists and enjoy the freedom of working on your own. Let's take a look at a few of the most common types.

GROUP PRACTICES WITHOUT WALLS (GPWWS): ONE-STOP CONTRACTING

Group practices without walls are the most common type of practice group today. Several or more practices, from solo providers to larger practices of 10 to 15 members, form a group. The individuals who work in most GPWWs maintain practice independence but offer a combined size that is appealing to contracting payors. Financial arrangements vary from group to group.

Some GPWW leaders decide to incorporate. They may consolidate support staff and standardize software, forms, and procedures. They operate with one tax identification number, standardize staff hiring and credentialing standards, and function as a large practice. Primary practice owners may hold controlling positions, issue stock, set up a profit-sharing plan, and so on. Individual practices within the group may become less distinct from one another.

There is joint liability in any GPWW. As a GPWW is formed, members should seek the guidance of both an attorney and an accountant. Each person involved needs to have a clear understanding of his or her duties and responsibilities.

Benefits to the Members. As a member of a GPWW, you may gain contracts and referrals that you would not obtain if you were not part of the network. You may also find that working with such a group provides more resources and a more professional atmosphere than working alone. There may be more opportunities to share resources, obtain supervision, and avoid isolation.

Benefits to Payors. Payors prefer to have a single contract with one unit that manages 30 or more providers covering a two- to five-county region. They also prefer to have one contract to negotiate, one phone number to dial, and one contact person to reach if there is a problem. At the time of publication, it costs $100 to $150 per provider to manage contracts and credential providers, so it is less costly for a payor to work with a GPWW than with an individual provider.

NETWORK OR ANCHOR GROUPS

A network is typically owned by one individual. The network may cover more than one region and may offer more than one specialty. Similar to GPWWs, these practices appeal to payors due to ease of contracting and lower costs. Practices with such contracts are known as *anchor groups*. Anchor groups are similar to GPWWs in that they are made up of several independent providers or practices. The group forms a network to provide services under a general contract type (e.g., behavioral healthcare), but there are separate contracts for each provider, practice, or site. Network models tend to be located in more rural or less provider-saturated markets, whereas anchors tend to be located in more urban and suburban venues.

CAVEATS WHEN JOINING A GROUP PRACTICE

If you decide to join a group practice, use caution. In the American Association for Marriage and Family Therapy (AAMFT) newsletter *Practice Strategies* (March 1997 issue), the following guidelines were suggested:

- Ensure that fee payments are within ethical and legal guidelines. Stay away from fee splitting or any payment method that could be interpreted as paying for a referral.
- Check out the other therapists in the group. Your reputation will be affected by their reputations.
- Have separate interviews with each member of the group. Try to learn as much as you can about their relationships with one another.
- Ask to see the record-keeping system and evaluate the level of confidentiality that is maintained.
- Find out how often clients are billed and what percent become delinquent.

9

- Find out where the group's referrals come from.
- Explore the group members' ethics. Ask them questions to learn how they handle various ethical situations.
- Find out about managed care contracts and ask whether you will be added.
- Find out whether you would be able to refuse referrals from a managed care firm with whom the group is affiliated.

INDEPENDENT PRACTICE ASSOCIATIONS (IPAS)

An independent practice association (IPA) is a megagroup that has evolved from one or more large provider groups. IPAs tend to be well financed and are often backed with venture capital or large financial contributions to cover start-up costs (see Chapter 2). IPAs are different from the other practice models in that they generally offer:

- Many professionals on staff
- Professionals experienced in several disciplines
- Multiple locations
- A single contract for payers
- Standardized services and procedures
- Comprehensive management information services

HYBRIDS AND MUTATIONS

There are a variety of species of practices today, and all are subject to the Darwinian forces of survival of the fittest in the marketplace. New types of practices are constantly emerging because the world is changing quickly. Some examples of these changes include:

- Changes in regulations (e.g., repeals of corporate practice-of-medicine laws)
- Changes in policy (e.g., the ability to take risk without an insurance license in direct contracting), with some states prohibiting provider groups from functioning as nonlicensed insurance entities and thus unable assume risk
- Changes in payment systems (e.g., capitation versus reduced fee for service versus case rate)

STORIES FROM THE REAL WORLD

From my experience as an organizational psychologist and as an intellectual property attorney working with psychologists and group practices, I've found that copyright, trademark, contract, and the Internet are often misunderstood. For example, here are some issues to consider:

- Who owns what when a group of psychologists join together to develop questionnaires and marketing pieces?
- Who owns the name of the group practice when it dissolves?
- Have you planned at the formation of a collective endeavor how it will terminate?
- Is there a written agreement among the members of a formal group practice, corporation, partnership, or even an informal office sharing?
- How do you choose a business name and marketing slogans that are within professional ethical guidelines and that don't infringe on others' rights?

Daniel Kegan, PhD, JD

- Changes in practice (prescriptive authority for nonphysician providers, expanding hospital admitting privileges, etc.)
- Changes in tax codes (e.g., service corporations versus private corporations versus limited liability corporations)

These kinds of changes will make life more complex for anyone in a mental health practice, and they also create opportunities for innovation.

PRACTICE BY DESIGN: MAXIMIZING YOUR APPEAL TO A GROUP PRACTICE

Many clinicians who have recently finished professional training work within an established practice when they are getting started in the mental health profession. This can be an excellent opportunity to get valuable on-the-job training. However, the marketplace in most parts of the country has a greater supply of clinicians than open positions. If you live in an area where jobs for mental health professionals are scarce, you can do several things to make yourself as attractive a candidate as possible.

You can maximize your appeal to almost any group practice if you have broad experience in the following four general areas:

1. Doing therapy with a variety of client populations is a plus:
   - Individual
   - Group
   - Family
   - Couples
   - All age groups
   - Inpatients
   - Outpatients
   - Residential cases
   - Diverse client demographics
   - Diverse client diagnoses
2. Having a specialty relevant to the practice that you hope to join can be very helpful:
   - A medical or health specialty
   - Children and adolescents
   - Families
   - Neuropsychological
   - Rehabilitation
   - Substance abuse
   - Eating disorders
   - Dual diagnosis
3. Being a member of a variety of organizations or networks demonstrates that you are committed to your profession and interested in current issues and developments. Active participation is even more impressive, such as serving on committees, volunteering, submitting articles, and so forth:
   - Membership in graduate student organizations
   - Membership in professional organizations (APA, AAMFT, NASW, etc.) at the national, state, and local level
4. You will be more marketable if you have a license to practice counseling, social work, or psychology. Even if you are seeking internship hours toward your psychology license, having a master's level license makes you more attractive as a potential employee of a group practice, clinic, or counseling center.

TIPS FOR SUCCESSFUL INTERVIEWING

If you decide to join a group as an intern or after you are licensed, you will need to interview for the job. As with any job interview, you will increase your chances for success if you follow these two guidelines:

1. *Be humble.* When you are interviewing for a position in a group practice, it is important to convey that you have skills and knowledge, but be careful to avoid bragging or sounding like a show-off.

2. *Do your homework.* Learning about your potential employer helps you assess whether there's a good fit between your professional needs and wants and those of the potential employer. Doing some research will also provide you with information that you can discuss in the interview to demonstrate that you have taken the time to learn about the practice or counseling center. You will be able to address the needs and priorities of the practice and offer your ideas for working with the group.

WHAT EMPLOYERS LOOK FOR

The following 15 areas are critical to the success of a mental health practice. Therefore, it is important that you demonstrate your competence in these areas (Salameh 1990):

1. *Availability.* You should be available to see clients at times that meet *their* needs, not yours. For example, if you are going to treat children, you'll need to be available during evenings and weekends, and not just during daytime hours.
2. *Balance.* You should be able to demonstrate your ability to manage both life and work demands without undue stress.
3. *Clearheadedness.* Absentminded professors may be charming, but this is not a positive quality for clinicians. Maintaining focus at all times is a must.
4. *Commitment and dedication.* Clinical practice is not a hobby for dilettantes or the underinvested. Professionalism is the rule.
5. *Diplomacy.* Many work situations require you to be able to consider alternative perspectives. Be flexible and willing to compromise.
6. *Ethics.* This is the sine qua non (essential element) of any clinical practice. Be ready to demonstrate your understanding of ethics if you are asked a hypothetical question ("What would you do if . . . ?") during an interview.
7. *Flexibility.* As with diplomacy, you should be agile and adaptable to changing needs.
8. *Goal directedness.* Distinguish yourself by describing what you plan to do in your career as a behavioral health professional and explain how joining this practice will help you achieve your goals.

13

9. *Innovation.* Describe the ideas you would bring that could be of genuine help to the organization or practice.
10. *Persistence.* Finishing graduate school is a good demonstration of persistence, but also be prepared to discuss how your persistence is relevant to your joining this group.
11. *Punctuality.* This quality is critically important in clinical practice. Demonstrate your punctuality during the interviewing process and always thereafter.
12. *Self-reliance.* Discuss how you are able to think on your feet and solve problems, even in ambiguous situations.
13. *Self-respect.* Demonstrate your professionalism by noting how well you manage yourself and your life's challenges.
14. *Simplicity.* Show how you keep your work and your relationships simple and straightforward and avoid creating disorder.
15. *Surefootedness.* Potential employers seek a stable and reliable professional to join their team.

Besides looking for these traits, a potential employer will be evaluating you and considering the following five questions (Howard and Howard 1990):

1. Would this person relate to our practitioners and fit in well with the group?
2. Are this candidate's goals compatible with the goals of our group?
3. Does this candidate bring expertise that will bring value to our practice?
4. Do the types of clients this candidate may attract fit within the current or desired client mix?
5. Would I trust this candidate's ability to manage a crisis or cover my clients for me if needed?

QUESTIONS TO ASK POTENTIAL EMPLOYERS

When you are interviewing for a spot in a practice, keep in mind that the interviewing process is reciprocal. You are being interviewed and you are also interviewing the employer. Be ready to ask questions with a clinical and theoretical focus, and prepare a list of nonclinical questions as well. Here are 24 examples of important things you will want to find out about:

1. What percentage of fees will you earn?
2. Is the employer willing to provide an initial minimal advance on a predetermined amount of the initial collections distributed over a predetermined period of time (e.g., X dollars of collections distributed like a salary to you over the first six months) to provide a steady source of income for you during the early months of employment?
3. Will the employer guarantee that you can complete the hours required to obtain your license?
4. Is there a pay differential for being licensed? If so, how much?
5. Does the employer expect you to work weekends, holidays, and evening hours? If so, how will you be compensated?
6. How is on-call or emergency coverage handled?
7. How many hours are considered full-time each week—40, 35, 37.5? Of these hours, how many are expected to be in direct client care and contact versus paperwork, marketing, and administrative tasks?
8. Will you be allowed time off to prepare for your licensure examination? If so, is it paid vacation time, personal time without pay, or some other arrangement?
9. To what degree are you responsible for handling billing problems?
10. Is the employer willing to renegotiate your agreement if it is not working out well for you?
11. What expenses does the employer cover (travel, office, testing equipment, etc.)?
12. Does the employer provide professional liability coverage? If so, what are the coverage limits? Who is the carrier? Is it occurrence or claims made?
13. Is life insurance provided? If so, at what level of coverage? Who is the carrier?
14. What about retirement benefits?
15. Will you be allowed to do additional work (teaching, part-time work at another practice, etc.)?

16. Does the practice do any marketing and soliciting of new clients for you, or is that solely your responsibility?
17. What provisions are there for continuing education (e.g., paid time off, paid registration fees, expenses)?
18. How are clients transitioned if you leave the organization or practice?
19. Are there prohibitions or restrictions concerning "client stealing" in your employment agreement or contract?
20. Are you considered a consultant or an independent contractor? (See the section on taxes in Chapter 6.)
21. Will the employer help you gain membership within PPOs and MCO panels? If so, are you paneled only as long as you are employed with this organization, or will you be independently credentialed? (It is better to be independently credentialed. If the panel identifies you with your personal Social Security number or tax ID, then it is independent. If it identifies only your employer, then it is not. When you leave the employer, it is likely that you will no longer be a provider on those panels.)
22. How many clinicians have remained with the employer in the past five years?
23. How are supervisor-supervisee conflicts reconciled?
24. What are the employer's policies concerning charting and chart ownership? For example, in the event of a future lawsuit, could you access the patient's chart even if you no longer work as part of this practice?

PRACTICE BY DESIGN: YOUR EMPLOYMENT STATUS AND THE IRS

It is important to properly identify your employment status with the Internal Revenue Service. In some cases, it is difficult to determine whether you are an employee, a consultant, or an independent contractor. While this may seem like a semantic distinction, it is very important. It impacts whether you, a payor, or the employer is responsible for payment of federal and state income and employment taxes.

If you have any question about your tax status when filing your taxes, consult with the Internal Revenue Service, your tax professional, or an attorney.

PRACTICE BY DESIGN: TYPES OF BUSINESS ENTITIES

The type of business entity you choose to be is a key factor in structuring your practice. Issues of tax and liability are key. First gain appropriate legal and tax consultation before making your decision to determine the best option for your circumstances.

The information in Table 1.1, compiled by the legal offices of Weiner & Eglit, Ltd., in Highland Park, Illinois (847-266-2040), is provided to help inform you about the possibilities and options available. *Please note that the law in your state may be different.*

HOW TO DECIDE WHAT TYPE OF PRACTICE IS BEST FOR YOU

When you consider the type of practice that suits you best, think about the advantages and disadvantages of being on your own. Mental health professionals who have been in solo private practice report the following pros and cons.

Advantages of Being On Your Own
- *Scheduling.* Freedom to set your own hours and time off.
- *Decision making.* Freedom to set your own policies, fees, and work environment; make your own decisions.
- *Flexibility and creativity.* The ability to choose which counseling methods to use with each client.
- *Financial freedom.* Potentially unlimited rewards.
- *Personal fulfillment.* Increased self-esteem from being on your own.

Disadvantages of Being On Your Own
- *Financial risks.* Start-up costs are high and success is difficult to attain.
- *Isolation.* Working on your own as a therapist can be lonely.
- *Multiple roles.* You must assume every role in your business, especially in the beginning.
- *Family impact.* Significant others may struggle with the demands of your business.

TABLE 1.1 Types of Business Entities

Factor	General Partnership	RLLP Partnership	Limited Partnership	Limited Liability Company	Sole Proprietorship	C Corporation	S Corporation
Limited liability	Partners equally liable	Yes—all partners	Only the limited partners	Yes	No limit	Yes	Yes
Management	All partners	All partners	By general partner	Members and/or managers	Self	Board of directors	Board of directors
Membership	No maximum Minimum of two	No maximum Minimum of two	No maximum Minimum of two (one general and one limited)	No maximum Minimum of two	One	No maximum	Maximum 35 (no corp, trust, pension plan, or non-resident alien stockholders)
Transfer of interest	Restricted—authorized by partnership agreement	Restricted—authorized by partnership agreement	Restricted—authorized by partnership agreement	Restricted—authorized by partnership agreement	Only upon liquidation	No restriction (usually)	No restriction

18

Different classes of ownership	Permitted	Permitted	Permitted	Permitted	No	Permitted	Only one class of stock permitted
Federal tax	Zero at partnership level	Zero at partnership level	Zero at partnership level	Zero at LLC level	Schedule C tax form	Corporate tax at 34% shareholder tax	Zero corporate-level tax (usually)
State tax	Zero at partnership level	Zero at partnership level	Zero at partnership level	Zero at LLC level	State 1040	4.8% corporate tax	Zero corporate-level tax
Personal property replacement tax	1.5%	1.5%	1.5%	1.5%	0	2.5%	1.5%
Annual franchise tax	No	No	No	No	No	Minimum $25, maximum $1 million	Minimum $25, maximum $1 million
Filing fee	None	$100 per partnership to a maximum of $5,000 partnership	$75 $15 renewal	$500 to organize $300 annual renewal	None	$75 to organize $15 renewal	$75 to organize $15 renewal

- *Unpredictable income.* As your client load fluctuates, so will your income.
- *Liability.* Many solo practitioners find operating on their own sometimes feels a bit like walking a tightrope without a safety net.
- *Lack of direction.* Without a boss to tell you what to do, you may feel lost.

What It Takes to Work Independently

If you are thinking about working independently, you will be more successful if you learn to think and act like an entrepreneur. The following list of attitudes, skills, and behaviors is typical of people who are successful self-employed businesspeople. Read through the list and circle Y (yes) or N (no) for each item. When you are finished, answer the questions that follow.

Y   N   1. You are able to tolerate uncertainty.

Y   N   2. You have excellent verbal and written communication skills.

Y   N   3. You are able to endure fluctuations in your income.

Y   N   4. You have good planning skills.

Y   N   5. You have confidence in your ability to succeed.

Y   N   6. You function well in social situations.

Y   N   7. You make friends easily.

Y   N   8. You can effectively organize your time without structure.

Y   N   9. You are a self-starter.

Y   N   10. You cope well with new situations.

Y   N   11. You prefer to be active.

Y   N   12. You can handle constant stress.

Y   N   13. You are comfortable promoting yourself.

Y   N   14. You are a persistent person.

Y   N   15. You like to be in charge.

Y   N   16. You make decisions based on available data and the systematic analysis of a situation.

Y N   17. You can ask for what you want.

Y N   18. You push for commitments from others.

Y N   19. You follow through on projects.

Y N   20. You have a high energy level.

Y N   21. You know how to motivate others.

Y N   22. You can set a schedule and follow it.

Y N   23. You know when to say no.

Y N   24. You don't allow disappointment and rejection to stop you from carrying out your plans.

Y N   25. You arrive promptly for appointments.

Y N   26. You make decisions easily.

Y N   27. You take responsibility for both successes and failures.

Y N   28. You are willing to give in order to receive.

Y N   29. Others would say that you are somewhat bossy.

Y N   30. You manage your time well.

Adapted with permission from Steve Bass, *Successful Private Practice*. Pasadena, CA: PCG Seminars, 1985.

Ask yourself the following three questions to assess how comfortable you may be as a self-employed businessperson.

1. What are your most significant strengths that will enable you to thrive on your own?
2. Aside from the items on the list, what additional characteristics do you possess that will help you succeed in solo private practice?
3. What areas do you think need development in order for you to succeed and be comfortable in solo private practice?

The answers to these questions will help you determine what type of practice setting is best for you: independent private practice, being part of a group, or as an employee of a counseling center, clinic, or large practice. None of these is better than the others; the important thing is for you to recognize which type of work setting best fits your personality and style.

Finance Your Start-Up Practice

Where to Get Money to Start Your Practice

Capital (money) makes it possible for you to open the doors of your clinical practice and help it grow. You may need funds for a variety of expenses, such as for leasing or buying office space, for paying monthly bills before you begin to obtain revenues from clients, and for paying yourself a salary during the early months of your business.

It is best to keep costs low and avoid borrowing money, but sometimes obtaining financing can mean the difference between starting a viable practice and never having a chance to succeed. The purpose of this chapter is to explain how business financing works so you can make an educated decision about what is best for your situation.

To obtain money for your practice, you will need to know what types of financing are available and how lenders evaluate potential borrowers. You will learn about both of these topics in this chapter. In addition, be sure to study Chapter 5, "Set Up Shop and Measure Results," which includes steps for planning and budgeting for the operation of your business.

There are many sources of capital available, from venture capitalists to life insurance companies. Each source has its advantages, and some are better suited to specific financing needs than others. You should assess your options to choose the most appropriate financing source.

Loans: Debt Financing

Several types of institutions provide debt financing (i.e., they lend you money and you are obliged to repay it):

- Commercial banks
- Leasing companies
- Thrift institutions
- Life insurance companies
- Commercial finance companies
- Other sources (loans from relatives, etc.)

Commercial Banks. Short-term credit from commercial banks is an extremely popular source of financing for all types of businesses, including mental health practices. In recent years, some banks have set up professional divisions with personal bankers who are experienced in meeting the needs of healthcare providers.

24

Bank borrowing may be the least expensive source of debt financing for secured and unsecured working capital loans, equipment loans, and real estate loans. A practice may develop a relationship with a local commercial bank that assists in the practice's financial planning process.

Short-term loans offered by commercial banks have several unique characteristics.

- They are usually extended for a period of 90 days or less and may be secured or unsecured, depending on the amount of risk the bank faces.
- When a bank loan is secured, the lender normally executes a security agreement in which the practice pledges a certain business asset as collateral.
- A practice may pledge its accounts receivable (billings to clients and third-party payors for services rendered but not yet collected) as an asset. The amount in accounts receivable is an asset that represents money owed to the practice.
- A commercial bank may also require your personal guarantee based on your personal assets.
- If the practice does not pledge any collateral against the loan, the bank may extend the loan on the practice's full faith and credit.

Leasing Companies. Leasing has become an increasingly popular source of debt financing. Almost any type of property can be leased:

- Computer systems
- Equipment
- Furniture
- Office space

As an alternative to normal debt financing, leasing offers you greater flexibility and convenience because the *lessor* (the institution, usually the bank, holding the lease) takes on some of the responsibilities of ownership, including maintenance and disposal. If you are reluctant to borrow, leasing can be an attractive alternative. The interest rate on the lease will most likely be somewhat higher than on a loan extended by a commercial bank, because the lessor assumes greater responsibility. Commercial banks and financial services companies are among the institutions that offer lease arrangements.

Thrift Institutions. Thrift institutions include savings and loan associations, mutual savings banks, and credit unions. These institutions have traditionally been a source of debt financing for borrowers purchasing homes or durable goods. These organizations were deregulated in 1982 and have become an alternative way to finance professional practices, office buildings, and equipment. Practices seeking debt financing from thrift institutions can expect an environment and terms similar to those of commercial banks.

Thrift institutions offer a wide range of services:

- Leasing
- Credit cards
- Electronic funds transfer
- Commercial lending

Life Insurance Companies. Life insurance companies offer limited financing to healthcare practices in the form of secured real estate loans. Some healthcare buildings are financed by mortgage loans granted by insurance companies. Low-cost loans are also available from life insurers based on the cash value of a provider's life insurance policies.

Commercial Finance Companies. These are alternative sources for borrowers with high-risk credit ratings. These companies generally finance credit sales as well as provide funds for short-term purposes. They borrow large sums from investors and bankers and then lend them directly to businesses. As a result, their interest rates will almost always be higher than those of banks, thrift institutions, and life insurance companies, and the terms of the loan reflect the borrower's risky credit rating. Here are some examples of these terms:

- Minimum cash balance requirements
- Collateral requirements, including personal assets
- Remedies for the finance company in the event of default

Commercial finance companies also provide other services, such as financing and factoring accounts receivable. Because your accounts receivable can be fairly accurately valued and are usually easily converted to cash, they are suitable assets to pledge. As accounts receivable

Venture Capital Firms

Venture capital firms are generally interested in equity investments in companies with extremely high growth potential and in entities that plan to go public (be traded on the stock market) at some time. If your plans include expanding the practice to fill unmet needs in the mental health market, venture capital may be a viable option; but be warned, it can be a tough sell and you may feel like you are losing control of your business. As compensation for the risk of the practice, venture capitalists may demand a voice in company management and a seat on your board of directors.

Venture capitalists are a diverse group. Targeting the right listing of venture capital companies is an exercise in and of itself. Venture capital firms vary by geography, industry specialization, stage of company development, and size of investment preferences.

Venture capitalists typically require a comprehensive business plan to serve as a road map of the practice development, financing, operations, and management (see Chapter 3). A venture capitalist may ask for the following information about your practice:

- Is the practice management team able to grow the business rapidly and successfully?
- Is there a market-driven need for the services?
- Is market potential large enough?
- Do barriers to entry exist? For example, is the area already saturated with therapists who provide services similar to yours?
- How much capital will be required and how will it be used?
- What exit strategies are possible? For example, could you sell your practice to a local hospital or merge with another group in a partnership?
- Does the practice understand how to interface in a managed care environment?

See References at the back of this book.

Angels are wealthy individual investors. Angels are often former entrepreneurs or executives who act as venture capitalists investing in entrepreneurial companies. Many investment clubs across the country serve as networks to reach this group of investors. The National Venture Capital Association (NVCA) publishes a list of these clubs.

are collected, the indebtedness is reduced. When the full value of the receivable is not pledged, collections made in excess of the borrowed amount are returned to the practice.

Receivables may actually be sold to a financial institution. Commercial finance institutions prefer the sale be made *with recourse,* meaning the risk of the account remains with the practice. If the accounts receivable are purchased from the practice without recourse, the process is called *factoring.* When a lending institution factors receivables, it assumes the credit risk, and the service is more expensive to the practice. Usually, a factor charges a performance commission on invoice amounts and interest at a 3 to 4 percent increase over the prime lending rate.

The advantages of receivables financing are obtaining funds quickly and having a more rapid cash flow. Factoring shifts the risk and inconvenience of credit collection to the factor, but both these practices are costly and may make the practice appear to be financially unsound and risky. Selling receivables is not advised unless you are making a large one-time repayment such as an IRS bill or working out a plan to recover from a catastrophic event such as a natural disaster. Providers who sell their receivables to cover monthly operating expenses are borrowing against their own future. It is like borrowing against next month's paycheck to pay this month's bills.

Choosing a Bank

Although many sources of financing are available, many behavioral health practices prefer to deal with a bank. Regardless of the type of lender you choose, it is important to seek one that can lend you money now and also in the future. You should look for a lender who seems to be responsive, understanding, and committed to your needs.

Three phases are involved in selecting a lending institution:

1. Research potential banking sources.
2. Interview bank officials who will service the account.
3. Evaluate the candidates.

Researching Potential Banking Sources

To determine which bank will best accommodate the needs of the practice, it is important to survey local banks and obtain information about their policies and experience in working with healthcare practices. Sources of information about local banks include the following:

- Other therapists
- Other healthcare providers
- Other professionals
- Your practice's accountant
- Your practice's attorney

Once several potential banks have been identified, you may contact each one to request financial information, such as annual reports, financial statements, and lending statements. Examine this information for

CHARACTERISTICS OF LARGE AND SMALL BANKS

Large Banks	Small Banks
More financial resources	Fewer financial resources
Less personal	More personal and involved relationships
More prestigious	More willing to help customer with community and professional introductions
May have professionals who work exclusively with healthcare providers and other professionals	Interested in customers who add value (professionals)
May have more healthcare expertise	May not have range of expertise in sophisticated financial instruments
Larger range in total services (executive tax planning, financial planning, investor advice)	May not understand the healthcare industry
May be more cautious when making loans	May not grow fast enough to continually meet the needs of a growing practice

evidence of financial stability and ability to render services, as well as stability, expertise, and independence:

- Does the bank have an officer dedicated to healthcare accounts?
- Has the bank been mentioned in the media recently? (Was it positive?)
- Are bank officials cooperative about sharing information with you?

INTERVIEWING BANK OFFICIALS

Arrange to meet with bank representatives, especially those who have the authority to guarantee specific services and the individuals who will be responsible for your account. Discuss practice expectations and what you need from the banking relationship. Ask about the bank's experience in dealing with healthcare (or better yet, *behavioral* healthcare) providers. Obviously, the more familiar lenders are with such clients, the better suited they will be for you and your needs.

You may also inquire about staff turnover, especially among senior staff. Having the same personnel over many years will ensure the bank's familiarity with the community, your practice, and your operations. Low turnover is also an indication that the bank maintains consistent policies and service offerings. You may want to provide the bank with your brochure or business plan so the bank officials understand the nature of the practice and what the bank may expect in terms of your needs.

EVALUATING CANDIDATES

The final step in lender selection is evaluation of the candidates. The practice compiles and analyzes all the information received from the bank interview and other sources. The bank that offers the best interest rate or the most favorable loan program may not necessarily be the best choice for the practice. Base your selection on the bank's ability to provide the most critical services required by the practice.

QUALIFICATIONS TO LOOK FOR WHEN SELECTING A BANK

You are going to have a relationship with your bank for a long time, so it is important to choose one that demonstrates the best qualifications. Look for qualities like these:

- *Competence,* as demonstrated by experienced and knowledgeable employees who are willing to accommodate the practice
- *Financial and managerial strength,* including adequate size and stability
- *Number and quality of programs* geared toward the healthcare industry, especially experience with mental health practices
- *Competitiveness* of interest rates and loan packages
- *Willingness to document* the practice's request in writing as a signal of good faith
- *Reputation* within the community

Once you have selected a bank, consider consolidating all accounts, including personal, business, savings, and pension accounts. By increasing the volume of business you offer the bank, you will increase your importance from the bank's perspective. This may result in preferential treatment for services or more favorable loan terms. Establishing a strong relationship and staying with a bank that provides superior service may be a valuable resource for you and your practice.

How Lenders Evaluate Borrowers

Lenders make decisions about loans based on their knowledge of the borrower and the business. You will make a positive impression on the lending officer with a well-prepared and complete set of informational documents. The principal document used to indicate your creditworthiness is the business plan, which is discussed in detail in Chapter 3.

Another key factor in the loan process is the lender's impression of your credibility. The lender gains this perception from face-to-face contact with you (and your associates if you have them) and with the information provided to support the loan request. If you are borrowing funds for the first time, you can expect to provide more information to the loan officer than if you have an existing credit history with the bank.

Once you have established credibility, you must work to maintain it. You must continue to produce results that are consistent with your business plan objectives and financial projections. If you repeatedly return to the lender for expenses that were not properly considered in the business plan, you will decrease your chances of getting favorable terms.

KEY INFORMATION FOR LOAN APPLICATIONS

Lenders consider three essential items when deciding whether to lend money:

1. How will the funds be used?
2. How much money is needed?
3. How will the money be repaid?

The data needed to answer those questions will depend on several things:

- Your previous relationship with the bank
- The purpose of the loan
- The amount of the loan
- The percentage of total expenditure being sought (e.g., a practice borrowing $5,000 to purchase office furniture valued at $15,000 is borrowing only 33 percent of the total expenditure, which will be more favorably considered than a loan request of $12,000 for the same purpose)

Different banks require different levels of detail. For example, if a sole practitioner or a group with less than three providers applies for a loan at a local bank, the lender may rely more on personal financial information than on the practice's operating information. On the other hand, if a large practice is financing real estate or a series of capital projects, the institution may require a projected or pro forma financial statement showing the capability of the practice's operations and ability to repay the debt. Therefore, it is important to have as much information as possible going into the process.

How the Funds Will Be Used. You may want to borrow funds to finance start-up or expansion. When you are starting or expanding a practice, you may need money for working capital, to purchase equipment, and to pay for improvements to the office. The lender needs to know how the funds will be used so the bank can obtain a security interest if property and equipment are being acquired. If the funds are to be used for working capital, the bank will require some other form of payment assurance.

Knowing how the funds will be used also helps determine the interest rate and term of the loan. For example, the term of a loan to purchase a computer system would probably equal the useful life of the equipment.

How Much Money Is Needed. The size of the loan depends on several factors.

- Determine the total planned expenditures and the amount that will be financed. This relates to the planning process discussed earlier. You may invest some of your own funds and borrow only a portion of the total.
- Include the expenditures in the business plan developed to support the loan application. This pro forma business plan shows your future needs as well as the level of debt you can repay.
- The bank must understand how the loan relates to your strategic plan. For example, if you are adding providers and need $100,000 to expand, will that amount be used for working capital and improvements? Will another loan be required for related issues? You may find it easier to repay excess funds than to obtain additional funding if the size of the first loan is insufficient.

How the Loan Will Be Repaid. You will be expected to demonstrate to the bank your ability to repay the loan. The main evidence is your business plan, which illustrates the ability to repay the debt from projected income in excess of expenses.

You may also need a contingency plan showing what steps you would take if the financial projections proved incorrect. The contingency plan may indicate a source of repayment other than practice income, such as a guarantee based on your personal assets.

THE SIX CS

Bankers consider several factors when evaluating your credit application. These are known as the six Cs:

1. Character
2. Capital
3. Capacity
4. Collateral

5. Circumstances
6. Coverage

Character. This is an intangible and subjective quality that con-
tributes to the lender's belief that you will repay the debt. The lender
attempts to measure character through analysis of the following:

- Your credit history
- References from your accountant, attorney, and others
- The level of preparation in forecasting your ability to repay debt
- Your attention to your budget and cash flow

The bank may consider all these factors and make a judgment about
your practice. The better the lending officer knows you, the more likely
he or she will judge your character favorably.

Capital. This is the amount of equity (in the form of cash) the practice
owners have contributed to the business. A practice with a large amount
of equity indicates a high level of commitment from the clinicians to the
future plans of the practice. As the risks associated with practice have
increased, banks have started to insist on a greater amount of equity
investment by the owner(s). The larger the equity, the less the practice
needs to borrow and the less financial leverage exists.

The proportion of debt to equity may be an important consideration
of the overall capital structure. The *debt-to-capitalization ratio* measures
the financial leverage of the practice. It is computed by dividing total
debt of the practice by total debt plus total owner's equity. Most banks
prefer a ratio of 75 percent or lower. For example, if a practice owes
$15,000 and has an additional equity of $10,000 in the practice, the
debt-to-capitalization ratio is $15,000 divided by $25,000, or 60 percent.

Capacity. This is your ability to use borrowed funds in a prudent and
profitable manner. The bank wants to determine whether the practice
can meet its debt service obligation over the life of the loan. To determine whether your practice has capacity, the bank may review your
business and marketing plans and judge your ability to sustain its current volume of clients and to attract new clients.

Collateral. This is the term used for assets with resale value that are pledged as security for a loan. Unless you own the building space in which you operate, the marketable assets (assets that are available to be sold) of a practice are basically limited to your equipment and accounts receivable. Both of these assets may be difficult to convert quickly into cash in the event of a default of a loan, so banks often discount their value heavily. Many behavioral health practices have low levels of collateral; therefore, banks often require that the therapists offer guarantees as a secondary source of funds. Your relatives can also make these guarantees.

Circumstances. This term refers to the ability of the practice to generate sufficient revenue to meet its debt service obligations. Circumstances depend on the target market and the demand for services. The criteria used are both current and long-term prospects. The bank appraises, among other things, the ability of patients to pay for the services rendered, and the amount and type of competition. The marketing plan may provide adequate documentation to enable the lender to judge whether the practice will be able to meet its obligations.

Coverage. This refers to the ability to meet debt obligations under unforeseen circumstances. An example would be carrying insurance to protect the practice in the event of a death of a key therapist or partner or the lack of client sessions in a natural disaster. A *debt-to-service ratio* can be computed to determine the level of coverage by dividing your practice's monthly net income (after compensation, interest, and depreciation expense) by the proposed monthly payment. The income statement and cash flow statement may be used to show the cash generated by the practice. You may also call on your accountant for assistance in developing the required evidence of coverage.

If the ratio is lower than 1.0, it indicates the practice is unlikely to produce enough cash to make the payments. The higher this ratio, the more confident the lender will feel in extending a loan. If you are just starting a practice, there may be no prior experience on which to judge your ability to cover the debt service requirement. In this case, the loan may be restructured to defer initial payments until your practice has an established clientele.

HOW A BANK WILL ANALYZE YOUR APPLICATION

The procedure a bank uses to analyze a loan application centers around two sets of documentation: the business plan and the financial statements for your practice. Other information, such as a personal financial statement, may be required to complete the overall assessment of the borrower's creditworthiness. The amount of information required depends on the bank, your practice, and your relationship.

Table 2.1 summarizes most of the items typically required in an application, along with the purpose it serves.

The bank will examine the financial statements closely and look for certain relationships that may affect your ability to repay the loan. The bank may explore any of the following:

- Receivables
- Equipment
- Your loans to other providers
- Your credit position

TABLE 2.1   Information Required by Banks When Lending You Money

Information Required	Why the Bank Needs It
Business plan	Overall background, indication of the use of funds in relation to long-range goals
Financial statements (balance sheet, cash flow, and income statement)	Broad perspective of business position, financial strengths and weaknesses
Income tax returns for 3 to 5 years	Broad perspective of business position, financial strengths and weaknesses
Credit check	Financial solvency
Collateral	Financial safeguard
Cash flow analysis, prior and future years	Assures practice has enough cash to repay the debt
Financial ratios	Business position, ability to repay debt
Evaluation of overall management capabilities	Relationship of management to profitability
Check that the practice is legally formed	Safeguard bank against fraudulent loans

Receivables. The bank may want to know the following information about your receivables:

- Amount
- Percentage of past-due accounts
- Average age
- Largest accounts and percentage of total

If you have a large amount of receivables or a high percentage of your business revenues in receivables, you may be less able to repay any loans. The age of a receivable is the length of time between the client session and when the bill is paid. The greater the age of an account, the less likely it is that it will be paid. The largest accounts and percentage of total are important because they show whether there are many small receivables outstanding or a few large ones that may affect the bank's determination of how likely you are to ultimately collect the money.

Equipment. The bank may want to know the following information about your equipment:

- Amount
- Type, age, and condition
- Appraisal
- Replacement schedule

This information helps the bank determine whether you will need to purchase or replace equipment soon, thus making it more likely that you will need another loan. This information also shows the bank what the equipment might be worth if you were to default on the loan.

Loans to Other Clinicians. Here the bank looks at its past experience with similar providers and may assume all behavioral practices will behave comparably to these previous borrowers.

Your Credit Position. Lenders use certain *financial ratios* to compare your performance with similar types of borrowers to assess your credit-worthiness. If you are already heavily in debt, the bank may determine

TABLE 2.2   Examples of Financial Ratios

Ratio	Computation	Target	What It Measures
Debt service coverage	Net income (after salaries) $\pm$ depreciation + interest/ (principal + interest) payment)	1.5+	Your ability to generate enough cash to repay the loan
Debt-to-capitalization	Total debt (including lease)/ total debt + equity	>75%	The amount of debt you have consumed
Return on equity	Net income × 2 (equity at beginning of year + equity at end of year)	>10%	Profitability
Current ratio	Current assets ÷ current liabilities	≥2:1	Ability to meet short-term requirements
Day cash balance	Cash × 260 ÷ annual operating expenses	> 20	Number of days cash available

that you are more likely to default on a loan. All ratios are evaluated together and in context with other factors in the financial analysis of the practice's operations and financial position.

Table 2.2 summarizes several commonly used ratios, shows their computation and the target number banks expect, and describes what the ratio measures.

YOUR PROPOSAL PACKAGE

Once you have decided on a funding plan (amount of loan, term, interest rate, collateral required, etc.), the formal funding proposal package is completed and submitted to the funding source.

Your proposal package will likely include the following information:

- A completed loan application form
- Your business plan
- Financial statements, including a thorough explanation of any losses or unusual events in the past three years
- Budgets and projections, as well as a comparison of actual financials to budgeted financials for the past year

- Information about your experience and education, or a copy of your practice brochure
- Market value and appraised value of investments and fixed assets (from balance sheet or accountant)

If collateral is required, a list of the pledged items is included in the proposal. If personal guarantees are made, the personal financial statements of those making the guarantees are included as well.

After you submit the application and other information, the loan officer evaluates the application. This process usually takes from one to four weeks. If you have not heard from the institution after four to six weeks, you should phone the bank and ask about the status of the application.

If the lender approves the loan, a preliminary contract or commitment letter is prepared spelling out the terms of the loan contract and requiring you to sign agreement to the conditions. The bank may also require a commitment or application fee as a sign of good faith and to offset the bank's administrative costs. You may ask the bank to reduce or eliminate the fee, but the bank may deny this request. After the lender receives the signed commitment letter, the formal loan agreement is executed.

STIPULATIONS

The loan agreement may specify certain conditions that you agree to meet. Here are some examples of typical stipulations:

1. You may not incur any additional debt.
2. You must maintain a minimum level of working capital.
3. There may be restrictions on dividend payments.
4. There may be restrictions on mergers or acquisitions.
5. There may be limits on capital expenditures within a specified amount.
6. If the practice is a corporation, loans may be limited to the officers.
7. The lender may require periodic appraisals of real estate collateral.
8. The lender may require an annual audit or review by an independent certified public accountant.

The loan structure is a critical issue when the loan is approved. You will be advised to establish a realistic repayment schedule that does not place unreasonable financial burdens on you, yet ensures prompt, regular payments to the lender.

If the lender rejects your loan application, you have a right to an explanation for the rejection. You may ask to provide additional data to rebut any negative information. You may want to apply for loans at other lending institutions, because different institutions have different criteria and standards and because the evaluation of credit is somewhat subjective.

MANAGING BANKING RELATIONSHIPS

The challenge of managing your finances does not end after you have obtained needed financing, credit lines, and checking accounts at a commercial bank. A good relationship with your bank helps ensure that you have access to the services you need.

Most banks require that their customers sign standard agreements for lockboxes and wire transfers. Because these agreements protect the bank and limit its liability for errors, your attorney may want to review the documents before the practice representative signs them.

You will achieve best results by being proactive with your banker. For example, develop a written agreement with the bank for all services provided and meet periodically with a bank representative.

(The information in this chapter was adapted from Lybrand and Coopers and APAPD in Stout, 1996; permission from the publisher.)

REPAYMENT STRATEGY FOR GRADUATE SCHOOL STUDENT LOANS

Many clinicians obtain loans in order to complete their graduate training programs. It can be difficult to begin the repayment process after graduation, because it can take years for the graduate to find a job that pays well or to build a successful private practice. One colleague made the following successful argument to delay repayment of his loans:

> The law in my state says that I cannot practice independently without supervision, even though I have completed my graduate education.

Although I have my Ph.D., I still need a year of supervised experience and then must pass my licensure examination. I cannot legally call myself a psychologist (in this case) until I earn my license. Therefore, it is not appropriate for me to start repaying my student loans until I have become licensed.

This psychology intern convinced his lender to delay the repayment process, giving the intern more time to establish himself in his new profession.

Create a Business Plan

WHAT A BUSINESS PLAN IS

Every new business needs a business plan to direct and monitor its progress. This is true for your mental health practice whether you work independently or are part of a group. Your business plan serves as a road map for the business of your practice. It is similar to a blueprint that a builder uses to build a building. Depending on the needs of your practice, your plan may be a simple, brief document or it may be fairly elaborate.

WHY YOU NEED A BUSINESS PLAN

A good business plan functions as the resume of your business. It can help you:

- Set goals for your practice
- Make decisions about the direction of your practice
- Determine whether an idea is feasible
- Determine whether an idea will be profitable
- Evaluate results compared to the goals you have set
- Provide information that will enable you to obtain loans for your practice

The process of creating a business plan helps you quantify important elements such as the following:

- How much money you will need to start your practice
- What your expenses will be
- How to maximize your money when setting up your office
- When you can expect to break even
- When you can expect to make a profit
- How much profit you can expect to make

As you design your business plan, you will consider where you are today and set goals for the future. Once you have defined your vision of the future, you will need to identify the specific steps necessary to reach your goals. After your plan is complete, you should refer to it regularly to monitor your progress and make adjustments. This will help you reach your goals.

PRACTICE BY DESIGN: HOW TO DEVELOP YOUR BUSINESS PLAN

Your plan may be a general guide to help shape the direction of your practice and formulate a strategy, or you may need a complex, well-researched document that contains plenty of specific numbers and facts. If your goal is to gain venture funding or capitalization, you may want to consider hiring a professional consultant to produce your plan.

There are two basic ways to develop a business plan: Do it yourself or hire a professional to do it for you.

SHOULD YOU DO IT YOURSELF OR HIRE A PROFESSIONAL?

There are several free templates available on the Internet to help you build your business plan. There are also several options available for purchase. An easy way to search for sample plans is to go to an Internet search engine (such as www.google.com or www.yahoo.com) and type "business plan" in the search box. You will discover plenty of information about business plans and many different templates. Look for the one that best fits your needs.

See the Reference section at the back of this book for a list of sites available at the time of publication. These sites change often, so we suggest that you also do your own search. You will also find a sample plan in the appendix.

You can hire a business consultant, CPA, or attorney to help you build your plan. At the time of publication, the fee for these services in the Midwest is up to $250 an hour, so a simple plan may cost up to $2,500. However, with all the tools available, most clinicians will be able to construct a basic business plan without the help of a consultant. Your plan should include everything from marketing strategies and detailed financial goals to being able to concisely state what you do.

BUSINESS PLAN ELEMENTS

Your business plan should have the following basic elements.

1. Describe the *business* you are in and the *need* it addresses.
2. Define who your potential *clients* are.

3. Explain *why* potential clients would purchase the service from you.

4. Develop a set of *concrete* goals that are in sync with your vision for your practice. Effective goals include:
   - Action verbs
   - Specifics
   - Ability to be measured
   - Challenges
   - Target completion dates

   For example, if you are interested in developing more therapy groups, then you might set a goal of "establishing three active groups with at least four members in each by *X* date."

5. Your plan should include specific *financial* targets. Saying "More money, more self-pay clients, less managed care," is too vague to be useful. A better description of your financial target might be, "I want to increase my net income by 10 percent over last year while reducing my managed care caseload from 60 percent of my practice to 40 percent."

6. Assess and track your *gross revenue* versus net income. Establish benchmarks for the number of clients, billable hours, and income you want. Include timelines so you'll be able to measure your progress. Analyze your financial history and identify which kinds of services are most profitable (note that *profitable* is different from *highest fee*). Be sure to include expenses as well as income in all your calculations (see Chapter 5).

7. Assess the *market*. If there isn't a need or demand out there, no matter how enthusiastic you are about doing something, you are just going to waste resources. Good sources for data include the U.S. Census Bureau, your local hospital(s), trade journals, professional associations, and colleagues.

8. Look at the *competition*. How many of your colleagues are doing the same things you want to do? What do you bring to the table—in terms of clinical skills or marketing prowess—that will allow you to successfully compete?

9. Create a *marketing plan*. Include a specific plan for generating referrals. (Unfortunately, the philosophy of "If you build it, they will come" works only in baseball movies.) See Chapters 9 and 10 for more information on this important part of your business plan.

10. Solicit trusted *feedback*. Ask your accountant, professional colleagues, and even potential referral sources to review your plan.
11. *Review* the plan every two or three months and evaluate how you are doing. Develop hypotheses to explain deviations in income or other factors. Develop a theory and then test it. Your business plan should be a living document that develops over time.

SWOT ANALYSIS

As you work on developing your business plan, you may also want to conduct a SWOT (strengths, weaknesses, opportunities, and threats) analysis of your practice (or your practice as you conceptualize it). This can provide a basic profile to help in planning further practice development and in your business plan.

Developing a SWOT analysis is fairly straightforward. List five items in each of the following categories that best describe your practice.

1. *Strengths.* What makes your practice effective, different, or special?
2. *Weaknesses.* In what areas does your practice need to improve?
3. *Opportunities.* Where are there opportunities for you to enhance your practice and improve your chances of achieving your goals?
4. *Threats.* Aside from internal weaknesses (item 2), what are real threats to the success of your practice?

Here is an example of a SWOT analysis conducted by a therapist in the Midwest.

Strengths: What makes your practice effective, different, or special?
1. I have lived in this city for my entire life, giving me an understanding of the people who live here and the challenges many of them face.
2. I have excellent credentials—a degree from a top school and training at a well-known clinic.
3. I specialize in working with families, which is a challenging set of skills.

4. I offer clients a sliding-scale fee structure.
5. I am on many managed care panels.

Weaknesses: In what areas does your practice need to improve?

1. I have done very little marketing in the past.
2. My office is located in an area that has gone downhill.
3. Parking is limited, making it difficult for clients.
4. I am the only therapist in my practice. This makes it difficult when I need to be out of town, and I sometimes feel a bit burned out.
5. I am getting fewer referrals from the local churches than in the past.

Opportunities: Where are there opportunities for you to enhance your practice and improve your chances of achieving your goals?

1. My lease ends in six months, and I could take the opportunity to move.
2. Two different students have approached me seeking internships. Bringing someone new into the practice could help me prevent burnout and provide better coverage to my clients.
3. A new medical practice is opening on Main Street that could be a good source of referrals.
4. I could develop a marketing plan to increase my visibility in the community.
5. A former colleague is ready to retire and has talked about selling her practice. This could be a source of new clients.

Threats: Aside from internal weaknesses you've listed, what are real threats to the success of your practice?

1. Managed care organizations are making it increasingly difficult to do business—because more time is required to complete the paperwork and because they pay providers less as each year passes.
2. The local auto manufacturing plant may close next year. Many of our town's residents work there, and this could ultimately threaten my practice.
3. The EAP that used to refer clients to me now refers only to therapists with alcohol counselor certification, which I lack.
4. I have heard several people say they are now seeing coaches instead of therapists.

5. The population in my town is aging. As people grow older, they go south for the winter, so my business in the winter months is down.

BUSINESS PLAN OUTLINE

According to the Small Business Administration (www.sba.gov), most business plans have the following elements:

- Cover sheet
- Statement of purpose
- Table of contents
- Information about the business
- A description of the business
    Your marketing plan
    A description of the competition
    A summary of your key operating procedures
    A list of the key people in the business
    A description of the insurance maintained by the business
- Financial information
    Information about loans
    A list of equipment and supplies
    Your balance sheet
    A break-even analysis
    Profit and loss statements
    Cash flow information
- Supporting documents
    Tax returns
    Personal financial statement (you can obtain the form for this from any bank)
    Lease or purchase agreements for office space
    Copies of licenses
    Copies of other relevant legal documents
    Curricula vitae (CVs) of the key people in the organization
    Copies of suppliers' letters of intent

CREATE A BUSINESS PLAN

PRACTICE BY DESIGN: MODEL BUSINESS PLAN

You will find a sample business plan in the appendix (Irwin 1995) that is modified for a behavioral healthcare practice. Yours may be longer or shorter, depending on what you plan to be doing in your practice. The size is relatively unimportant as long as you include all relevant details. You can tailor and vary this model to your individual needs, goals, and circumstances. It is offered here as an aid for getting started, not as a substitution for professional assistance. Italicized or bracketed text and blank lines are to be substituted with your own information. All names and numbers herein are fictional and hypothetical, employed only to make the model business plan more easily read and understood.

Set Your Fees

HOW TO DECIDE WHAT TO CHARGE FOR YOUR SERVICES

When you are setting fees for your counseling services, there are three kinds of fees to consider:

1. Fees for managed care clients.
2. Fees for clients who pay out of pocket (fee for service).
3. Discounted fees for clients who have financial hardship.

MANAGED CARE CLIENTS

When you see clients whose fees are paid by a managed care organization (MCO), you must follow the guidelines of the agreement you signed when you became a provider for that MCO. Refer to Chapter 7 for information about working with MCOs.

CLIENTS WHO PAY OUT OF POCKET

Some of your clients will pay your full usual-and-customary (U&C) fee themselves, out of pocket. This arrangement is called *fee for service* or *out of pocket*. These clients may ask for a receipt for each session and, in some cases, will obtain their own insurance reimbursement. (Please see Chapter 5 for a sample receipt form.)

CLIENTS WITH FINANCIAL HARDSHIP

You may wish to offer sliding-scale fees for uninsured, low-income clients. It is wise to establish and post this scale. It should be based on annual household income, as demonstrated by client's past two years' income tax returns and number of dependents. (See Table 4.5 later in this chapter for an example.)

HOW TO ESTABLISH YOUR FULL FEE

When you are deciding how much to charge for your counseling services, *you* are the one who determines what your fee should be. After setting your full fee for one session (typically 50 minutes), you may also wish to set fees for other services, such as group therapy. In addition, you may want to consider establishing a sliding scale for clients with financial hardship. We will discuss this later in this chapter.

When setting your full fee, consider the following questions:

1. What is the average fee or going rate for a 50-minute hour of psychotherapy in your community? Consider the fees charged by other therapists with similar licenses and experience.
2. What fee would you feel comfortable charging?
3. What fee do you think the average client expects to pay for psychotherapy?
4. How much have you paid for your own therapy?
5. What are the current fees charged by therapists with your license in your part of the country? For current information, consult the website or other publications of your professional organization for information. (Depending on which license you hold, you will find information at www.AAMFT.org, www.APA.org, www.NASW.org, etc.)

HOW MUCH DO THERAPISTS EARN?

According to a survey in *Psychotherapy Finances* (October 2000), therapists' median professional income is:

Professional counselors: $47,350
Marriage and family therapists (MFTs): $59,405
Social workers: $61,164
Psychologists: $80,000
Psychiatrists: Not reported

The median hourly full fee for therapy was reported as:

Professional counselors: $79
MFTs and social workers: $80
Psychologists: $100
Psychiatrists: $132

Source: Psychotherapy Finances, October 2000.

How Much Money Do Psychologists Earn?

The American Psychological Association (APA) conducts an annual survey of its members to determine the earnings of psychologists in various work settings. The most recent data available at the time of publication indicated that the net income of licensed clinical psychologists employed full-time in 2001 was $72,000. Net income for licensed counseling psychologists was $66,500.

Many psychologists have additional sources of income from other work activities; therefore, these data may not represent total income.

Source: Darnell Singleton, Antoinette Tate, and Garrett Randall, *Salaries in Psychology 2001: Report of the 2001 APA Salary Survey.* APA Research Office, January 2003.

MANAGEMENT METRICS: INCOME AND FEE SETTING

Knowing your costs is critical to successfully managing your practice. This section provides you with the tools necessary to do so.

WHAT SHOULD PSYCHOTHERAPY COST?

Many behavioral health professionals of every discipline tend to base their fees on other professionals' fees, without any thought about their own expenses, costs, overhead, marketplace, and so on. In establishing what you will charge, or in evaluating what you currently charge, it is important to consider certain factors as they may apply to your practice. These are listed in the worksheets that follow.

When it comes to establishing your usual-and-customary (U&C) fee, it is important to factor in your costs and overhead, and also the value of your expertise and specialty training in the context of your local marketplace. It is important to be aware of marketplace issues. For example, if you practice in an impoverished area or in a location that is highly penetrated by managed care, you may need to adjust your fees downward.

The research conducted by *Psychotherapy Finances* can be invaluable as a general guide for regional and practice area fee structures. (Visit www.psychotherapyfinances.com, or call 800-869-8450.) APA publishes a biennial survey across almost every imaginable practice aspect on its website (see research.apa.org/99salaries.html). This information can be accessed by APA members.

Costs of Getting Started

License examination costs	$ _____
Study material for licensing exam	$ _____
Rent (security deposit and first month's rent)	$ _____
Furnishings	$ _____
Telephone service and equipment	$ _____
Answering service/system	$ _____
Business stationery	$ _____
Computer	$ _____
Software	$ _____
Internet services	$ _____
Website design	$ _____
Website hosting and maintenance	$ _____
Office supplies	$ _____
Liability insurance	$ _____
Attorney fees	$ _____
Consultant fees	$ _____
Total	$ _____

Ongoing Costs (Monthly Operations)

Rent	$ _____
Utilities	$ _____
Telephone service	$ _____
Answering service/system	$ _____
Pager	$ _____
Insurance	$ _____
Professional	$ _____
General liability	$ _____

Fire	$ _____
Disability	$ _____
Health	$ _____
Life	$ _____
Office expenses (photocopy lease, cleaning service, etc.)	$ _____
Professional dues	$ _____
Taxes	$ _____
State	$ _____
Local	$ _____
Federal	$ _____
Consultants	$ _____
Practice	$ _____
Tax/accounting	$ _____
Business	$ _____
Attorney	$ _____
Supervision	$ _____
Commuting costs	$ _____
Train	$ _____
Parking	$ _____
Tolls	$ _____
Gas	$ _____
Continuing education	$ _____
License renewal	$ _____
Secretarial services	$ _____
Billing services	$ _____
Books and publications	$ _____
Networking and business entertainment costs	$ _____
Marketing costs	$ _____
Retirement funds	$ _____
Student loan(s)	$ _____

Miscellaneous	$ _____
	$ _____
Total	$ _____
Grand total practice costs	$ _____

Note: These lists do not include any expenses for travel, political contributions, clinical materials (test kits, forms, etc.), office equipment (wireless phone service, fax machines, calculators, etc.), business application fees (Doing Business As (DBA) notice, service marks, incorporation costs, etc.), or any other specialty equipment (neuropsychological test equipment, biofeedback equipment, etc.).

Source: C. E. Stout (1996). "What Should Psychotherapy Cost?" *Illinois Psychologist,* spring, 24–26.

DO THE MATH: PRACTICE COSTS

Add up the applicable factors from the worksheet that apply to your particular situation. This is referred to as *practice costs,* or PC. Then include your factors in the following formulas to determine your costs:

$$(X \text{ clinical service hours}) \times (Y \text{ number of weeks worked annually})$$
$$= \text{total annual hours worked}$$

$$(\text{Total annual hours worked}) \times (20\% \text{ for bad debt})$$
$$= \text{total billable annual hours}$$

$$\frac{\text{Total billable annual hours}}{\text{Practice costs}} = \text{hourly cost}$$

For example:

Costs of Getting Started

License examination costs	$ 250
Study material for national licensing examination	1,200
Rent (security deposit and first month's rent)	800
Furnishings	3,000

Telephone service and equipment	250
Business stationery	200
Computer and printer	1,200
Software	500
Office supplies	200
Attorney fees	1,000
Consultant fees	1,000
Total	$9,600 (or $800/month)

Ongoing Costs (Monthly Operations)

Rent	$ 400
Utilities	40
Telephone service	40
Answering service/system	25
Pager	15
Insurance	15
Professional	63
General liability	17
Fire	8
Disability	83
Health	450
Life	10
Office expenses (photocopy lease, cleaning service, etc.)	75
Professional dues	85
Taxes	
State	875
Local	N/A
Federal	1,875
Consultants	
Practice	150

Tax/accounting	50
Business	150
Attorney	100
Supervision	150
Commuting costs	
Train	96
Parking	48
Tolls	N/A
Gas	40
Continuing education	200
License renewal	7
Secretarial services	250
Billing services	200
Books and publications	75
Networking and business entertainment costs	85
Marketing costs	200
Retirement funds	350
Student loan(s)	450
Miscellaneous	200
Total	$6,877
Grand total practice costs	$7,677 or $92,124 annually

For example, assuming you have initial annual practice costs of $92,124 and you plan to work 30 clinical hours per week for 48 weeks per year (figuring four weeks of vacation) minus 20 percent (bad debt, uncollectible fees, missed sessions, etc.), you would have 1,440 billable hours minus 20 percent, which equals 1,152 revenue-generating hours annually. Annual practice costs of $92,124 divided by 1,152 suggests that to cover your costs for the first year, you need to generate at least $79.97 per hour. If you add a modest 5 percent profit margin, it becomes $83.97 per hour; and a 10 percent profit margin will bring it up to $87.97 per hour.

Subsequent annual practice costs will decline somewhat, since everything noted in the start-up costs will have been paid for and will occur only once. Thus, subsequent annual practice costs will be roughly $82,524 in this hypothetical, yielding an hourly cost of $71.64. With a 5 percent profit margin, this grows to $75.22 per hour, and with a 10 percent margin of profit, to $78.80 per hour.

You may also wish to also solve the equation in the following ways to determine how many hours you would need to work (solving for Y) or to adjust your hourly rate (solving for X).

$$\frac{\text{Monthly expenses}}{X \text{ dollars per hour}} = Y \text{ billable hours per month}$$

For example, $82,524 in annual practice costs is $6,877 per month, and if you charge (and, more important, get) $125 per hour, the equation would read as follows:

$$\frac{\$6,877}{\$125} = Y \text{ billable hours per month} = \text{about 55 hours per month}$$

If you had $82,524 in annual practice costs resulting in $6,877 per month of expenses and you speculated that you could generate 140 billable hours per month (or 35 per week), then:

$$\frac{\$6,877}{X} = 140 \text{ billable hours per month}$$

Solving for X,

$$X = \frac{\$6,877}{140} = \$49.12 \text{ per hour}$$

In gaining an understanding of costs versus productivity, you can readily understand how those with busy practices but also with high practice costs and insufficient fees can quickly get into financial trouble. The mix and interplay of costs, fees, and productivity are tightly interwoven. Your success is incumbent on being able to understand, track, and manage these in such a way as to strike a sustainable balance of economics and practice time.

There are many ways to save money as you set up your practice. For example, you may not need to purchase a computer for your practice if you already have one, and costs such as office rent and utilities can be reduced drastically by subleasing or sharing expenses with suitemates. It is likely helpful for your economic peace of mind to calculate what-if scenarios with such economies factored in. This will help you discover potential areas for savings and thus lead you to prioritize them and pursue them first. Many clinicians start out with a part-time practice initially and then build to a larger independent practice as time passes and cash flow increases.

DO THE MATH: TARGET NUMBER OF CLIENTS TO MEET INCOME GOALS

Pressman (1979) devised some simple yet helpful models to use as one's practice gets started. Say you want to calculate the number of hours you would need to be seeing clients per week in order to hit a certain revenue target. Divide your weekly gross revenues by your hourly rate and multiply the quotient by 1.25 (to accommodate missed sessions, cancellations, and bad debt). For example, if you wish to gross $600 per week at an hourly rate of $45 per session, you would need to conduct approximately 17 sessions per week:

Target weekly gross revenues per hourly session rate) × 1.25
= sessions needed per week

$$\left(\frac{\$600}{\$45} \right) \times 1.25 = 17 \text{ hours per week}$$

Table 4.1 is a handy reference showing various rates. It also vividly depicts the impact that your rate has on the amount of income generated versus hours worked (of course, this doesn't include your costs).

61

TABLE 4.1   Number of Hours Scheduled at Various Hourly Rates

Weekly Net Income*	$45/hour	$75/hour	$90/hour	$125/hour
$200	6	3.5	3	2
$300	9.5	5	4	3
$400	12.5	7	5.5	4
$500	15.5	8.5	7	5
$600	19	10	8.5	6
$700	22	12	10	7
$800	25	13.5	11	8

*Adjusted for cancellations and bad debt.

Another helpful model (Pressman 1979, p. 11) deals with acquisition of client load. This is a very unreliable area of prediction, as it is contingent on widely differing practice variables (short- versus long-term treatment, payor mix, referral flow and load, etc.). Table 4.2 should be used as a rule of thumb with those caveats in mind.

TABLE 4.2   Acquisition of Client Load

Month	Referrals per Month	Total Client Hours Scheduled by the Week	Rate of Attrition*	Net Client Hours by the Week†
1	2	2	0	2
2	2	3	1	2
3	2	4	1	3
4	3	6	1	4
5	3	8	1	6
6	4	10	2	8
7	3	12	1	9
8	4	15	1	11
9	3	16	2	12
10	4	19	1	14
11	3	21	1	16
12	4	23	2	17
13	3	24	2	18
14	4	27	1	20

*Allowance for clients terminating therapy.
†Based on addition of referrals less attrition and cancellation rate of 25 percent per week.

PRACTICE BY DESIGN: WHAT DOES THE MARKETPLACE SAY?

Clinical billing is managed within a system of codes known as Clinical Procedural Terminology (CPT) codes. (A listing of these appears in Chapter 5.) *Psychotherapy Finances* (800-869-8450 or www.PsychotherapyFinances.com) has produced an informative periodic survey across clinical disciplines and geography since 1979. Its most recent survey (2000) of more than 1,500 therapists from all U.S. states produced the information in Table 4.3.

The Association for the Advancement of Psychology (AAP), in its summer 2001 issue (p. 5) of *Advance* summarizing the survey, noted that,

TABLE 4.3   Industry Pay Scales

Most Frequent *Direct/Self-Pay* Fees Paid for Individual Therapy (CPT 80806)

Profession	Fee
Marriage and family therapist	$80
Professional counselor	$79
Psychiatrist	$132
Psychologist	$100
Social worker	$80

Most Frequent *Managed Care* Fees Paid for Individual Therapy (CPT 80806)

Profession	Fee
Marriage and family therapist	$60
Professional counselor	$60
Psychiatrist	$95
Psychologist	$70
Social worker	$60

Most Frequent *Indemnity Insurance* Fees Paid for Individual Therapy (CPT 80806)

Profession	Fee
Marriage and family therapist	$80
Professional counselor	$80
Psychiatrist	$120
Psychologist	$95
Social worker	$80

with the exception of psychiatrists, all other behavioral healthcare disciplines have had a decrease in the amount of their managed care fees.

Overall, clinicians are receiving just over 30 percent of their total clinical income from MCOs.

Clinicians in solo practice do markedly less managed care work than do those in groups (29 percent versus 34.1 percent).

Psychologists tend to gain more of their income from third parties (i.e., MCOs and indemnity insurance) than does any other discipline.

Clinicians with master's degrees (e.g., social workers, counselors, marriage and family therapists) generally make less than doctoral-level clinicians (e.g., psychiatrists and psychologists).

Since the last survey conducted by AAP in 1997, psychologists' private practice income has decreased 1.7 percent; psychiatrists, on the other hand, had a 13.7 percent increase over the same time period.

Clinicians in solo practice reported that they spent 35.8 percent of their gross revenues on practice expenses (up 0.9 percent from 1997).

Group practices reported that they spent 34.7 percent of their gross revenues on practice expenses (up 3 percent from 1997).

The American Psychological Association conducts a biennial survey called *Salaries in Psychology.* A survey published in 2000 is available at http://research.apa.org/99salaries.html. For example, this rich resource reviews salaries for various faculty (i.e., differing university departments,

TABLE 4.4 Average Number of Sessions by Region for Direct Pay and Managed Care

Region	Direct/Self-Pay *Mean* Number of Sessions	Direct/Self-Pay *Median* Number of Sessions	Managed Care *Mean* Number of Sessions	Managed Care *Median* Number of Sessions
East	29.0	20.0	20.6	15.0
South	19.2	12.0	13.0	10.0
Midwest	25.0	15.0	11.9	10.0
West	21.2	14.5	10.3	8.0
Pacific	32.1	20.0	10.7	8.5

two- and four-year colleges, medical schools, professional schools, research, applied), notes the impacts of managed care on net income for licensed practitioners and median salaries adjusted for cost of living for selected metropolitan areas, and much, much more. (See Table 4.4.) It offers much of interest to nonpsychologists as well, showing the costs of living for 25 selected metropolitan areas.

HOW TO ESTABLISH A SLIDING-SCALE FEE STRUCTURE

Many therapists offer a discounted fee to clients who are unable to pay the full amount. The ethics codes of most professional organizations in the mental health field suggest that fees should be discounted for clients who need our services but who are unable to pay the full fee because of financial hardship.

Some therapists find negotiating a lower fee to be awkward or uncomfortable for both themselves and clients. However, it is important to decide what your fee policy will be before you begin seeing clients on your own. From a risk management perspective, it is wise to treat every client the same when it comes to fees.

The following solution is fair to both the client and the therapist.

1. For clients who can pay the full fee out of pocket, charge your regular fee.
2. If the payor is a managed care organization (MCO) or health maintenance organization (HMO), you must follow the organization's guidelines and charge the fee specified in the contract.
3. For clients who pay out of pocket and ask for a reduced fee because of financial hardship, follow your sliding-scale fee structure. Apply your schedule uniformly to every client with financial hardship.

EXAMPLE OF SLIDING-SCALE FEES

Many therapists in every type of practice setting establish sliding-scale fees. The policy is printed and discussed with new clients at the first session. The rates may be updated annually. Having the policy in writing

65

STORIES FROM THE REAL WORLD

In the early 1960s, my first patient in private practice *should* have taught me a lesson. I was so eager to have this very first patient that I charged her a remarkably low fee, based on her *alleged* finances. She was a married student and worked part-time. We agreed on $6.00 per session, which was all that she claimed she could afford. After nine months, she informed me that she was leaving on a two-month summer vacation in Europe. "How can you afford it?" I asked. "Oh, I economized and saved a lot of money this year," she said.

Many years later, a local professional school referred a PhD candidate for the required experience in personal psychotherapy at a discounted (student) fee. My custom was to charge a low fee to such students if they couldn't afford to pay standard fees and if they agreed that they would do the same when they were in a position to do so. (It turned out that this patient was *not* economically disadvantaged. Her husband was a well-paid professional.)

At the termination of her required therapy hours, I learned that she had been working as a psych assistant to a highly paid psychologist. She had been earning more per session as a psych assistant than she had paid for her own therapy with me. On hearing this I said, "I'm sorry that you've not learned enough from your therapy to treat others fairly." She shrugged her shoulders, smirked, and probably felt good about cheating me.

Later, when I was an examiner for the psychology licensing exam, this client's name came up. Of course I couldn't examine her and had no input in determining her value as a psychologist. However, I caution new psychologists to question the validity of their patients' statements about their economic situations before reducing fees.

Sandra Levy Ceren, PhD

---

helps prevent awkwardness and embarrassment for both the client and the therapist.

Know your professional association's ethical guidelines. AAMFT Ethical Guidelines state, "Therapists must establish a clear fee policy which is communicated clearly to clients and third-party payers. The fee rate should be the same for insured as well as uninsured clients. Therapists who wish to have sliding scale fees should ensure that they adjust the billed fee equally for insured and uninsured clients." (The American Association for Marriage and Family Therapy, *Family Therapy News*, December 1999.)

The key is to present facts truthfully to the insurance company and then advocate for the best outcome you can get. Ethical practice does not require financial martyrdom. In fact, it is highly ethical to seek appropriate compensation for professional services, in part so you can maintain self-care and the continued ability to offer those services. Just be honest in how you go about it.

Table 4.5 shows an example of a sliding-scale policy based on a full fee of $125 for a 50-minute session. This policy is included in the paperwork given to the client at the first session. By locating a client's annual household income and the number of family members in his or her home at this time, you can set the rate accordingly for each 50-minute session.

In order to qualify for this fee adjustment, clients need to provide copies of the first page of their 1040 for the last two years. If a client cannot afford this fee, I will make every effort to refer that client to a nearby community mental health center.

INSURANCE REIMBURSEMENT AND MANAGED CARE LISTS

If you decide to enter the insurance and managed care arena, be prepared for a lot of hard work and frustration. Many independent practitioners are looking for ways to find clients who are able to pay their fees

TABLE 4.5   Sliding Scale for Psychotherapy Services

| Annual Household Income | Number of People in Your Household | | | | | |
	1	2	3	4	5	6
<$30,000	$70	$70	$60	$50	$40	$40
$30,000–$44,000	$80	$80	$70	$70	$60	$60
$45,000–$59,000	$100	$100	$90	$90	$80	$80
$60,000–$74,000	$125	$125	$110	$110	$100	$100
$75,000+	$125	$125	$125	$125	$125	$125

privately, without insurance or managed care involvement. The best way to do this is simply to make it your policy to request payment of your fees up front, session by session. If a client wishes to bill his or her insurance company, provide the client with statements on a regular basis.

If you decide to build your practice by sitting on managed care panels, get some expert advice. Subscribe to a newsletter such as *Psychotherapy Finances*, at www.psyfin.com, or phone (561) 624-1155.

You will find additional information about fees in Chapter 5 ("Set Up Shop and Measure Results"), Chapter 6 ("Minimize Risk"), and Chapter 7 ("Manage Managed Care").

Set Up Shop and Measure Results

This chapter explores two phases of operating your business: setting up your shop and evaluating the results of your efforts once you are up and running. Both are critical to the success of your practice.

Choosing an Office Location

Choosing an office location is one of the most important decisions you make for your practice. It means making a commitment, usually of a year or longer, so it's obviously important to take your time choosing the right place. You must consider two issues: what feels right to you and its impact on your clients.

Which Town?

The first decision to make when you set up an office is in which part of your town or metropolitan area to locate. In Chapter 9, you will learn how to work with target market demographic information and identify the kinds of clients you want to work with. When choosing an office location, you will need to consider the key demographic factors of the clients you are targeting. You will also need to decide how much of a commute you can live with and find a town within that distance that houses your target clients.

Since therapists meet their clients face-to-face on a regular basis, it's critical to choose an office where your clients feel comfortable. Your location can have a positive or negative impact on bringing clients to your practice. Don't even think about locating in an area that feels even slightly unsafe. This is especially important in the counseling business, since we often work during evening hours.

What about Working from Home?

According to the AAMFT publication *Practice Strategies*, fewer than 10 percent of marriage and family therapists see clients in offices at home. The number of home-based therapists may be increasing because it is an easy way to reduce overhead. The July/August 1999 issue of *Practice Strategies* outlined a number of issues to consider if you think this may be an option for you:

1. Consider what your clients will think about the arrangement. Seeing you on your home turf alters the power balance and may make them feel uncomfortable. An office in a professional office building is a neutral setting, and many clients may prefer it. On the other hand, many clients say the home atmosphere is much more comfortable and conducive to doing therapeutic work. They enjoy it and do better work in such a warm environment.

2. Consider the impact on your neighbors. They may object to the increased car traffic, possible parking problems, and seeing strangers walking to and from your house. If your business becomes a nuisance for your neighbors, you will have to deal with it, so it's best to talk to them up front.

3. Check to see if you need permits from your city or township, especially if you are making alterations to the house or property.

4. Think about how you will protect the privacy of your family, your neighbors, and your clients.

5. Consider the kinds of clients you see and think about whether there is an issue of security for your family. If you see clients who may be violent, this may not be a good option for you. Also consider the spouses and families of your clients and whether they may be violent as therapy progresses. In the home office setting, your clients impact your family and neighbors as well as you.

6. With an office away from home, it is fairly easy to keep your home address private. If your office is in your home, you lose that security and privacy.

7. It may be awkward for your children and spouse to see your clients as they come and go. Try to set your hours so your clients and family members avoid crossing paths.

8. Therapists who see clients at home say they are very careful when they screen new clients. But even the most experienced therapists say that it can be difficult to determine over the phone who may pose a threat at some point in the future. Some clients are more appropriate for agency settings and should not be seen at home.

9. You have to be comfortable with your clients knowing a lot more about you than they would if you saw them in an office setting. In some cases, having clients seeing you in a real home setting

can be good for the therapeutic process. On the other hand, some clients will be envious or disapproving of your home, your neighborhood, or your car. Working at home may bring up issues that would not be present if you saw your clients away from your home.

10. Some therapists say that it is not a good idea to see clients at home when children live in the house. If you decide to do it anyway, be sure there is an adult watching them when you are working with clients.

11. Make sure the house and property are safe for clients.

12. Check with your insurance company to be sure they approve your plan. Find out if your homeowner's insurance covers accidents in your home office. Many insurers exclude it if you do more than a certain amount of business from your home.

13. If you plan to have a bookkeeper or other office employee working at your home office, you may need to obtain workers' comp coverage.

14. Many therapists miss being around people. There are no colleagues, and it can be very lonely. You have to go out of your way to create opportunities to mix with other professionals on a regular basis.

15. Since there is no commute, you are available to your family for more hours than if you had to drive to and from an office.

16. It is convenient to work where you live. However, a downside is that it can leave you with little time to shift gears after a stressful day.

17. Some people who work at home say they sometimes feel trapped and need to get away, if only for a walk around the block at lunchtime.

18. You have to be able to deal with the distractions when you work at home. The laundry, chores, and refrigerator are always there calling to you. You have to be disciplined and resist the tendency to get off track.

19. If you are on one or more managed care lists, check with the MCO to make sure it approves your working from home. Some companies may ask to visit your home office to make certain it meets their guidelines.

STORIES FROM THE REAL WORLD

Shortly after I moved into my new office, the toilet overflowed. As I stood over it, plunger in hand, my office suitemate looked in and saw what was going on. She said, "Ah, now there's a situation not included in those books on 'how to succeed in private practice.' "

This is what I learned early in my private practice experience:

1. A plunger is a handy piece of office equipment.
2. On-call plumbers and other people with tools are important resources when you are opening an office.

Stephanie Pratola, PhD

---

20. If you are considering seeing clients at home, be sure to see Woody Allen's movie *Deconstructing Harry*. Look for the scene with Kirstie Alley seeing therapy clients at home.
21. For more information, read *Working from Home: Everything You Need to Know About Living and Working Under the Same Roof* by Paul and Sara Edwards (Jeremy Tarcher, 1999). It provides lots of information and guidelines for all kinds of professionals who work at home.

LOCATING IN A GROUP PRACTICE OR COUNSELING CENTER

Rather than going out on your own, you may want to consider joining a group practice, counseling center, or clinic (see Chapter 1). Consider the advantages and disadvantages of making such a move.

Advantages of Working in a Group Setting
1. Colleagues are always nearby and available for sharing ideas, asking for supervision, and meeting your social needs.
2. Expenses are shared in a group setting.
3. In many cities, you may be able to find a practice or center where you may be able to rent blocks of time to see clients. You may be able to find an arrangement where you pay only for the time you use.

4. Your association with the group may add to your credibility.
5. Working in a group setting may provide you with greater opportunities for referrals.

Disadvantages of Working in a Group Setting

1. You may have to share your therapy rooms and furniture with other therapists. They may or may not be as neat and careful as you are.
2. There may be friction between therapists. Be sure you understand what kinds of clients your colleagues normally see, and think about how that will affect you.
3. Most counseling centers have specific policies that you will be expected to follow. This may not be compatible with your working style.
4. You may not be able to use the facilities as freely as you'd like. There may be scheduling conflicts and mistakes, where two therapists are expecting to use the same room at the same time (or worse yet, where another therapist walks in on your therapy session).
5. Clients may prefer a private setting to a large, busy waiting room or impersonal staff.

CITY PRACTICE OR COUNTRY PRACTICE?

Advantages of Working in the City

1. There are usually more clients in urban areas because the population is denser.
2. Many other professionals nearby may refer clients to you.
3. Many nearby businesses and organizations present marketing opportunities for your practice.

Advantages of Working in the Country

1. The smaller population means that you are more likely to see your clients around town. This may not bother you, but some therapists would prefer not to run into their clients in between sessions.
2. You may find that the country offers a quieter, less stressful life for you and your clients.

3. Suburban and rural locations tend to be less expensive, and your office would require less overhead.

Should You Sublease an Office or Rent Your Own?

It all depends on what you can afford. Renting space from a colleague will save you money during the early years of your practice. Subleasing is also a good way to make the transition from intern therapist to independent professional. You can look for another therapist from whom to rent space by looking in the classifieds of the local paper or in the classifieds of your professional publication. The AAMFT, the APA, the National Association of Social Workers (NASW), and other professional organizations have classifieds in the back of their monthly publications, and you may be able to find the perfect office there.

When sharing space with another professional, it is important to make certain that you feel completely comfortable with that person. You are linking your name and reputation to his or hers, for better or worse.

Other Considerations When You Look for an Office

1. Choose an office that allows you to be flexible. When your practice is new, it is difficult to predict what your needs will be in a year or two. Choosing a space that can grow with you is ideal. When you are starting out and trying to keep expenses down, it is tempting to choose the smallest space you can find. But you may quickly outgrow it.
2. Choose an office where you can see more than two clients at a time. There will be occasions when you will want to see an entire family, even if that isn't your specialty.
3. Your waiting room should be large enough to accommodate twice the number of clients you see on average in a session during prime-time hours.
4. Choose a location near main streets and freeways. Clients value convenience, and easy access is important.
5. If you choose a space in an office building, it is better to be near medical practices.
6. There are advantages and disadvantages to having other therapists in your building. If you are the only therapist, people who

STORIES FROM THE REAL WORLD

When I had just subleased office space in a popular building in a southern California city, I mentioned it to another therapist. The therapist said, "I used to have my office there, but I was held up at knifepoint in the parking lot." There wasn't much I could do at that point, since I'd already signed an agreement, but I wish I had asked around more thoroughly before jumping at the first thing that came along.

Laurie Cope Grand, M.S.

work in your building will be more likely to choose you and refer clients to you. If there are other therapists in your building, chances are you won't be the only one working in the building at night.

7. Choose a building with plenty of parking available, both for the people who work in the building and for the clients.
8. Choose a building where there is plenty of light in the parking lot at night. Ask the landlord how late the lights stay on at night. Drive around at night during hours you plan to be seeing clients and see whether you feel safe.
9. Before you sign a lease, ask local businesspeople and other therapists what they know about your building.
10. Have your lease reviewed by an attorney before you sign it.
11. Ask to see the restrooms before you sign the lease. What you see is what you are going to have to put up with.
12. Knock on doors and ask other tenants their opinion of the quality of building management. Are repairs made quickly? Are there any potential problems you should know about (e.g., the air-conditioning that is difficult to regulate during the summer, making the office feel like a meat locker most of the time . . . or the thin wall between your office and the man in the office next door, who gets on the phone every morning at 10 A.M. and yells . . . or the security guard who sleeps at her station on Saturday mornings . . . or the housekeeping staff who steals small appliances)?
13. Look for an office with a window. It may not bother you now, but never seeing the light of day will get on your nerves.

COMMUNICATING WITH CLIENTS

We communicate with our clients in many ways. Beyond the office session, this section provides ideas for secure and professional means to do so.

PHONES, VOICE MAIL, AND FAX MACHINES

You will need a separate telephone line for your practice. Most therapists prefer to use an answering machine or voice-mail service through their telephone company. The advantage is that it provides a greater sense of control over how your phone is answered. Therapists who use answering services prefer them because they provide a human contact. The answering service can reach you in cases of emergency, while a machine can only take a message.

If you can afford it, you will be easier to reach if you also have a fax machine with a dedicated line and a pager. Both are becoming necessities these days, and people expect you to have both. However, they are expenses and must be included in your start-up costs.

STORIES FROM THE REAL WORLD

One of the best things I did many years ago was to surround my practice with a layer of confidentiality and privacy for my clients, even though it was often inconvenient for me. Two examples are my phone answering system and my office staffing process. I went to great lengths and expense to find an automated phone system that did not involve any human taking messages from clients, even in emergencies. This ensures that my clients talk only to me, even in a crisis.

Similarly, I make my own appointments, greet my clients myself, and am the contact person for billing matters. This guarantees the privacy and confidentiality of my clients, allowing them to trust me more and work more efficiently and effectively in their therapy. Further, in the long run this style has led to fewer billing and collection problems, has increased referrals, and, ironically, saves me time.

John E. Mayer, PhD

ONLINE THERAPY

A new way of doing therapy has emerged during the past several years: online therapy. While it is still very new, increasing numbers of therapists are trying it, first with one or two clients. There are certain benefits, such as having the ability to send and receive e-mail messages 24 hours a day. Some people also enjoy having the luxury of taking their time writing messages and thinking about them before sending them. Those who have tried this method also say they feel less inhibited in expressing their feelings and thoughts. They also like having a record of their messages and the other person's responses.

There are plenty of cautions, however. Both senders and receivers must be extremely careful to send messages to the correct address. An error could result in a breach of confidentiality. Privacy is also a primary concern, especially when the therapist or client is using a computer that is shared with others.

According to *Psychotherapy Finances* (May 2003), many therapists are thinking about adding online therapy to their services. In an article titled "The 'Just-Do-It' Approach to E-mail Therapy," the newsletter advises therapists to answer the following questions when they are considering whether to offer online or telephone therapy:

1. *How do I charge clients for online therapy?* First of all, few, if any, insurance companies cover online or telephone therapy. The article recommends using your basic hourly fee and charging for the time you spend reading and responding to each e-mail. To receive payment for your services, you can accept credit cards by setting up a merchant account through your bank. An alternative is to use PayPal, which is a service available through eBay. With PayPal, clients can pay with credit cards and checks that are processed online.

2. *Is it ethical?* Check the ethical standards of your state licensing board and your national professional association (APA, AAMFT, etc.). See www.metanoia.com for a discussion of whether this type of therapy is in fact therapy and whether it is ethical. Make certain that you protect the privacy of the client by using a password-protected e-mail account (not accessible to anyone but you) and that your computer has firewall software.

3. *Is it effective?* Distance therapy using e-mail or telephone can be a way to reach clients who live in underserved areas — places where there are no therapists. It can also be an option for clients who have previously avoided therapy because they are reluctant to meet in person. For a variety of reasons, these clients may be unwilling or unable to visit a therapist in person.

4. *Is it difficult to do?* Online therapy requires some skills that are different than those used in traditional face-to-face therapy. Doing therapy with a person who is not in the room means that you lose the ability to see the client's body language, hear the tone of voice, and read other nonverbal reactions.

5. *Could it lead to malpractice problems?* It is important to understand the guidelines of your state licensing board and your national professional association. It is also important to have the client complete a detailed information form and sign an agreement (see www.personal-counselor.com for an example). It is unclear whether the laws of the therapist's state or those of the client's state apply to this type of therapy.

ONLINE THERAPY PRECAUTIONS

According to the guidelines of the International Society for Mental Health Online (http://ismho.org/), "The client should be informed before he or she consents to receive online mental health services. In particular, the client should be informed about the process, the counselor, the potential risks and benefits of those services, safeguards against those risks, and alternatives to those services."

If you decide to add online therapy to your practice, it is important that you follow the same procedures online as you would in person. The International Society for Mental Health Online offers these guidelines:

1. Limit your practice to areas in which you are competent and that are within the scope of your license.
2. Establish and communicate clear policies and procedures about how and when you will communicate with the client, how much it will cost, and how the client will pay for your services.
3. Carefully evaluate all potential clients before providing services.

AAMFT legal consultant Richard S. Leslie, JD (2002) advises that therapists examine the following issues before providing online therapy:

- Does your state have a telemedicine law? Whom does the law cover and what does it require?
- Does your state licensing board have guidelines for online therapy? What are they?
- What are the legal aspects of obtaining verbal and written informed consent for online therapy?
- What are the potential benefits and risks of online therapy?

4. Have a plan for emergencies. Since the client is likely in a different city or state, you need to know what to do if he or she requires emergency services. Obtain the name and phone number of a qualified professional (such as the client's medical doctor) who could see the client in case of an emergency.
5. Follow rules of confidentiality just as you would with any client. Make sure the client understands the guidelines.
6. Keep records of your work with the client.

KEEPING RECORDS

If you are a licensed therapist, you most likely learned basic record-keeping systems during your internship. If not, here are a few key points.

You will need a way to keep track of the following information:

- Client personal information
- Client diagnosis and treatment information
- Record of client visits
- Your income
- Business expenses

You can keep track of this information on paper or on your computer. If you prefer to stay with paper, visit your local office supply store and look around in the section where record-keeping systems are sold.

STORIES FROM THE REAL WORLD

If you have employees, a payroll service is a must. There is way too much to manage: making tax deposits, filing quarterly tax returns, changing deductions, and tracking unemployment compensation rates, to name a few. Our payroll service is the most cost-effective vendor we use for our practice. I wish I had discovered this five years earlier than I did. I would have spared myself a lot of headaches.

Daniel J. Abrahamson, PhD

SETTING UP AND MAINTAINING CLIENT RECORDS

It is important to have the proper forms for your practice. The proper forms can help you:

- Make your practice run efficiently
- Standardize routine procedures, such as seeing new clients
- Standardize documentation
- Comply with the rules of third parties such as MCOs and other payers, as well as with the Joint Commission on the Accreditation of Healthcare Organizations (JCAHO) and other regulator bodies

You can easily obtain a variety of helpful and customizable paper forms and software-based templates from Medical Arts Press (www.medicalarts.com or 800-328-2179), which offers a number of useful forms and organizing tools. Ask for the Mental Health Edition. (See the appendix for several sample forms.)

STANDARDIZATION MAKES FOR LESS HASSLE

Each time you join an MCO provider panel, the MCO provides forms required for clinical documentation. After signing up with many panels, you may be faced with a confusing variety of different forms that ask for basically the same information. Each MCO requires its own form, leading to a paper blizzard for the clinician to manage. Finding the right form to go with the right MCO and the proper client can become a confusing waste of time. By reviewing all the clinical forms and incorporating the necessary elements into a single form, you can streamline paperwork requirements while leaving more time and energy for clinical work and growing your practice.

As MCOs continue to shift more of the utilization management to providers, more standardization is needed to simplify the entire process. If you design your own standardized clinical documentation, you will need to get each of your MCOs to accept it. This is difficult to do, but you can accomplish this by writing, telephoning, and/or meeting with the appropriate representative of each company and obtaining approval for your form. You may have to make adjustments to your form, since each company may request unique data.

Before therapy can begin, you must attend to a few details. You must explain the details of the therapy contract and obtain information from the client. Some of the key topics to be addressed include:

- Your contract with the client
- A description of the services you provide
- When you will meet and for how long
- Your professional fees
- How the fees are to be paid
- Insurance reimbursement
- How to contact you in between sessions
- A description of what records are kept of the sessions
- Information about treating minors
- Confidentiality guidelines

A simple way to convey much of this information is to provide a form for the client to read at home after the first visit. The client can review the information, sign it, and bring it to the next session. The client should receive a copy for his or her records. If the client has any questions, he or she should ask them before signing.

The American Psychological Association Insurance Trust has a model form (see Psychotherapist-Client Contract in the appendix) that you may adapt to fit your practice. The form covers the key points listed and is quite comprehensive.

The Psychotherapist-Client Contract. The sample psychotherapist-client contract in the appendix has been prepared for two reasons.

1. It enables you to obtain informed consent from your clients (for psychologists, this is required and stated in *Ethical Principles of Psychologists and Code of Conduct*, 1992, Standard 4.02).
2. It allows you to establish a legally enforceable business relationship with the client and avoid risks of such business issues that may become the bases for malpractice suits and ethics or licensing board complaints. Full, informed consent is an ethical necessity and a good risk management strategy.

The sample form is designed for psychotherapy practices. You can modify it to include other practice areas such as psychological evaluations, testing, neuropsychological assessment, family therapy, group psychotherapy, and so on, if they are a part of your work.

There is great diversity of business practices among therapists. You should revise the contract to fit your business practices rather than adjusting your practices to fit the contract. Since regulations and laws governing institutions are different than those governing private practitioners, the forms may need modification before they can be used in hospitals, clinics, or other institutional settings.

The document includes some general language about the risks and benefits of psychotherapy, but it should be supplemented verbally or in writing by the therapist on a case-by-case basis. We chose this approach because the risks and benefits of therapy can vary considerably from case to case. It is difficult to design a single form that is appropriate for all situations. For example, it is probably important to have a more thorough discussion of risks and benefits with those clients considered most difficult or risky. If you are a group or family therapist, other issues may need to be included. You may verbally provide additional information and make a note in the record about what was said. Of course, this will not be as protective as a signed agreement, but it generally makes clinical sense.

The sample contract was originally developed for Massachusetts psychologists, but most of it can be used anywhere. There are two possible exceptions:

1. *Client access to personal records.* The sample provides sufficient alternative sections to cover almost all variations regarding record access. However, there is so much variation from state to state in laws governing privilege, confidentiality, and exceptions to both that you should edit the form to suit the laws in your state.

2. *The laws and regulations governing therapeutic confidentiality, testimonial privilege, and exceptions to these protections of the psychotherapist-client relationship.* We strongly advise you to have your own attorney review the document before you begin using it. It should comply with state and local statutes regulating the practice of psychology (or your license) and should be free of language that could be interpreted as a guarantee or implied warranty regarding the services rendered.

Informed Consent When You Work in a Practice Group.

Informed consent statements should include the following statement in order to minimize vicarious liability exposure for loosely organized groups, associations of independent practitioners, and management services organizations (MSOs) that manage maintenance and billing services:

> As you know, I work with a group of independent mental health professionals, under the name [name of practice]. This group is an association of independently practicing professionals that share certain expenses and administrative functions. While the members share a name and office space, I want you to know that I am completely independent in providing you with clinical services, and I alone am fully responsible for those services. My professional records are separately maintained and no member of the group can have access to them without your specific, written permission.

Management services organizations should include the following information bills and other official communications to consumers:

> [Name of group] is a corporation that provides administrative and management services to mental health professionals. As an independent practitioner, your provider is solely responsible for all matters concerning your clinical care, and all questions about that care should be addressed to her/him.

The preceding information was developed by American Psychological Association Insurance Trust (APAIT), 750 First Street NE, Suite 605, Washington, DC 20002-4242, phone (800) 477-1200, fax (800) 477-1268. Copyright 1998.

Initial Treatment Plan Form. The Initial Treatment Plan (see sample in the appendix) covers both the initial assessment and the treatment plan. This form is based on the Assessment Form used by MCC Behavioral Care, Inc. The form is tailored for outpatient practice, but can be modified to fit other practice models.

These are the key points on page 1 of the Initial Treatment Plan:

- The first page of the form contains the client's name, date of birth, date of referral, and date first seen.
- Other demographic data are included in a face sheet that is placed in the client's chart.
- Tracking date of referral and date first seen are occasionally requested by MCOs, as they want to know how long it takes for a client to be seen.
- The first page also includes the full diagnosis based on the criteria of the *Diagnostic and Statistical Manual of Mental Disorders* (DSM-IV; American Psychiatric Association, 1994). It is placed here so the diagnosis can easily be found in the chart by a clinical supervisor or utilization coordinator if needed.
- The narrative sections on page 1 ask the reason for seeking treatment and a description of symptoms. Some MCOs want to know, "Why now?" Others want to see the symptoms that support the diagnosis.
- The histories requested by the MCOs can be brief and usually are needed only to support the diagnosis.

These are the key points on page 2 of the Initial Treatment Plan:

- This page includes a section describing prior treatment efforts.
- You can also include the client's family history of psychiatric and alcohol and drug problems here.
- Medical history and a listing of current medications are an important part of any assessment and so are incorporated here.

- A checkoff mental status exam is also provided, so every component of the assessment is addressed.

CPT Codes. Clinical Procedure Terminology (CPT) is the coding terminology that clinicians must use when billing a third party (e.g., insurance company). These codes change periodically, so it is important to stay up-to-date with them in your practice billing forms. The American Medical Association publishes the *CPT Coding Manual.* You can access this information at www.ama-assn.org, or call (800) 621-8335.

Table 5.1 lists the most commonly used CPT codes in behavioral healthcare.

These are the key points on page 3 of the Initial Treatment Plan:

- This is the initial treatment plan. Will medication, psychological testing, or a physical examination be necessary? Most MCOs require a rationale for such interventions, so the form provides room to explain.
- You will generate a problem list along with achievable, specific, and objective goals and planned interventions. By structuring the plan

TABLE 5.1   CPT Codes

Activity	CPT Code
20–30 minutes, individual psychotherapy, office/outpatient setting	90804
With medical evaluations and management services	90805
45–50 minutes, individual psychotherapy, office/outpatient setting	90806
With medical evaluations and management services	90807
75–80 minutes, individual psychotherapy, office/outpatient setting	90808
With medical evaluations and management services	90809
20–30 minutes, individual psychotherapy, inpatient/partial hospitalization/residential setting	90816
With medical evaluations and management services	90817
45–50 minutes, individual psychotherapy, inpatient/partial hospitalization/residential setting	90818
With medical evaluations and management services	90819
75–80 minutes, individual psychotherapy, inpatient/partial hospitalization/residential setting	90821
With medical evaluations and management services	90822
Psychological testing	96100

this way, you follow the focused approach required for brief therapy, structuring treatment to help the client get maximum benefit.

- You will also specify the mode of treatment and the frequency and length of sessions.
- You will estimate the length of treatment in the "number of sessions to complete goals" line. This can be quite a challenge. While traditional psychotherapy is open-ended, with no clear ending points, you must incorporate the time-limited nature of treatment in your plan and look ahead to the termination of treatment.
- The signature and date make the plan official.

These are the key points on page 4 of the Initial Treatment Plan:

- Many clinicians want a more detailed history, so the last page, "Additional Notes," is available for this purpose.
- Another advantage to this page is confidentiality. There may be information that you do not want revealed to anyone that will be important in treatment but not needed to justify medical necessity. That information can be placed on page 4.
- This page is kept in the chart and is *not* sent to the MCO.

Client Risk Profile. The Client Risk Profile (see the appendix) is adapted from a Medco treatment plan form. Medco asked its providers to determine the level of risk that each client presented. The risk profile helps a practice manage its cases by alerting the clinical supervisors to clients who need close monitoring. Clinicians find it helpful by reminding them of the type of potential problem a client might present during the course of treatment. The form also helps monitor consultations for medications. The risk profile should be completed at the same time as the initial treatment plan.

Progress Notes. The Progress Notes form (see the appendix) helps keep both you and the client focused on goals and outcomes. The presenting problem and goal are listed at every session along with the interventions used and the client's progress to date. You should make your notes specific and focused. You must consider the client's level of risk at every session, along with a description of the risk. The treatment plan is also included to keep you focused. It also informs clinical supervisors (if you have students) of the direction of the treatment.

One way to use the plan cue is to record the client's next appointment. This can serve as a check for you or the client in case of confusion over scheduled appointments.

Listing the session length and type of service helps ensure proper billing.

Listing the visit number alerts the clinician about whether recertification is required and helps track utilization.

Client Receipt Form. The Client Receipt form (see the appendix) can be used as a receipt for the client for billing purposes, as a record of payment, and the client may submit it to his or her insurance company for reimbursement.

Treatment Update Form. In the interest of keeping paperwork at a minimum, the Treatment Update form (see the appendix) can also double as a progress note. It requests the same information as a progress note but adds a checklist to obtain continued visit certification.

Closing Summary Form. The Closing Summary form (see the appendix) includes information that you or your group practice can track to document basic outcomes data, such as the following:

- Global assessment of functioning
- Prognosis
- Length of treatment (by time and by number of sessions)
- Reasons for terminating treatment

Include your recommendations for further treatment to aid another therapist if the client returns to treatment.

While you may be focused mostly on bringing in new clients, it is also important to attend to the termination process—including terminations where the client is ready to leave treatment as well as clients who terminate prematurely. In cases where it is appropriate for a client to leave, clinical case notes generally document the termination. However, many therapists fail to properly document situations where clients leave therapy prematurely. This creates a risk for clients still in need of care, as well as posing a professional liability risk for the therapist.

For example, consider the case of the client who stops coming to therapy sessions. Months later, the client attempts suicide with a drug overdose. The client suffers brain damage. In such a case, the therapist could be sued for negligence. As a defense, the therapist could say that the client dropped out of treatment and had not been seen for the previous few months. Such a defense would not serve the therapist well because a simple subpoena of clinical notes would show the following:

- The treatment was not finished.
- The clinician had planned to see the client again for the next session.
- The therapist did not follow up to encourage the client to resume treatment or offer help in finding another therapist.

A formal letter of termination is a necessary clinical tool. First, it is important for effective liability risk management. It also indicates to the client a professional opinion that he or she still is in need of treatment (if indeed that is true) and that you would be willing to again see the client (if you indeed are) or that you could refer the client to another professional if he or she so wishes.

Note: The forms mentioned in this section were adapted from Graham, in Stout 1996, with permission from the publisher.

Record of Client Visits. You can use various software systems to keep track of client visits. An alternative is to buy a book of ledger cards.

Confidentiality. The ability to keep information private and confidential is, of course, a key element in your choice of any record-keeping system. If you track any client information by computer, it is important to make certain that information is secure.

KEEPING TRACK OF YOUR INCOME AND EXPENSES

The *Dome Bookkeeping Record* is an example of a simple, inexpensive system where you can record all expenses and income in one place. If you prefer to keep track of this on your computer, you can use software such as Quicken or Microsoft Money. You can also set up your own record-keeping formats with affordable applications such as Microsoft Works.

PRACTICE BY DESIGN: BUYING AND USING TECHNOLOGY

The latest technology can help you provide excellent client care. It can also help your practice run cost-effectively. However, Holtman (1996, p. 114) notes that "automating a bad process not only ensures that we can do a bad job every time, but we can do it faster and with less effort than before." When planning technological solutions, it is important to focus on process design and keep in mind that no technology solution can fix a bad process.

Consider the following points when you consider purchasing technology for your business (Garrity 2001, pp. 26–27):

1. *Identify gaps in the current system.* Review the operational structure of the system you are considering replacing, including design, system interfaces, manual versus automatic processes, workaround solutions. Rather than taking the time and resources to fix a fundamental problem, use newer technology to solve the problem — for example, instead of linking all computers via expensive running of cable, use a wireless router and a wireless wide area network (WAN). This is the discovery phase. Outline the process in a series of steps. For example, "How many steps are involved in completing a typical client record?" Break down each step and question everything. Find out how much you are spending to maintain your current procedure. Missing information or process-complicating steps can be identified as gaps in your operational structure.

2. *Determine the source of the gaps.* Are the performance gaps caused by systems, by procedures, or is there some other cause?

3. *Set benchmarks.* Once you understand the problems, compare your operations with those of others in similar businesses. Have other practitioners in similar practices faced the same dilemmas? Contact other practitioners directly. They will most likely be happy to share their experiences in selecting vendors and implementing new systems. This is an excellent opportunity to learn from the mistakes of others and to avoid potential pitfalls.

4. *Be flexible.* Stay open to change.

5. *Establish a buddy system.* After you choose a solution, pair up those in your practice who embrace new processes and equip-

ment with those who are less excited about learning new technology.

Remember, the purpose of technology is to simplify record keeping. Take the time and, if necessary, consult with professionals before purchasing new systems.

PRACTICE BY DESIGN: CAN YOU AFFORD TO BE ON YOUR OWN?

Part A: The Future. Take a day or two to think about the following questions. After fully considering them, write in your answers. Be realistic. You will likely refer back to this page as you consider your answers to other questions in the book. (You may also find it interesting to refer back to these questions at some point in the future to gauge how you are progressing.) *The goal of this exercise is to help you detail the critical aspects of establishing a clinical practice.*

1. What is the time by which you expect to achieve the following: ___/_____ (Identify a month and year somewhere between two and five years from now. The more specific you are, the more useful the information will be.)
2. How many days a week are you working? _____
3. How much are you grossing annually? $_____
4. How much are you netting (after professional expenses and taxes) annually? $_____
5. List the professional activities you are engaged in (*Idea Starters:* individual client sessions, groups, families, testing, evaluation, testifying, teaching, consulting, marketing, supervision, writing, etc.) and the amount of time with each in the average week:

Example: 2–14 hours of individual sessions per week
      1 psychological assessment per week (8 hours of time [testing, scoring, interpretation, and report writing])
      2 couples per week
      2 groups per week (90 minutes each = 3 hours)

3 hours marketing activities
2 hours paperwork/billings, etc.

Total: 30–32 hours/week

Hours	**Activity**
_____	_____
_____	_____
_____	_____
_____	_____
_____	_____
_____	_____
_____	_____
_____	_____
_____	Total

6. List your fees by activity and service time duration:

Example: My full fee for *individual psychotherapy* is *$125* per *50-minute session.*

My full fee for *full psychological testing battery* is *$1,500* per *evaluation.*

My full fee for *couples therapy* is *$125* per *50-minute session.*

My full fee for *group therapy* is *$45* per *90-minute session.*

My full fee for _____ is $_____ per _____.

My full fee for _____ is $_____ per _____.

My full fee for _____ is $_____ per _____.

My full fee for _____ is $_____ per _____.

My full fee for _____ is $_____ per _____.

My full fee for _____ is $_____ per _____.

My full fee for _____ is $_____ per _____.

Part B: The Present. Now do the exact same exercise, but for *today,* not for some point in the future. If you are already in full- or part-time private practice, just list your averages. If you are not yet in practice, list your most conservative and realistic estimates of what your numbers will be when you start your practice.

1. What is today's date? ____/_____
2. How many days a week are you working? _____
3. How much are you grossing annually? $_____
4. How much are you netting (after professional expenses and taxes) annually? $_____
5. List the professional activities you are currently engaged in:

Example: 6 hours of individual sessions per week

1 psychological assessment per month (8 hours of time [testing, scoring, interpretation, and report writing])

1 couple per week

1 group per week (90 minutes)

8 hours marketing activities

4 hours paperwork/billings, etc.

Hours   **Activity**

_____   _____

_____   _____

_____   _____

_____   _____

_____   _____

_____   _____

_____   _____

_____   _____

_____   Total

6. List your current fees by activity and service time duration:

Example: My full fee for *individual psychotherapy* is *$75* per *50-minute session.*

My full fee for *full psychological testing battery* is *$700* per *evaluation.*

My full fee for *couples therapy* is *$75* per *50-minute session.*
My full fee for *group therapy* is *$20* per *90-minute session.*

My full fee for _____ is $_____ per _____.

My full fee for _____ is $_____ per _____.

My full fee for _____ is $_____ per _____.

My full fee for _____ is $_____ per _____.

My full fee for _____ is $_____ per _____.

My full fee for _____ is $_____ per _____.

My full fee for _____ is $_____ per _____.

Take a look at how close (or far apart) A and B are. This is an indication of how close (or far away) *you* are from having your desired practice. Continue reading for ideas on how to narrow the gap.

DO THE MATH: PRODUCTIVITY AND REVENUE

The hypothetical situation shown in Tables 5.2 and 5.3 builds on the examples in the previous exercise to fill in the blanks.

At first glance, the projected total amount shown in Table 5.3 may sound quite sizable. However, keep in mind that the projected figures are *gross* revenues and *gross* income. This means that in order to calculate what will actually go in your pocket, you must also factor in expenses (rent, utilities, etc.) and other costs such as missed appoint-

TABLE 5.2   Current Weekly Productivity and Revenues

Activity	Productivity	Gross Income
Individual therapy	6 @ $75	$450
Psychological assessment	.25* @ $175	$175
Couples therapy	1 @ $75	$75
Group therapy	1 @ 5 @ $20†	$100
Marketing	N/A	0
Paperwork/billings	N/A	0
Total weekly gross income		$800 (or $3,200/month or $38,400 annually)

*This is based on *one* psychological assessment per *month,* hence .25 is used to calculate a weekly figure.
†One group with five members each paying $20

94

TABLE 5.3   Projected Weekly Productivity and Revenues

Activity	Productivity	Gross Income
Individual therapy	13 @ $125	$1,625
Psychological assessments	1 @ $1,500	$1,500
Couples therapy	2 @ $125	$250
Group therapy	2 @ 7 @ $45*	$630
Marketing	N/A	0
Paperwork/billings	N/A	0
Total weekly gross income		$4,005 (or $16,020/month, or $192,240 annually)

*Two groups with seven members, each paying $45.

ments, vacation time away from the practice, bad debt, and so on. These factors will be addressed later in this chapter.

PRACTICE BY DESIGN: FIND THE GAP AND NARROW IT

Look back at the exercise you have just completed. When you compare the future (Part A) to the present (Part B), you can address how close (or far off) you are for each item. For example:

- You may be productive in terms of clinical hours and productivity but miss the mark in terms of gross income. If this is the case, you may want to consider increasing your fees (see Chapter 4).
- If you find a discrepancy between gross and net income, you should take a look at your operating costs and overhead expenses (also see Chapter 4).

Let's take a line-by-line look at how you can maximize your income. Refer to the six questions you answered on worksheet, Part A, as you analyzed the *present* state of your practice.

Line 3 deals with annual gross revenues.
Line 4 deals with annual net income.
Line 5 deals with productivity.
Line 6 deals with fees.

If:	*Then the problem likely is:*	*So consider doing this:*

Line 3 is high
Line 4 is low
Line 5 is high
Line 6 is high
  or okay
	Expenses, overhead,
	  and/or taxes
		Critically examine your
		  costs. If your gross
		  income is quite high,
		  also seek the advice
		  of a tax expert.

Line 3 is low
Line 4 is low
  (based on line3)
Line 5 is okay or
  high
Line 6 is low
	Case mix, fee structure,
	  and/or bad debt
		Examine your mix of
		  payors (managed care,
		  sliding scale, bad
		  debt, etc.)
		Consider increasing fees,
		  decreasing bad debt
		  and write-offs,
		  decreasing the number
		  of reduced-fee clients
		  while increasing the
		  number of full-fee
		  clients.

Line 3 is low
Line 4 is low
  (based on line 3)
Line 5 is low
Line 6 is okay
	Productivity
	  and/or activity
	  mix
		Increase marketing
		  activities; conduct an
		  analysis of your
		  activity mix.

Line 3 is low
Line 4 is low
  (based on line 3)
Line 5 is low
Line 6 is high
	Overpriced in
	  the market
	  and/or low
	  productivity
		Examine your
		  fees vis-à-vis
		  the local marketplace;
		  consider reducing
		  fees (but ensure that
		  costs plus profit are
		  covered); increase
		  marketing to increase
		  client flow/
		  productivity.

Line 3 is high
Line 4 is high
Line 5 is low or
  okay
Line 6 is high
	No problem, yet
	  (is your fee structure
	  sustainable in differing
	  market conditions?)
		Examine your vision
		  of current pricing in
		  the context of
		  marketplace
		  predictions.

If:	*Then the problem likely is:*	*So consider doing this:*
		For example, is there any concern that managed care may further penetrate your market and thus place you at risk for declining referrals? If so, what can you do now to prepare for this?

You will learn more about these issues in the next few pages, but first let's Do the Math on some hypothetical situations to get a better feel for how varying factors can affect your bottom line.

Knowing where to focus your time and energy is critical. For example, let's say that your income is inadequate, although you are quite busy with plenty of full-fee clients. In this case, it would *not* make sense to increase your marketing efforts. Instead, it would be better to work on improving cash flow with more efficient billing procedures and claims management.

The following five examples illustrate how to apply these concepts to a variety of situations.

EXAMPLE 1

If your . . .	*Is . . .*
Gross revenue	High
Annual net income	Low
Clinical productivity	High
Activities	High
Fees	Acceptable
	↓

Then you should . . .
Check overhead expenses.
Seek the advice of a qualified accountant to look for ways to minimize taxes.

EXAMPLE 2

If your . . .	*Is . . .*
Gross revenue	Low
Annual net income	Low
Clinical productivity	Acceptable or high
Average fee	Low
	↓

Then you should . . .
Examine your case mix.*
Review your fee structure.
Review all bad debt and
   uncollectible fees.

*To examine your case mix, do the following:

1. Review the number of clients you see for reduced fees (managed care, sliding scale, etc.)
2. Consider the feasibility of restructuring your client mix.
3. Consider increasing your usual and customary fees.
4. Look for ways to reduce the number of cases for which you will not be paid.
5. Assess the costs versus the benefits of seeing reduced-fee and sliding-scale clients.
6. Set a limit on the extent to which you are willing to lower fees.
7. Develop marketing plans to increase the number of full-fee, private-pay clients.

EXAMPLE 3

If your . . .	*Is . . .*
Gross revenue	Low
Annual net income	Low
Clinical productivity	Low
Average fee	Acceptable
	↓

Then you should . . .
Review clinical productivity and
   look for ways to increase.

Increase marketing activity to generate new referrals and increase revenue.

Review activity mix and increase the most profitable (psychological evaluations or court consultations) and decrease the least profitable (individual therapy sessions at sliding-scale rates).

EXAMPLE 4

If your . . .	*Is . . .*
Gross revenue	Low
Annual net income	Low
Clinical productivity	Low
Average fee	High
	↓

Then you should . . .

Review your average fee; you are most likely overpriced for your market.

Look for ways to minimize expenses.

Increase marketing activity to generate new referrals and increase revenue.

Review activity mix and increase the most profitable and decrease the least profitable.

EXAMPLE 5

If your . . .	*Is . . .*
Gross revenue	High
Annual net income	High
Clinical productivity	Acceptable or low

If your . . .
Average fee

Is . . .
High
↓

Then you should . . .
Even though all is well, be
  prepared for shifts in your
  marketplace.
If you have a direct contract with
  a local business, a business
  downturn or merger could result
  in a termination of your
  contract that leaves you
  high and dry.
Monitor the general business
  climate of the companies with
  whom you do most of
  your business.

MANAGEMENT METRICS: MAXIMIZE STRENGTH AND MINIMIZE WEAKNESS

There are a few key metrics (measures) that you should keep close tabs
on for two important reasons: (1) to maximize the current functioning of
your practice and (2) to discover its strengths and potential areas of
weakness. These metrics include payor mix, activity mix, clinical productivity, return on investment (ROI), and quality of referral.

EVALUATING YOUR PAYOR MIX

Payor mix refers to the variety of payor sources you may have in your
practice. These typically will include:

Payor Sources
Third-party payers

Examples
Managed care organizations, or
  MCOs (e.g., Magellan,
  ValueOptions)

	Health maintenance organizations, or HMOs (e.g., Rush HMO, Prudential HMO)
	Third-party administrators, or TPAs (e.g., Prairie States)
	Traditional indemnity payers (e.g., insurance companies like Blue Cross/Blue Shield)
Direct payment	Clients who pay you directly (out of pocket) at the time of service. This could be at your full (usual and customary) fee, at a negotiated reduced-fee rate, and/or at your sliding-scale rate.
Contracted services	Direct contracts with businesses, hospitals, and the like.

Table 5.4 shows an example of how you can analyze your payor mix. List the various payors in the left column and evaluate each according to the factors along the top of the chart.

EVALUATING YOUR ACTIVITY MIX

Activity mix is the combination of the various types of services you provide. These could include any of the following:

Individual psychotherapy
Initial evaluations
Group psychotherapy
Couples therapy
Family therapy
Psychological testing
Neuropsychological testing
Psychosocial evaluations
Social histories
Disability evaluation
Mental status examinations

Psychiatric evaluations
Medication management
Business coaching
Personal coaching
Supervision
Consultation
Speaking
Writing

TABLE 5.4   Payor Mix Analysis

Payment Type	Service: CPT 90806 Fees	Mean Client Flow*	Mean Number of Total Sessions	Mean Monthly Income	Hassle Factor[†]
U&C private pay	$100	3	15	$1,200	Low
MCO 1	$85	5	10	$1,700	High
MCO 2	$90	2	5	$720	Low
MCO 3	$75	5	8	$1,500	Okay
MCO 4	$75	5	10	$1,500	Okay
Sliding-scale private pay	$65	3	15	$780	Okay

*The average number of clients in your practice at any point in time.
[†]Hassle factors:
Okay = Paperwork is manageable and billing is normal.
Low = Prompt payment, little hassle, minimal paperwork.
High = High hassle factor examples

MCO issues	• The MCO has a utilization review department that is difficult to connect with.
	• There is a long accounts receivable process even when you present a clean claim (i.e., error-free and complete claim form).
	• The MCO is notorious for giving too few sessions regardless of clinical justified need.
	• The MCO is too prescriptive.
	• The MCO demands too much unnecessary paperwork.
U&C or sliding-scale private-pay client issues	• Long aging of accounts.
	• Clients manipulative regarding payments.
	• Present various other hassles.

(Feel free to alter or create your own metrics for the hassle factor.)

Evaluating Clinical Productivity

Clinical productivity is the frequency (and time) involved in the various clinical activities in your activity mix. Each activity consumes a different amount of time. For example, medication management may only be 15 minutes; group psychotherapy may be 90 minutes; psychological testing may take two to three hours to administer and then many more hours in scoring, interpretation, report writing, and so on. Thus, you may want to evaluate the amount of time you spend on activities that actually generate income. For example, for a psychiatrist, four 15-minute medication management sessions are much more productive (and thus lucrative) than one 60-minute therapy session. For a psychologist or other therapist, one 90-minute group session with 10 clients, each paying $25, generates more income than one individual therapy session at $125.

Measuring Return on Investment (ROI)

Return on investment refers to the return (payback) on your investment of time and/or money in practice-building activities. For example, you may find that it takes you just as much preparation and presentation time to lecture at a national professional conference as it does to participate in grand rounds (a periodic opportunity for specialists to lecture to peers of similar and like disciplines; for example, a neuropsychologist lectures to neurologists and neurosurgeons, or a family therapist lectures to pediatric specialists) at a local hospital, but you find that you get many more referrals from the grand rounds than the national conference. You should examine your ROI for all activities, including newsletters, mailings, websites, phone directory ads, and so on. This will help you make better decisions about how to spend your marketing dollars (see Chapter 8).

Table 5.5 shows how you can calculate the ROI of your marketing activities.

Evaluating the Quality of Your Referrals

Quality of referral is a measure of how appropriate your referred clients are vis-à-vis the services you offer. If you receive a high number of child therapy referrals but you provide only ADHD evaluations, you must

TABLE 5.5   Calculating the ROI of Your Marketing Program

Activities in the Past Month	Number of Referrals in the Past Month	Resulting Average Gross Revenues	Cost*	ROI	Decision
Website maintenance and updates	2	2 clients @ $125/hr @ 4×/month = $1,000	$100/month	+$900	Keep doing
Direct mail newsletter	0	0	$2,000 printing, $150 list, $750 postage, 6 hours of my time valued @ $70 = $420	−$3,320	Stop doing
Presentation at SPA annual meeting on treating obesity	0	0	$175 registration, $25 parking, 3 hours preparation valued @ $70 = $210, 6 hours of lost billable clinical hours @ $100 = $600	−$1,010	Keep doing for national exposure to peer group, networking, CV development, and giving back to the profession
Grand rounds at ABC General Hospital on treating obesity	6	5 clients @ $100/hr @ 4×/month = $2,000	$15 parking, 3 hours preparation valued @ $70 = $210, 6 hours of lost billable clinical hours @ $100 = $600	+$1,175	Keep doing

refer those clients to another therapist. An analysis of the quality of your referrals should also include a referred client's ability to pay. This is important, for example, if you receive many referrals of clients who cannot afford your fees or who are covered by MCOs for which you are not a provider. Such referrals will inevitably result in clients who leave therapy before they have completed their treatment.

Let's look at how variations in each of these areas can influence the success of your practice. Table 5.6 shows an example.

TABLE 5.6   **Referral Analysis Worksheet**

Referral Source	Average Number of Monthly Referrals	Appropriateness of the Type of Case Referred	Ability to pay (Non-Managed Care)	Appropriateness of MCO Network	Adequate Length of Care	Overall Quality of Referral
Dr. Jeff Smith, pediatrician	3	Good for the most part	Very good, all pay U&C promptly w/o use of MC or sliding scale	N/A	Yes	Very good
Dr. Liz Steele, child psychiatrist	4	Mixed	N/A, all managed care	Yes	Okay, but much UR to deal with	Good/okay
Dr. Joy Hersh, pediatric neurologist	1	Okay	Varies, but many need sliding scale	When MCO payor, paneled provider	Okay, mostly evaluations	Okay
Ms. Mary Jones	6	Good	Varies, but many need sliding scale	Some need referral to appropriate MCO provider	Okay	Good

105

"Balance your billable time with marketing time. Being too busy with billable work is as dangerous as being nonbillable. If you're always busy working, you're not out there maintaining your network, writing your articles, and hosting your seminars. You're invisible except to current clients, which means outside forces could rob you of your seeming success."

Sarah White, *Marketing Basics*.

Minimize Risk

When you are in almost any profession, you can be sued even when you have done nothing illegal or unethical. This is certainly true in the mental health profession. Every person who offers mental health services has liability risk. This chapter will help you identify and prevent legal and ethical pitfalls in your clinical practice and provide guidelines for responding to a lawsuit.

UNDERSTANDING THE LAW

Each branch of the mental health field (psychologists, marriage and family therapists, counselors, social workers, etc.) is governed by its own set of legal and ethical principles. In addition, each state has its own laws and guidelines for each of these professional groups. While it is impossible to outline all of these rules here, it is critical that you understand the laws that govern your license in your state. Be aware of these critical areas so you can minimize risk:

- Advertising
- Confidentiality
- Consent to treatment
- Dangerous patients
- Disclosure
- Dual relationships
- Informed consent
- Insurance

- Legislation
- Psychotherapist-patient privilege
- Record keeping
- Scope of competence
- Scope of practice
- State licensing requirements
- Therapist-patient sex

Stay informed of the laws and guidelines by reading the publications and visiting the websites of your professional association and state licensing board on a regular basis. The largest associations in the United States are as follows:

American Academy of Child and Adolescent Psychiatry (www .AACAP.org)
American Art Therapy Association (www.arttherapy.org)
American Association for Marriage and Family Therapy (www .AAMFT.org)
American Association of Pastoral Counselors (www.AAPC.org)
American Counseling Association (www.counseling.org)

American Medical Association (www.ama-assn.org)
American Mental Health Counselors Association (www.AMHCA.org)
American Psychiatric Association (www.psych.org)
American Psychiatric Nurses Association (www.APNA.org)
American Psychological Association (www.APA.org)
California Association of Marriage and Family Therapists (www .CAMFT.org)
National Association of Social Workers (www.NASWdc.org)

DEFENDING YOURSELF

For mental health practitioners, the cost of mounting a legal defense can easily be $100,000. This amount represents the cost of the defense and does not include a judgment.

MOST FREQUENT CLAIMS AGAINST MENTAL HEALTH PRACTITIONERS

Table 6.1 shows the types of claims that are made against mental health practitioners. *Occurrence* is the frequency of the alleged offense (sexual misconduct comprises 19 percent of the cases). When a therapist is sued for a given offense, the *percent of losses* column shows percentage of cases lost (50 percent of sexual misconduct claims are lost).

TABLE 6.1   Claims against Mental Health Practitioners

Claim	% of Occurrences	% of Losses
Sexual misconduct	19	50
Incorrect treatment	15	13
Loss from evaluation	11	5
Breach of confidentiality	7	3
Incorrect diagnosis	6	6
Suicide-related claims	6	11
Defamation: libel/slander	4	<2
Loss of child custody and visitation	3	<2
Improper meeting of clients	2	<2

Note: Reported in VandeCreek and Stout (1993).

The Triple Crown of Lawsuits

Clinicians are at risk for the "triple crown" of lawsuits when three things go wrong in the process of working with a client:

1. First, there's a misdiagnosis.
2. This leads to a failure to treat (because the treatment plan was based on an erroneous diagnosis).
3. A failure to refer follows (e.g., misdiagnosing a thyroid dysfunction as major depression and treating it with cognitive therapy instead of referring the client to a physician).

Because clinical judgment and diagnostic ability are the most critical aspects of accurate treatment planning, making a diagnostic error amplifies the risk of liability. "Where there's a trauma, there's a tort" has long been a saying in forensic practice. In the mental health field, you might add to that, "Where there's a disgruntled client, there's a risk."

Practice by Design: Client Risk Factors

One way to minimize risk is to pay attention to warning signs. Kull (1989) lists the following 10 warning signs that may indicate liability risks:

- A disgruntled client
- A dissatisfied family
- A deteriorating client-clinician relationship
- Adverse reports from a client representative (in some inpatient treatment units)
- A dissatisfied payor
- A routine outpatient review that challenges the comprehensiveness and appropriateness of diagnosis and treatment
- Medication errors
- Incomplete medical records
- Clients whose behaviors violate hospital procedures for passes, privileges, unauthorized leave, and other activities
- Incident reports, or injuries occurring while hospitalized (a slip and fall, infection, etc.)

PROFESSIONAL LIABILITY INSURANCE

It is essential for all clinicians to have adequate liability insurance coverage. In recent years, insurance carriers have developed many new plans, but they have also created a bit of confusion. The American Psychological Association's Insurance Trust (APAIT) has developed a guide for clinicians in selecting an insurer and a plan. You may obtain the guide by calling APAIT at (800) 477-1200, or visit www.APAIT.org. Other professional organizations have information about liability insurance as well.

Two Types of Liability Insurance Coverage

Claims-made coverage provides coverage as long as your payments are up-to-date and coverage is in force. If you terminate coverage and are sued later by a client whom you treated while you were insured, you would not be covered. However, you can buy what is called a *tail*, which allows you to pay a percentage (usually 175 percent) of your previous year's premium to be covered forever after for every client seen during the time of your claims-made coverage.

Occurrence coverage provides coverage for all of your cases while you are insured and forever thereafter, even when you are no longer paying premiums. You are covered forever for all clients seen during the time you were covered.

MANAGED CARE RISKS: DUTY TO APPEAL

Legal case precedents and clinical and legal responsibilities resulting from managed care utilization review procedures are a growing threat. Numerous legal cases (e.g., *Wickline v. State of California, Warren v. Colonial Penn Franklin Insurance Company, Hughes v. Blue Cross of Northern California, Harrell v. Total Health Care, Inc., Raglin v. HMO Illinois, Inc., Boyd v. Albert Einstein Medical Center,* and *Wilson v. Blue Cross of California*) support the opinion that the clinician is responsible for determining the course of treatment. This means that *if something goes wrong, you will most likely be held responsible.*

This risk-laden position led to Applebaum's (1993) discussion of a clinician's *duty to appeal.* This idea holds that the clinician must take steps to appeal any decision or utilization review that he or she believes is not in the best interest of the client.

Applebaum notes that "clinicians can discharge their fiduciary [in trust] obligations to clients only by seeking to persuade others to approve [certain services for] that case" (p. 253). This does *not* mean that the decision must be overturned before the clinician's risk is lessened. It just means that the clinician has to exert appropriate effort to try to appeal the decision. This is not necessarily a difficult task, since many clinicians have appealed utilization reviewers' decisions in the past, and most clinicians feel comfortable in the role of client advocate.

PRACTICE BY DESIGN: INSURANCE FRAUD RISKS

Perhaps one of the most common pitfalls in clinical practice is unclear documentation regarding who actually conducted a clinical procedure or, if testing was conducted, who interpreted the results and who authored the report. There is no risk of fraudulent billing when a licensed and appropriately trained clinician conducts all of these procedures. Problems arise when students, interns, or psychometricians conduct the testing and/or author the report and when their role is not clearly disclosed on the billing statement or report.

Therapists can avoid accusations of fraudulent billing or unethical practices by making detailed notations of who did what in the clinical situation and by signing the report as the *supervisor* of the author (not as the author). (Supervising a student or technician is fine; it's the issue of billing inappropriately that creates insurance fraud risk.)

PRACTICE BY DESIGN: RECOMMENDATIONS FOR DOCUMENTATION

Because a clinician can never be certain that a report, data, or file may not be used against him or her in litigation, it is important to keep the following recommendations in mind:

1. Never, under any circumstances, alter a client's record or report. Not only is it illegal and unethical to alter client records, it is usually futile to try. Since the 1980s, the Internal Revenue Service has required that inks manufactured in the United States be formulated with trace chemicals that vary from year to year. A simple forensic chemical analysis of a written document can pin

down, with considerable certainty, when it was written (and whether it was later altered). Electronic or computer-based files are also easily evaluated for authenticity or alteration. (Some addenda are appropriate if they are written in a legitimate and timely fashion.)

2. Some things are not appropriate to include in a report, file, or clinical note. Taboo topics (Bales 1987; Kull 1989; Negley 1985; Soisson, VandeCreek, and Knapp 1987) include:

   - Hunches
   - Value judgments
   - Emotional statements by the clinician (e.g., "The client's mood today was quite trying/upsetting/infuriating")
   - Personal opinions that are irrelevant to diagnosis or treatment
   - Illegal behavior (on the client's part) that is not homicidal or suicidal
   - Sexual practices that are irrelevant to the clinical picture
   - Sensitive information that holds little clinical utility and that could, if made public (via court order or proceeding), embarrass or cause harm to the client or others

PRACTICE BY DESIGN: RECORD-KEEPING GUIDELINES

Some managed care companies require you to provide information about clients, thus raising concerns about breaching confidentiality. It is important to carefully review contracts and consent forms for information about releasing information to a managed care company or to a utilization reviewer (clinical evaluations, psychological testing reports, computer-generated reports, etc.).

The American Psychological Association (APA) recommends that clinicians keep their records of all cases, including raw data and notes, for at least three years. The APA also recommends that you keep a summary of each record for 12 years.

It is our recommendation that you keep the entire test record, including raw data, indefinitely. The statute of limitations does not actually start ticking until it is clear to the client that harm has been done. In an extreme example, 20 years could pass and a clinician could then be involved in a suit. Having archived records could mean the difference

Cummings and Sobel (1985) noted a case in which a therapist was sued by the son of a woman he had treated some 20 years before. The son claimed that the therapist had ruined his childhood because the therapist was unable to successfully treat the mother's depression. The therapist had never seen or treated the plaintiff.

between being prepared and being in trouble. The volume of materials versus available storage space and costs may require some special arrangements for off-premises archiving.

Practice by Design: Exceptions to Confidentiality

Therapists must maintain client confidentiality in order to protect the client's right to privacy. Most states clearly spell out the parameters for confidentiality, but there are several exceptions. For example:

1. *Workers' compensation law.* This law supersedes mental health law in most states. The reason is best explained with an example. If a workers' compensation claim is lodged against an employer for something that has involved psychological testing, the employer's not having access to the report would be the same as a denial of the employer's constitutional right to prepare a defense (i.e., due process).

2. *Client request.* If a client requests a copy of any type of test report, you may release it to him or her. This does not include raw test data or any type of personal notes per se. (It is unethical to release any type of raw test data to anyone who is not properly trained to be able to interpret those data.)

   Some people consider computer-generated reports to be a form of raw data and not the same as completed psychological reports. The best policy is not to release a copy of a computer test report to the client or to untrained clinical individuals.

3. *Consent of the client.* This varies from a request in that a client can offer consent for a psychological report, or any part of a clinical record, to be sent to a third party. It may not be in the client's

best interest, and the clinician can make that known to the client. Nevertheless, the client has the final say regarding any reports sent out with that client's consent.

4. *Laws requiring disclosure.* In certain circumstances, state law mandates breach of confidentiality. For example, child abuse or elder abuse must be reported. In Illinois, it is a Class A misdemeanor if a clinician has not reported suspicion, evidence, or allegations of any type of child abuse to the appropriate authorities within 24 hours of learning of it.

5. *Medicare and Medicaid laws.* These laws supersede confidentiality acts for reporting of information.

6. *If the client is a litigant.* If a lawsuit is filed against a clinician, the client cannot claim that confidentiality has been breached when the clinician must disclose information relevant to his or her defense of the suit.

7. *Duty-to-warn or duty-to-protect laws.* Although not every state recognizes the Tarasoff ruling established in California, most states have a duty-to-warn law. These laws state that a clinician must inform the target if a client reports a homicidal ideation. Similarly, duty-to-protect laws require informing appropriate individuals that an identified client is perhaps homicidal or suicidal and that measures may need to be taken for involuntary hospitalization.

8. *Future criminal behavior.* This is a remarkably vague area and is potentially a legal minefield for clinicians. A clinician is best advised to rely on duty-to-warn and duty-to-protect concepts (such as the Tarasoff doctrine) when a client is likely to exhibit future criminal behavior that may create risk of harm to other individuals or self-harm to the client. You may encounter this situation if you have clients who sell and distribute drugs and who are being tested or are in treatment for drug or substance abuse. If it is difficult to predict a client's future criminal behavior, it is strongly recommended that you seek clinical consultation and legal advice.

9. *Any type of emergency.* If an individual is in need of immediate medical care, or if there is a medical emergency or a need for commitment procedures, the situation takes precedence over confidentiality concerns.

10. *Within the context of supervision.* Most laws allow individuals in a supervisor-supervisee relationship to share confidential client information.

11. *Court order.* This intervention varies from state to state.
    - Some states require breaching confidentiality at the subpoena level if accompanied by a valid client consent.
    - Some states do not allow release of information in response to a subpoena unless it is accompanied by a signed client consent.
    - In some states, the only circumstance in which a record can be released is when a court order is obtained. In effect, it is a subpoena signed by a judge.

12. *Federal grand jury subpoena.* If a client is the focus of an investigation and a clinician's records are judged to have possible bearing in the matter, then this type of subpoena may be issued. The clinician must release what is requested.

13. *IRS subpoena.* As with a federal grand jury subpoena, if the IRS suspects that a client is conducting illegal tax activities, and if the clinician has information relevant to the investigation, records must be released.

PRACTICE BY DESIGN: PLACE HIGH VALUE ON CLIENT SATISFACTION AND AVOID TROUBLE

Every smart businessperson understands that it is important to have satisfied customers. Even though the mental health business is unique in many ways, it is your job to help clients achieve their goals. Look for ways to actively seek feedback and let clients know that their opinions and perspectives are valued.

Several writers (Bales 1987; Kull 1989; Negley 1985; Soisson et al. 1987) have recommended ways to maximize your clients' satisfaction and avoid lawsuits. Some of these points may be at odds with your clinical orientation, but they will help you stay out of court:

- Clarify clinical procedures and activities. Note the risks and rewards of treatment. Where clinically appropriate, encourage the client to actively participate in treatment.
- Understand your own personal limits and expertise. Do not practice

outside of your professional scope. Refer clients to other professionals when appropriate.

- Consult periodically with colleagues on difficult cases. Note the consultation in the clinical record but maintain client confidentiality and anonymity.
- Stay up-to-date with current practices and diagnostic techniques. Incompetence is never an acceptable defense.
- Ask the client for feedback about ways to improve his or her satisfaction with the treatment experience.
- Keep complete, accurate, appropriate notes. Never alter them after the fact.
- Obtain informed consent from the client if he or she is competent, or from a guardian if the client is judged incompetent.
- When any unusual incidents occur involving your clients, discuss them thoroughly and openly. Keep a record of the incident and what you did about it.
- Pay close attention to your attitude and communication with the client. Pay equal attention to the client's attitude and communication with you.
- Be cautious with any client who responds or reacts in the extreme, either positively or negatively.
- Avoid making personal disclosures in conversations with clients.
- Avoid touching your clients.
- Do not try to collect on past-due bills with borderline clients.
- If you need to talk to a client's previous therapists or obtain past reports or clinical notes, obtain the client's written consent before doing so.
- Document all diagnostic decisions and rationales for ruling out certain diagnoses.
- Use extreme caution in the evaluation or treatment of clients diagnosed with repressed traumatic memories, posttraumatic stress disorder (PTSD), borderline personality disorder (BPD), dissociative personality disorder (DPD), paranoia or paranoid-dependent personality disorder, personality disorders, or sexual problems.
- Take notes and write reports as if they will someday be read as evidence for the prosecution.
- Retain records forever.

PRACTICE BY DESIGN: TIPS FOR AVOIDING MALPRACTICE SUITS WHEN TESTING

Malpractice issues obviously do not lie solely in the domain of treatment. Pope and Vasquez (1991) note that "figures compiled by the APA Insurance Trust comprising all malpractice suits closed over a twelve-year period indicate that incompetent or improper assessment techniques are the fifth most frequent cause of suits against clinicians, accounting for about 3.7 percent of the total costs and about 5.4 percent of the total number of claims" (p. 2). Pope offers these seven recommendations to help mitigate clinician risk in evaluation or testing situations:

1. Keep current; failure to do so can lead to malpractice.
2. Make certain that the client's reading level is adequate for the instrument.
3. The norms commonly used with a test may not fit a particular assessment task or client. This may or may not be due to the client's cultural and/or linguistic background.
4. Test administration must be adequately monitored.
5. Standardized tests should be used in a standardized manner. Cutting corners can impact the test's validity.
6. Factors that may affect the meaning of test findings must be formally reported. For example, "The client was 30 minutes late due to a flat tire," or "There was construction noise outside that was distracting." If the situation is too upsetting, testing should be rescheduled, if possible.
7. Test results are hypotheses, never final edicts. Findings should help inform treatment planning.

PRACTICE BY DESIGN: WHAT TO DO IF A SUIT IS FILED AGAINST YOU

As noted earlier, there is not always a correlation between wrongdoing and lawsuits. Some clinicians who have done nothing wrong may find themselves in the awkward, upsetting role of defendant. *Psychotherapy Finances* (February 1994) recommends the following steps:

1. Recognize this is a common occurrence.
2. Don't panic, but don't underreact, either.
3. Contact your attorney.
4. Contact your liability insurance carrier.
5. Follow their instructions precisely.
6. Do not talk about it to others—period. Although this may seem antithetical to clinicians not to share, lawsuits become public quickly enough, and loose talk can damage your reputation. Moreover, the friends you speak with could be brought into court as plaintiff's witnesses if you have given them details relevant to the case. Keep in mind that from the time you are served until the case is resolved or ruled on, anything you say can and will be brought into the courtroom by the plaintiff's attorney.
7. Collect all records that relate to the case, including files, calendars, clinical notes, reports, raw data, billing records, and so forth.
8. Never alter anything.
9. Develop a witness list for the attorney, not you, to follow up on.
10. Do not go to the plaintiff and attempt to work things out. This usually backfires and only makes things worse.
11. Be prepared for the long haul to get to the case's end. It sometimes takes years.

HOW TO RESPOND TO AN INVESTIGATION

Every clinician faces the risk of litigation. Although the steps outlined in this chapter will help reduce the risk of lawsuits, nothing can fully ensure that a claim will never be filed against you. Therefore, it is important to know what to do should an investigation be initiated against you. Crick (1990) has outlined the following 10 steps (pp. 4 to 5, reprinted with permission):

1. Do not provide any information via telephone. Even with caller ID technology, it is not possible to know exactly who is on the other end of the line. It is best to limit all communications to any opposing party to either written correspondence or in person.

2. Verify the identity of the investigator and the agency. Ask for some type of identification (a business card, badge, identification card, or driver's license). Find out the position or title of the person (server, investigator, attorney, state employee, etc.).

3. Determine if you are the focus of the investigation. You may be involved as a witness, not the ultimate defendant.
   - If you are the focus of the investigation, seek legal counsel before responding to any questions.
   - If you are not the focus of investigation, ask for a letter (or some type of document) stating this fact.

4. Ask to have another person present in the interview.

5. Try to learn exactly what the inquiry or investigation is about. If at any time you feel that you are at risk in any way, stop the interview and consult your attorney.

6. Never lie. If you are unsure or do not know the answer to a question, do not answer with an assumption. If you are unsure about something, just say so. You may feel that every question should be answerable, but not all are. Do not feel pushed into a corner and do not think that a little lie will not come back to haunt you.

7. If at any time during the investigation you are told "you have the right to remain silent," do so, and immediately obtain legal counsel. You have just been given a Miranda warning and are subject to criminal investigation procedures. It would be best to avoid saying anything more until your counsel arrives. You may ask if you are free to go or if you are under arrest.

8. If you are the focus of investigation, unless instructed otherwise by counsel, do the following:
   - Do *not* provide original or copies of any documents, files, notes, etc., unless you have been served with a court order or a search warrant.
   - Do *not* identify, acknowledge, or provide comment or opinion on any documents shown to you.
   - Do *not* provide or sign any written statements.

9. If any documents, computers, disks, or other materials are seized by a court order or search warrant, obtain a detailed receipt for them.

10. Be wary of any so-called informal or informational conferences you are asked to attend. Specifically ask the nature, structure, intent of the meeting, and who else is to be attending.

PRACTICE BY DESIGN: THINGS TO REMEMBER IF YOU ARE ACCUSED OF WRONGDOING

- *Use your attorney.* If you are accused of malpractice or unethical conduct, you may have strong feelings of panic and fear. However, the opposing party may misjudge your emotional responses as signs of guilt. Therefore it is important to work through an attorney, since he or she is trained to be your advocate.
- *Understand the law.* It is different from psychology or science in its approach to arriving at truth. In science, it is presumed that truth is discovered through replicability and probability (e.g., 95 percent certainty, or $p = 0.05$). In law, a truth of the past 50 years may change tomorrow via a new case precedent.
- *Protect yourself.* The adversarial process of law is alien to the collaborative, compromising, consensus-seeking style of most clinicians. Although it is natural to seek emotional support during an ordeal such as a lawsuit, always remember that any conversation may be introduced as testimony in court. As unfair as this seems, it is a distinct possibility, and you must safeguard yourself.
- *Be assertive.* If you face a legal threat, you must react strongly. Immediately assume a fact-finding, defensive posture. Frivolous cases are more quickly quashed with immediate, strong, defensive responses.
- *Stay in ongoing supervision.* It is always a good idea to participate in a supervisory or peer review process from which you can gather feedback, new ideas, and suggestions from peers or a mentor. Being involved in such a group or relationship enables you to obtain outside perspectives and be alert to early warning signs for high-risk cases. If a case becomes a legal problem, your documentation of other professionals' input can provide valuable support for your clinical and diagnostic decisions. Such documentation should focus only on the clients' circumstances and not their identities.

- *Know your stuff.* It is important to be able to justify (if ever necessary) all of your diagnostic decisions. This means that you must have adequate *general* training in psychopathology and diagnostics as well as *specific* knowledge of the types of clients you normally see (children, substance abusers, people with medical issues, etc.). It is important to have thorough knowledge of the DSM-IV and be able to verbalize a differential diagnostic process and a theoretical orientation.
- *Maintain appropriate limits, boundaries, and roles.* Although most clinicians are friendly, warm, and empathic, they must make certain that the client does not misperceive those attributes as anything more. There should *never* be any social, business, or any other contact with clients outside the therapeutic setting.
- *Be willing to write off some fees.* Psychotherapeutic services and consultations are often expensive, and within managed care, they are frequently not fully paid for (if at all). Billing clients who do not intend to pay for the consultation, or sending a case to collections, often triggers the client to file a frivolous suit as a countermeasure. In such a situation, the client's manipulative strategy is that if the bill is dropped, the suit will be dropped. This is similar to blackmail. Such a tactic is an example of the cliché, "The best defense (against paying a bill) is a good offense (file an unfounded suit)."
- *Get signatures.* You should be aware of this possibility as you decide how and whom to bill. If you use a collection agency, the client may file a suit charging a breach of confidentiality. You can prevent this with an office policy requiring all clients to sign a document acknowledging that unpaid bills may go to a collector.

It is your responsibility to practice within strict parameters, and do not hesitate to seek legal counsel when needed. Applying the principles in this chapter and staying current with ethical, legal, regulatory, and assessment/diagnostic standards may not prevent a lawsuit, but it should help promote a solid defense.

CHAPTER 7

Manage Managed Care

WHAT YOU WILL LEARN:

Practice by Design: Guidelines for Signing Contracts

Practice by Design: How Managed Care Has Evolved
    Health Maintenance Organizations (HMOs)
    First Generation of Managed Care: Service Limitations
    Second Generation of Managed Care: Preferred Provider
       Organizations
    Third Generation of Managed Care: Automation
    Fourth Generation of Managed Care: Outcomes Management
    Fifth Generation of Managed Care: Capitation and Risk Sharing
    Generational Overlap

The Impact of Managed Care on Clinical Practice

Practice by Design: How to Grow Your Practice within Managed Care

Practice by Design: Managed Care Matrix

Practice by Design: Managed Care Organizing System

Two of the most baffling aspects of managed care are the specialized vocabulary and contract issues. This chapter will serve not only to demystify some of the confusing aspects of managed care, but also to help you understand the issues that will enable you to deal successfully with MCOs.

PRACTICE BY DESIGN: GUIDELINES FOR SIGNING CONTRACTS

As we discussed in previous chapters, contracts can be complex and intimidating to deal with, and contracting with managed care panel obligations is no different. The following are some suggestions for you to consider.

The following information is adapted from Chris Stout's interview with Lisa Rabasca, in the APA *Monitor on Psychology* (February 2000, pp. 60–62).

Care standards. Providers should not sign contracts that call for the "highest standard" of care, because one could argue that such a standard would require a complete psychological evaluation, social history, blood workups, and psychiatric consultation—all for the cost of what may have been calculated by the provider as psychotherapy alone.

One-sided indemnification. By signing a contract with a one-sided indemnification clause, you agree to be responsible for everything that happens to the client, including problems that might occur in billing or with another provider. You are signing a contract that indemnifies (covers) the company. You may want to consult an attorney to learn how to alter the contract so you are responsible only for actions over which you have control within the scope of your practice as a licensed professional. The contract should also stipulate that the managed care company is responsible for all the activities involving the business aspects of care.

Note: The information in this chapter is *not* a substitute for legal advice. Any specific questions with any MCO contract you may consider signing should be posed to the organization and/or trusted legal counsel.

Confidentiality. Managed care contracts are often *not* in synchrony with state confidentiality laws, yet state law always takes precedence. If this is true in your state, ask your attorney to draft language that says client medical records will be provided in accordance with the state's confidentiality laws.

"Say-no-evil" and "gag" clauses. According to these clauses, which many states now prohibit, if you say something negative about the managed care company, your contract could be terminated. You may wish to delete this clause or not sign a contract that includes such wording.

Restrictive covenants. Be wary of any contract that limits you to a geographic area or type of service, since it might keep you from contracting with other companies. You may wish to negotiate an exemption or not sign the contract.

What a Contract Should Include

1. *Term-of-contract considerations.* Many contracts are written for only one year, but it is generally better to negotiate a longer contract so the terms do not change annually. Providers also need to stay on top of renewal dates for their contracts so they can be ready to renegotiate terms. Some contracts have automatic rollovers known as *evergreen clauses.*

2. *"With cause" and "without cause" clauses.* Most contracts include both of these clauses.
   - "With cause" allows the company to terminate providers from a network if they do something that breaches their contract, such as inadvertently billing a client incorrectly or failing to send the managed care company an updated copy of their license. In such instances, the contract allows for appeal and due process to determine whether the provider could have prevented the error.
   - "Without cause" allows either the provider or the company to terminate the contract at any time for no reason as long as notice is given, typically 60 or 90 days.

3. *Contract termination.* Providers should be aware of circumstances that would cause their contract to be terminated. For example, a managed care company might seek termination if you fail to send the company an updated copy of your malpractice insurance. Or

you could seek termination because the managed care company isn't paying you within 45 days, as stipulated in the contract.

4. *Liability for client care.* The contract should outline how cases will be handled if the contract is terminated by either party. For instance, the contract should state that the insurer will pay for a set number of sessions while the client makes the transition to another provider.

5. *Appeals process.* Not all contracts spell out an appeals process for utilization review decisions, but they should. Better companies typically provide independent, third-party peer reviewers.

6. *Provider evaluations.* The contract should delineate how providers are evaluated on their performance.

It is important to read the contract carefully and be sure you understand it. If you want to be part of it, sign it or negotiate changes and then keep track of what you have obligated yourself to do (see "Managed Care Organizing System" at the end of this chapter). You should not be afraid to negotiate reasonable changes to a contract. It happens often.

PRACTICE BY DESIGN: HOW MANAGED CARE HAS EVOLVED

Managed care has had a dramatic influence, both positive and negative, in the practice of behavioral healthcare. Clinicians, consultants, professional groups, and hospital administrators have argued against many managed care procedures. Even though you may dislike having to work with managed care, you will have the most success if you are proactive and persistent. If you accept managed care referrals, you should work as effectively as possible within the system to benefit your clients and run your practice with the highest level of professionalism.

To understand the managed care system of today, it helps to review how the system has evolved:

- Health maintenance organizations
- First generation: Service limitations
- Second generation: Preferred provider organizations
- Third generation: Automation

- Fourth generation: Outcomes management
- Fifth generation: Capitation and risk sharing

HEALTH MAINTENANCE ORGANIZATIONS (HMOS)

In the beginning, managed care was identified with health maintenance organizations (HMOs). The HMO model provides enrollees with a variety of healthcare services, including behavioral healthcare, for a set fee per month. HMOs are often regulated by state insurance commissions.

The three most common practice models within HMOs are the staff model, the group model, and the network model. (See Chapter 1 for further discussion.)

Staff Model HMO
- Clinicians are paid employees of the HMO.
- Care is provided at clinic sites that are owned and operated by the HMO.

Group Model HMO
- Clinicians are in large private practices, independent practice associations (IPAs), or group practices without walls (GPWWs). A group has broad geographic coverage through its various offices.
- Clinicians are not HMO employees (unlike the staff model).
- Office sites are owned and operated by practice owners, not by the HMO.
- In some instances, a degree of exclusivity is provided to large group practices that receive the majority of referrals (known as *anchor groups*).

Network Model HMO. This is similar to the group model, but it uses a number of smaller practices to service clients instead of a few large anchor groups or IPAs/GPWWs.

FIRST GENERATION OF MANAGED CARE: SERVICE LIMITATIONS

The first generation of managed care provided reduced services. For example:

- Payors paid for fewer days in inpatient and residential facilities.
- The number of covered outpatient sessions was limited.
- Psychological assessment was limited. Psychological testing or assessment was often not covered by a client's insurance agreement.
- The fees paid were smaller.

Payment Dilemmas. Clinicians who conduct testing evaluations — clinical psychologists, educational or school psychologists, educational specialists, and others — faced dilemmas of many varieties when it came to managed care cases. In some instances, regardless of which battery test was administered, these clinicians would be paid a flat fee. However, some managed care companies would pay for only certain types of tests; others would not pay at all. If a utilization reviewer or case manager thought that psychological testing was not indicated (even if testing was a covered benefit), then testing would not be approved, even after it had been ordered by the doctor in charge of the case.

Within the managed care environment, psychological testing is sometimes paid for at a reduced hourly rate for an unlimited number of hours. A variety of payment schemes have been developed, such as limiting the amount paid for a full battery or paying for only selected tests.

Examples of Payment for Tests. The most frequent methods of pricing and payment for testing are as follows:

1. *Flat rate (or fee for battery).* If approved within a policy's benefit structure, a testing battery is paid for at a total set fee, regardless of the number and types of tests administered or the amount of time taken. There is usually an implicit (if not explicit) minimum expectation of an intelligence test, an objective personality measure, and an interview or screening device or two. Fee rates may range from $250 to $500, depending on the payor, the geographic region, and the minimal tests included.

2. *Fee for test.* Reimbursement is based on a predetermined selection of approved tests at approved fees. There is usually no option to bill for the additional time involved in interpretation or in writing the report. Thus, if an examiner wishes to administer the Wechsler Adult Intelligence Scale, third edition (WAIS-III), and Minnesota Multiphasic Personality Inventory, second edition (MMPI-2),

and conduct a clinical interview (assuming all are approved), payment would be based on the total of the sum of each test's predetermined reimbursement level. If the managed care organization reimburses $75.00 for WAIS-III, $50.00 for MMPI-2, and $100.00 for a clinical interview, the battery would yield $225.00.

3. *Fee for service.* Reimbursement is based on an hourly rate. For example, if five hours are billed for administration and scoring, the five hours are multiplied by the customary managed care rate for testing (e.g., $70 per hour) to yield the total fee allowed ($350).

4. *Inclusive/per diem/capitated rate.* Facilities, group practices, or other types of provider entities may contract for a variety of services bundled together. If psychological testing is part of that bundle, it is unlikely that any independent contractor examiner would be referred to the case. These arrangements typically occur within hospitals or other systems of care. A staff psychologist who is on salary (or retainer, or a similar employment arrangement) conducts the referred testing and bills no one. There is usually no preapproval and no regulation or restriction regarding test selection or battery composition. Such choices are within the discretion and clinical judgment of the assessor.

Some plans may limit the total hours per battery (or per testing episode), even though testing may take longer. Other plans may not limit hours, but may require preapproval and may possibly dictate which tests are to be administered. (The preapproval process of the flat rate is similar.)

More generous plans may pay for the time it takes to write the report. Examiners must be aware of a possible requirement for using different Clinical Procedural Terminology (CPT) coding in such instances (e.g., CPT 96100: Psychological Testing). See Chapter 5 for more on CPT codes and billing. When examiners bill for their services, it is very important to use the appropriate CPT code to avoid any risk of nonpayment or any question of insurance fraud. (Such risks are discussed in detail in Chapter 6.)

Comparison of Payment Models. Table 7.1 compares the various reimbursement models for psychological assessment under current (2004) managed care options.

TABLE 7.1   A Sample Comparison of Standard Testing Battery Reimbursement Models

Battery components	Flat Rate Test/Activities Included		Fee for Test Test/Activities Included		Fee for Service* Test/Activities Included		Capitated Test/Activities Included	
	Yes	Amount	Yes	Amount	Yes	Amount	Yes	Amount
Clinical interviews	X	N/A	X	$75	X	$70	X	$0
Bender Gestalt	X	N/A			X	$20	X	$0
WAIS-III	X	N/A	X	$75	X	$100	X	$0
MMPI-2	X	N/A	X	$50	X	$50	X	$0
TAT	X	N/A			X	$50	X	$0
Rorschach	X	N/A					X	$0
Aphasia screen	X	N/A			X	$25	X	$0
Scoring and interpretation	X	N/A					X	$0
Report write-up	X	N/A					X	$0
Total paid		$300		$225		$315		$0†

*Amount based on fraction of $70 per hour.
†Psychologist is paid per member per month (PMPM), not per discrete clinical activity.

SECOND GENERATION OF MANAGED CARE: PREFERRED PROVIDER ORGANIZATIONS

The preferred provider organization (PPO) is the second generation of managed care. In this model, select providers contract to provide specific types of services at preset, reduced fees. The client has the option to use an independent provider, but there are financial disincentives for going outside the payor/insurance network. For example, there could be a higher co-pay or deductible or less reimbursement for that clinician. There is currently no federal regulation of PPOs.

Utilization Review and Management. The additional component of second-generation managed care is the initiation of utilization review/ utilization management (UR/UM). Under this system, PPO staff members interface with facilities or providers in approving treatment plans or procedures such as psychological testing.

Historically, there has been a great deal of friction and frustration between clinicians and utilization review managers. Initially, some utilization reviewers of managed care companies were not clinically trained. Fortunately, as things have evolved, individuals in these positions have become more sophisticated, and managed care companies increasingly use psychiatric nurses, psychiatrists, psychologists, and professionals in this capacity. Thus, UR/UM is now a peer-to-peer model.

Information Needed for Applying to PPOs. The application forms used by PPOs are not standardized, which can create a confusing array of paperwork for clinicians seeking to join. However, most managed care organizations (MCOs) require the following documents:

- Proof of malpractice insurance (usually a copy of the face sheet and amounts in the range of $1 million per occurrence/$1 million per annual aggregate, or $1 million per occurrence/$3 million per annual aggregate)
- Copy of professional license
- Copy of diploma or terminal degree
- One to three letters of recommendation
- Copy of National Practitioner Databank Query results (visit www.npdb-hipdb.com or call 800-767-6732 or 805-987-9476)
- Documentation of any malpractice history
- Sample report and/or treatment plan
- Description of treatment or clinical philosophy
- Current vita
- The MCO's own application

You may find it helpful to keep copies of these documents on hand in order to expedite processing applications.

THIRD GENERATION OF MANAGED CARE: AUTOMATION

The third generation of managed care involves a greater number of automated systems. There has been rapid improvement in the sophistication and utilization of these systems. Managed Health Network was one of the first to use an innovative combination of "bubble" forms and bar coding to expeditiously process paper claims. Some MCOs partnered with AT&T for an innovative, on-site data entry system that is being used throughout the United States. A variety of utilization tracking methodologies are being employed. Some of the more sophisticated methods use provider profiling, diagnosis cross-validation, and computer-administered therapy.

FOURTH GENERATION OF MANAGED CARE: OUTCOMES MANAGEMENT

The fourth generation focuses on efficacy and outcomes management systems. Outcomes management includes:

- Evaluation and quantified measurement of client satisfaction
- Symptom resolution (treatment outcome)
- Functionality measures
- Demonstrated efficacy (outcome follow-up)

The increasing focus on outcomes makes quality a more significant part of the managed care equation. MCOs evaluate outcomes by examining clinical performance data in relation to clinical procedures. A variety of psychological assessments (screening tools, specific instruments, health status measures, batteries, etc.) are used to evaluate outcomes.

FIFTH GENERATION OF MANAGED CARE: CAPITATION AND RISK SHARING

Most of the industry considers capitation and risk sharing to be the fifth generation of managed care. A prenegotiated, fixed payment (or premium) is prepaid on a per member per month (PMPM) basis to the provider or facility. Enrollees receive a predetermined set of services for a contracted time period. The fee is paid regardless of the services provided. It was predicted that most managed care arrangements would have shifted to capitation within the past few years, but the shift has not been as dramatic as some in the industry predicted.

GENERATIONAL OVERLAP

Healthcare payment models are evolutionary, and as such there are no discrete steps of progression. Quite the contrary occurs in the healthcare marketplace: Most of the five evolutions coexist simultaneously, with ever-changing proportions of penetration in each part of the country. Each geographic region follows its own evolution, with California being the trendsetter that the rest of the country follows.

THE IMPACT OF MANAGED CARE ON CLINICAL PRACTICE

The Practice Directorate of the American Psychological Association commissioned a focus group research project (APAPD 1994, p. 1) on managed care using the Widmeyer Group, Inc. The project was conducted in four cities with six focus groups. The findings indicated a consensus among those surveyed, noting the following:

1. *Eroding self-confidence.* Psychologists and other behavioral healthcare professionals have felt demoralized when having to defend themselves and their work to third parties.
2. *Loss of control.* Psychologists perceive threats to their identity as healthcare providers and to their ability to function and practice independently.
3. *Feeling vulnerable.* Those surveyed reported experiencing economic erosion within the practice of psychology. Concerns included public perceptions and misperceptions of how psychologists practice.
4. *Disturbed by trends.* Some psychologists are considering leaving the field in response to unforeseen changes and shifts in their psychological practices in particular and in healthcare delivery in general. Actual feelings of loss and mourning were noted with regard to these changes.

133

The APAPD study also explored respondents' direct opinions concerning managed care. The psychologists polled felt that (p. 2):

1. *Cost is more important than quality.* Psychologists pointed to what they felt was a lack of treatment quality within managed care plans. Cost containment was a greater worry than quality, and the medical model was a poor fit with psychological problems and treatments.

2. *Confidentiality is being eroded.* Ethical and legal issues are involved when patients' reports and other clinical data are discussed with a utilization reviewer. The expertise and training of reviewers were related issues.

3. *Serious ethical issues are created by managed care.* Respondents described problems using diagnostic codes, along with the perceived "not-too-sick-but-not-too-well" balancing act—a contrived means of keeping a client in care. Some respondents said that both improvement and lack of improvement are causes for a treatment's termination.

4. *Doing more work for less money.* Many psychologists perceive that treatment expectations are waxing while concomitant payment levels are waning.

5. *Utilization reviewers are not credentialed.* Respondents complained that many utilization reviewers lack proper credentials and training. These problems seem to result from reviews that are not peer-to-peer.

PRACTICE BY DESIGN: HOW TO GROW YOUR PRACTICE WITHIN MANAGED CARE

It is important to realize that being in a preferred provider network may result in a less income. Some capitated, shared-risk contracts are possible exceptions to this. On average, you will make about 10 to 35 percent less per service (depending on the market). As mentioned earlier, annual practice income is usually reduced by two factors:

- Lower fees for usual and customary procedures.
- Fewer clinical activities (i.e., fewer therapy sessions, testing limitations, or denials of requests to conduct assessments).

What can you do about this?

More sophisticated MCOs are now moving toward asking providers to identify their clients according to their zip code, diagnostic group, age group, client satisfaction, and various outcome measures. They are also asking them to track their continuing education credits.

It is likely that the information required for credentialing and recredentialing will become even more sophisticated in the future. Once your application is approved, you will receive a provider agreement or a contract. You can expect to be asked about the following issues:

- Which geographic areas you can serve
- Your medical and professional staff membership status at local hospitals and medical centers
- Your system for promptly returning phone calls and your ability to manage crisis calls and emergencies
- Your availability for client appointments
- Your capacity for accepting new referrals (and any limitations)
- The number of networks, PPOs, and HMOs in which you are currently a provider
- Sample reports or treatment plans for various diagnostic categories and populations
- Your treatment philosophy or theoretical orientation
- Your liability history and outcomes
- Your fee structure by CPT code and procedure
- Level of automation (computer, electronic data interchange (EDI), fax, Internet, voice mail, etc.), and HIPAA compliance

Think about how you can build these factors into your practice to make yourself more attractive to MCOs.

PRACTICE BY DESIGN: MANAGED CARE MATRIX

Many clinicians find it useful to develop a list or matrix of the managed care and insurance companies they belong to. The list or matrix includes information about each company, including the criteria, contracts, phone numbers, and so on for precertifications, payment types (fee for service, reduced fee for service, flat rate, etc.), payment levels, and other relevant data. Keep your list updated and refer to it often to make cer-

TABLE 7.2   Sample Managed Care Matrix

MCO/Ins. Co.	ABC Group	DEF Company	GHI Association
Precertification required?	No	No	Yes
Contact person (discipline)	Ms. Smith (LCSW)	Jorge Martinez (MFT)	Sam Fisher (psychologist)
Position	Utilization Reviewer	Utilization Reviewer	Utilization Reviewer
Phone number	888/555-1234	888/555-1234	888/555-1234
Fax number	888/555-9876	888/555-1234	888/555-1234
Billing address	222 Maple Yourtown, ST 98765	2500 Eastern Pkwy. Anytown, IL 60012	8374 Western Ave. Somewhere, CA 91199
Payment type	Contracted rates	Contracted rates	Contracted rates
Payment level	$75 for CPT 90806; $750 for CPT 96100	$65 for CPT 90806; $650 for CPT 96100	$85 for CPT 90806; $750 for CPT 96100
Additional information	None	None	Make sure you get precertification

tain that you are meeting the requirements of each company. This will help you avoid denial of payment for services provided. Table 7.2 is an example of a matrix.

PRACTICE BY DESIGN: MANAGED CARE ORGANIZING SYSTEM

It may be helpful to have a system to manage the care provided for the various contracts you (will) hold. The following is an example of such a system. If you are in solo or group practice, using this (or your customized version of it) will be helpful in tracking contractual obligations and specific procedures and protocols of the differing companies you are contracted with. You may use it to set up your system and keep it in a binder or on your computer.

Sample Contract Organizing System

MCO: Aetna Health Plans (AHP)

Description	The network has been revised effective 1/1/2002 and is referred to as "the behavioral health network of Aetna Health Plans (AHP)" and Human Affairs International (HAI). AHP/HAI referrals may have coverage through any of the following products:

1. AHP's Open Choice (PPO)
2. AHP's Managed Choice/Elect Choice
3. HAI's Employee Assistance Program
4. HAI's Managed Behavioral Health

Membership in the AHP/HAI behavioral health network does not necessarily mean that we can provide care for every AHP/HAI covered member. For instance, AHP has an HMO product in Illinois called Select Choice, but the membership in the Select Choice product will not be using the AHP/HAI, the HMO will be managed by Blue Cross/Blue Shield effective 3/1/03.

Any questions about a client's plan or benefits should be referred to the toll-free Member Services telephone number listed on the AHP/HAI member's health insurance identification card.

Participating providers	S. Smith	Eff. 1/1/02	All products
	M. Jones	Applied 2/2/02	
	L. Doeff	1/1/02	Waiting for contract copy

Participating hospitals	Memorial Hospital	All plans
	Park Hospital	All plans

Referrals	Open Choice — No precertification of referrals is required; members usually just look in the published directory for an approved provider.

AHP Managed Choice — The primary care physician or the member must call the toll-free 800 Member Services ID number on the member's card to discuss the referral with an AHP reviewer to determine medical necessity and eligibility and to coordinate a treatment plan and contact a participating network provider.

Outpatient precertification
AHP Open Choice — Members may select a provider from the published directory and directly access ("self-refer") to our office. Members in Open Choice are not required to precertify office visits.

HAI Employee Assistance Program — We are not providing EAP services for AHP/HAI; however, we are eligible to receive referrals for treatment beyond the EAP benefit. Upon referral we will receive a confirmation letter certifying a particular number of sessions. The letter will tell us specifically what benefits have been approved and where to call with questions.

HAI Managed Behavioral Health Program — When a referral is made to us, we will receive a confirmation letter certifying a particular number of sessions. The letter will tell us specifically what benefits have been approved and where to call with questions.

Inpatient precertification
Call the toll-free member services number listed on the front of the client's ID card. A certification number will be issued when an admission has been properly precertified.

NOTE: Failure to do so may result in a 20% negotiated fee reduction.

Utilization review
Focused Psychiatric Review — Precertification, concurrent review, and case management.

Managed Choice:
(800) 733-0433.
PPO — Check client's ID card.

Referrals
Clients can be referred to anyone in the Chicago Directory for Partners National Health Plan.
No paperwork.
No approval needed from primary care physician.

Weekend admission	Precertify prior to planned admissions. Certify the next business day for emergencies. Managed Choice: (800) 733-0433. PPO—Check client's ID card.
Nonnetwork admissions	Nonemergencies—Network only. Emergencies—Fully covered, but client will be transferred to Network hospital, if possible.
Claims	HCFA-1500 form. Do not send a statement to the client. Claim Centers different for each employer group, check client's ID card.
Co-payments	Varies for each employer group, check client's ID card.
Concurrent care	Case-by-case basis depending on medical necessity. Call (312) 372-0209 UR can approve.
Number of inpatient visits required per week	Once within 24 hours of admission and once per day thereafter. All other arrangements on a case-by-case basis.
Notes	Provider Relations (312) 372-0209. Baxter in-network 90%, $100 deductible, out-of-network 70%, $400 deductible. Send all Baxter employee's claims to:

Aetna Life Insurance Company
P.O. Box 7006
Rockford, IL 61126-7006
Claim Information: (800) 448-5181
Precertification for Baxter clients: (800) 879-7691
12/31/01—Executed contracts being sent per provider relations.

After 2/28/03, out-of-network providers must transfer their cases to in-network providers or have their clients contact the Aetna Access Line to discuss (AHP/HAI may make an exception).

1/27/01 — Per Mary S. in AHP Provider Relations, we are currently approved for the HMO product.

3/17/91 — Per Karen H., okay to replace providers that have terminated. Can only add provider with same level of training.

Major employer's insurance   Baxter Healthcare

CHAPTER 8

Market Your Practice

WHAT YOU WILL LEARN:

Why Marketing Is Such a Challenge for Therapists

What Your Clients Are Really Buying

Practice by Design: How to Analyze Your Marketplace
> Define the Competition
> Define the Demographics
> Look at Current Trends

Analyze How Clients Choose a Therapist

Identify Your Target Clients
> What Do Your Clients Value?

Practice by Design: Tailor Your Marketing to Your Target Clients
> Tailor Your Services to These Clients
> Set Your Fees Based on These Clients

Practice by Design: Develop a Marketing Plan and Short-Term Objectives

What Should You Name Your Practice?

Emphasize the Benefits of Your Service

Practice by Design: How to Design a Promotional Strategy

Practice by Design: Measure Results and Continuously Fine-Tune Your Program
> Case Study: Evaluating Results of Promotional Activities
> Seven Keys to Effective Marketing

Why Marketing Is Such a Challenge for Therapists

If you are like most therapists, you don't like the idea marketing your practice. There are several reasons for this.

Fear of seeming unprofessional. The thought of placing an ad in the local paper or networking with the Rotary Club may make you feel like a used-car salesperson; all you lack is the plaid sports jacket. The idea of promoting your services may feel unprofessional, tacky, or egotistical.

Lack of knowledge. You may not know what to do or where to begin. After all, very few clinical training programs include a course on practice marketing, perhaps because those in the world of traditional academia look down on the idea of self-promotion. Most university training programs focus on clinical skills, not practice-building skills. The same is true for most internships. As a result, most mental health professionals (MHPs) begin their professional lives lacking the basic skills for building and growing a practice.

Avoidance. Because you have never learned to market your practice, you avoid it and focus on developing your clinical skills. You may think, "If I build it, the clients will come," but you quickly learn that the philosophy that worked for Ray Kinsella, Kevin Costner's character in the 1989 movie *Field of Dreams*, will *not* help you build a thriving practice.

Speaking the language of your profession rather than the language of your clients. Many smart, well-credentialed clinicians think that marketing simply means listing their credentials in an ad or brochure. If you think this way too, conduct a little experiment: Ask a random sample of nonacademic and nonclinical individuals what the letters that follow a therapist's name (PhD, PsyD, MA, MS, LCPC, CACS, MDiv, ABPP, etc.) mean. It is very likely that you will learn that few potential clients care whether you are boarded in something, belong to some professional club, or practice a specific flavor of therapy. Most clients call you because they have a problem and think you can help them.

The information in this chapter (and those that follow) will help you conquer your aversion to and anxiety about marketing your practice. You will learn the basics of marketing and you will see that it is not a mystery. This is what you will learn:

- Dozens of tools that you can use right now to build your practice
- The basic principles of marketing your practice
- Why marketing it is so important to your practice
- How to develop a marketing plan
- How to find your marketing niche
- Ways to get people to refer clients to you
- How to get free publicity
- How to design ads that will increase your visibility and attract new clients
- How to stand out through a combination of newsletters, exceptional business stationery, and maybe even a website
- How to increase your visibility by giving presentations and workshops
- How to attract and keep clients by paying attention to some details you may not have thought of

WHAT YOUR CLIENTS ARE REALLY BUYING

When people are looking for a therapist, they aren't really looking for a *therapist*. They are looking for a solution to a problem. Your challenge is to discover problems that need solving. The mistake many business and professional people make is focusing mainly on selling themselves or their practice. As Jay Conrad Levinson (1993) writes in *Guerrilla Marketing Excellence*, prospective clients "don't care about *your company;* they care about *their problems.*"

Think about what people want in life. Lacking these things is what motivates them to seek professional services like yours. Chances are, they aren't looking to satisfy their basic needs like shelter and physical security—most of your prospective clients already have those needs met.

> "One study revealed in *Advertising Age* that price was only the fifth most important reason to patronize a business. More important than price were selection, service, quality, and confidence in the business."
>
> Jay Conrad Levinson (1997), *The Way of the Guerrilla.*

143

Remember Abraham Maslow, the psychologist who theorized that people's behavior is motivated by the drive to satisfy a hierarchy of needs? You probably remember that Maslow (1998) conceptualized people's needs as a pyramid, with the basic needs at the bottom.

Your potential clients are most likely interested in meeting needs that are a bit higher up Maslow's hierarchy:

- To be happy
- To enjoy life
- To feel attractive
- To be successful
- To have satisfying relationships
- To feel good about themselves

Your marketing efforts should focus on how you can help people have what they want.

If they look in the phone book, something must catch their eye for them to decide to make the phone call. A statement that appeals to them, a friendly photograph, or a reference to their problem may motivate a person to call.

Throughout this process of thinking about consulting a therapist, most people are doing two things: (1) hoping the problem will go away by itself and (2) looking for ways to find a solution on their own. Very often, your greatest competition is the choice between do-it-yourself

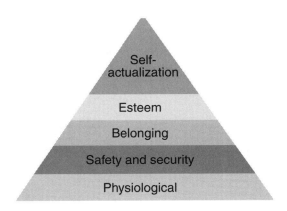

FIGURE 8.1 Maslow's hierarchy of needs.

therapy or doing nothing at all. This means that if this prospective client ever appears in your office, he or she may very well continue considering the do-it-yourself approach into the first few sessions.

What does this mean to you? Two things:

- You must be able to demonstrate that using your service will lead to better results than taking the self-help track.
- Instead of criticizing the self-help option, just acknowledge it as an alternative and concentrate on providing excellent, productive service.

PRACTICE BY DESIGN: HOW TO ANALYZE YOUR MARKETPLACE

Can you imagine starting a new business without first understanding who lives in the surrounding geographic area? It's amazing, but many therapists do exactly that when they set up their first practices. Let's look at what such an analysis involves and why it's a crucial step.

To really understand your marketplace, you will need to define it in terms of (1) competition, (2) demographics, and (3) current trends.

DEFINE THE COMPETITION

One important part of your market analysis involves taking a look at who else is practicing in your area. You will want to find out the following information:

- How many other therapists are within a two- to five-mile radius?
- What licenses do these therapists hold? How many of each type of license?
- What can you learn about the practice specialties of these competitors?
- What kinds of marketing are your competitors doing?
- How visible are they? Are they more than just listings in the Yellow Pages?

It's a good idea to get in your car and take a drive. Check out the office buildings in which your competition is located. Make some notes.

Mark their locations on a map. See where they cluster. What challenges and opportunities do you see?

Next, it is important to take the time to analyze your competition.

First, define who your competition is. Look in the Yellow Pages and other listings and be sure you understand who is out there vying for the same clients you are. Get creative. You want to find out what those competitors of yours are really like.

- How do they do business?
- How do they treat clients?
- What is it like in their offices?

One way to do this is to go "therapist shopping." It's a bit like being a mystery shopper in a department store. Choose a few therapists whom you'd like to know more about. Call their offices and ask if you can meet with them. Say you're doing a survey of the market area and you want to get to know the other professionals.

Second, make a list of questions you'd like to ask, covering areas such as these:

- Hours of availability
- How they work with clients
- Areas of specialty
- Fees

If possible, visit a few of these therapists. Note how you feel as you walk into the office building, the waiting room, and the therapy room.

- How might a client feel?
- What impression do you get as you meet with each person?
- What do you think he or she does particularly well?

Now comes the critical question: Based on what you've seen of your competition, what are your challenges and opportunities? You will find ways in which you are at a disadvantage. For example, you may not have a PhD, or you may lack the 20 years' experience of the social worker on Main Street. You can feel like a minor player when you walk into a busy practice with 15 different stacks of business cards in the waiting room. This is especially true if you are just starting out. But every factor has its flip side. Your challenge is to find your hidden strengths and create ways to build on them.

Third, identify the ways in which your practice is superior or unique. After you've met with a few of your competitors, make a list of what you've learned. What do most therapists do especially well? What opportunities do you see to excel? Evaluate your findings in terms of the following factors:

- How long licensed
- Special training
- Specialty areas
- Affordable fees
- Comfortable, nonintimidating office
- Feeling of safety in the parking lot and building
- Conveys a feeling of confidence
- Conveys a feeling of warmth
- Office feels private
- Confidential atmosphere: files locked and conversations private

Add your own factors and look for opportunities. How can you stand out?

DEFINE THE DEMOGRAPHICS

Demographic data includes facts about the people who live in your area. It includes things such as:

- Average age
- Income
- Education
- Occupation
- Marital status
- Gender
- Family size
- Percent who are homeowners
- Average home price

This information can be found in places such as the following:

- Chamber of Commerce
- Public library (ask the librarian)
- Local business publications
- Real estate offices
- Websites (e.g., the U.S. Census Bureau)

This information is important, especially when you are deciding where to open a practice.

Many people consider psychotherapy to be an expensive service, and demographic factors will help you decide the most favorable locations in which to open such a business. Demographics will also help you decide which specialty areas to market, based on the population living in your market area.

LOOK AT CURRENT TRENDS

Current trends are important to consider when you are designing a marketing plan for your practice. Here are a few examples of relevant trends:

- More young families moving in
- Senior citizen population expanding
- Large companies expanding or downsizing
- Mergers and closings
- More of certain ethnic groups moving in or out
- Recent disasters (earthquakes, tornadoes, wildfires, etc.) that have impacted the economy as well as people's psyches

You can learn about such trends in the following ways:

- Read the paper
- Surf the Internet
- Walk through the mall or down the street
- Watch TV news shows

ANALYZE HOW CLIENTS CHOOSE A THERAPIST

How do people choose a therapist? Here are a few of the most common ways:

- Yellow Pages ads
- Asking doctors or clergy
- Asking school psychologists
- Asking friends or relatives

- Attending seminars or workshops given by therapists
- From managed care lists

Most referrals are based on someone's knowledge about the therapist. Therefore, it is important that you do the following:

- Make contact with as many potential referrers as you can — by networking.
- Make it as easy as possible for people to refer to you — also by networking.
- Make it as easy as possible for potential clients to choose you — by being visible and active in your community.

Your key task is to make yourself as *accessible* to as many people as possible. There are many ways to increase your accessibility. Here are some examples:

- Include your photo in your advertisements (Yellow Pages, newspaper, flyers, etc.).
- Participate in numerous networking events for as long as you are in business.
- Offer to speak to groups.
- Give free seminars and events at your office or in hotel meeting rooms.

IDENTIFY YOUR TARGET CLIENTS

You may have heard the marketing term *target market*. Have you identified yours? Doing so can help you build a strong practice because you know to whom you are really marketing your services. Most therapists market their services to two groups:

- People who will be their clients
- People or groups who will refer clients to the practice

This is an important distinction. Be sure to identify who belongs in each of these categories for your practice, and include both in your marketing strategy. For example:

If your target clients are . . .	*Possible referral sources are . . .*
Kids with ADD	School psychologists; psychiatrists who work with kids; pediatricians
People who are infertile	OB-GYNs, reproductive endocrinologists
Single adults seeking to find mates	Fitness centers and health clubs; members of the clergy
Couples thinking about divorce	Divorce attorneys; members of the clergy

WHAT DO YOUR CLIENTS VALUE?

In *The Guerrilla Marketing Handbook* (a must-read, along with the entire *Guerrilla Marketing* series), authors Jay Conrad Levinson and Seth Godin (1994) say that one key to success in your practice is to deliver more than the customer expects. They write, "Act on the knowledge that customers value attention, dependability, promptness, and competence" (p. 348).

Compare yourself to your competition in terms of those four elements — attention, dependability, promptness, and competence — and find five ways to create more value for your clients. You will soon have more clients.

PRACTICE BY DESIGN: TAILOR YOUR MARKETING TO YOUR TARGET CLIENTS

Your target clients have certain specific traits, such as their demographic profile, geographic location, and type of lifestyle. Target marketing is different from general marketing in that you identify a specific segment or niche and design all of your marketing activities to appeal to clients belonging to that group. Examples of target clients include:

- Upper middle class, married, $150,000 income and above, living in zip code 91107, no children, age 30 to 39.
- Middle class, divorced, single parents, $30,000 to $50,000 income, living in zip codes 22405 to 22407, age 25 to 40.

TAILOR YOUR SERVICES TO THESE CLIENTS

How might the services for these two groups be different? Here are some ideas:

1. The first group would be most interested in couples groups, marital therapy, career issues, and workshops on personal growth issues.
2. The second group would be interested in workshops on survival skills for single parents, evening availability, family therapy, and brief therapy.

In *Rocking the Ages: The Yankelovich Report on Generational Marketing*, authors J. Walker Smith and Ann Clurman (1998) describe how effective marketing campaigns can be designed based on understanding the generation to which the target client belongs: Generation X, the baby boomers, and what the authors call the Matures.

The authors state that the values, preferences, and behaviors of consumers can be understood in terms of "three distinct elements: (1) life stage, (2) current social and economic conditions, and (3) formative cohort experiences."

If you identify the generation of your target clients, you can better target your services to meet their needs and values.

SET YOUR FEES BASED ON THESE CLIENTS

When setting your fees, you should consider the following factors:

- What your competitors are charging
- What your clients consider reasonable
- Trends in your area and in your profession
- Your target client

See Chapter 4 for more information on fees.

It is challenging to set fees for psychotherapy because your service is intangible. Some experts say that those who purchase services see price

---

"Create the possible service; don't just create what the market needs or wants. Create what it would love."

Harry Beckwith (1997), *Selling the Invisible: A Field Guide to Modern Marketing.*

151

> "There is one thing each of us has that no one else has. There is one thing you can do that nobody else can. Find it, and foster it. You will never die at your business if you are doing what you are meant to do."
>
> Deepak Chopra (1995), *The Seven Spiritual Laws of Success.*

as an indicator of quality, so a lower fee has a negative impact on how potential clients might see you.

In *The Guerrilla Marketing Handbook,* authors Levinson and Godin (1994) write, "When a customer tells you that your price is too high, what he's really saying is that you don't give enough value for what you're charging. Time and time again, aggressive businesses have shown that people will pay for quality and service. . . . Your price is rarely the problem. Worry instead about benefits, positioning, and service."

PRACTICE BY DESIGN: DEVELOP A MARKETING PLAN AND SHORT-TERM OBJECTIVES

It is critical to put your marketing plan in writing and refer to it often. You need both a long-range plan, covering the next one to three years, and short-term objectives for the coming 6 to 12 months. Just as in your clinical work, objectives are effective only if they are specific, concrete, and measurable. For example:

Specific: I will conduct an all-day parenting workshop on the second Saturday of every month in 2005.
Not specific: I will offer parenting workshops.

Concrete: Three weeks before each of my presentations, I will send out press releases to five newspapers in the northwest suburbs.
Not concrete: I will publicize my presentations.

Measurable: I will have 18 weekly clients by December 31, 2005.
Not measurable: I will be seeing more clients by the end of 2005.

Once you've developed a killer set of objectives, don't stick them in the drawer and forget about them. Do just the opposite: Put them to work and keep them up-to-date.

> "Being interactive means being connected, giving and taking, responding . . . [therapists] who realize that interactivity leads to lasting relationships with customers are also hitting the interactive trail when they offer free consultations, a potent marketing weapon if ever there was one, with free seminars that invite questions and are set up to close sales, and with speakers who talk to groups for free and then distribute brochures and establish relationships."
>
> Jay Conrad Levinson (1997), *The Way of the Guerrilla: Achieving Success and Balance as an Entrepreneur in the 21st Century.*

- Put them on your bulletin board right next to your desk
- Make an action calendar with subgoals and checkoff lists
- Reward yourself when you accomplish what you set out to do.

WHAT SHOULD YOU NAME YOUR PRACTICE?

Many clinicians consider adopting a name for their practice. Doing so is really a matter of personal taste, but strategy can also play a role.

Check your state and professional regulations. In some states and professions, you may not use anything but your own name if you are a solo practitioner. Be careful to avoid giving your practice a name that implies that it is larger than it actually is. For example, if Dr. Tyrone Palmer has a solo private practice in Pasadena, in some states and professions it would violate the guidelines to call himself Palmer Associates, Palmer Clinic, Pasadena Counseling Center, or anything else that gives the impression that anyone besides Dr. Tyrone Palmer is a member of the practice.

Here are some other things to keep in mind when choosing a name for your practice:

1. If you are part of a group practice, a long and growing (or changing) string of names can be hard to remember, awkward, and not very creative.
2. If you choose to adopt a company name other than your own, it is very important to be able to be satisfied with it for the long term. (Watch for pitfalls like rhyming with a profanity or inadvertently creating an obscene acronym.) Then check with your local Cham-

ber of Commerce or appropriate state regulatory agency and see what papers need to be filed for an "assumed name" also known as "doing business as," or DBA. There is usually a minimal filing fee, an annual fee, and a requirement to post your real name and DBA name in a local paper for a few editions, none of which are difficult, expensive, or complicated.

3. If you practice under you own name, or with others, named or not, you need not bother with DBA procedures (such as "Dr. Smith and Associates" or "Jones and Jones Counseling Services," or "Mary Periwinkle, MSW, Family Therapy").

4. You may wish to use a catchy practice name or a special phrase with the name of your practice (a tagline) and restrict others from using it (think "Weight Watchers" versus "Jenny Craig"). You can learn about service marks and trademarks by consulting an attorney, or do the research yourself to save on fees. Just check with your appropriate state agency, get the forms, fill them out, and return them with the required fee. This enables you to use the trademark symbol (™) following the word or phrase that has been registered.

EMPHASIZE THE BENEFITS OF YOUR SERVICE

To help you differentiate your counseling services from those of your competitors, you must learn to spell out the features and benefits. There are four steps to this process:

1. Define your service.
2. List the features of your service that are different from your competitors' services.
3. Identify the benefits your services offer your clients.
4. Stress these benefits in all of your marketing efforts.

Let's look at each of these.

First, *define your service.* Describe what you do in terms that potential clients will understand and relate to. Two examples:

- "I help clients define how they want their lives to be different and identify the steps that will help them reach their goals."
- "I help couples create the kind of relationship they want."

154

Second, *list the features of your service* that are different from your competitors' services. Features include things like:

- "I see clients weekly for 50-minute sessions."
- "I use a family systems approach when I work with clients."
- "I am available evenings and Saturdays."
- "My hourly fee is based on the client's ability to pay."

Third, *identify the benefits* your services offer a client. For each feature, identify the benefits of your service. Benefits answer the question, "Why is this important to me?" Another way of looking at your list of benefits is that it answers the question, "How does my service make my client's life better?" For example:

- "My convenient hours make it possible for clients to schedule appointments without the added stress of taking time off work."
- "My affordable fee makes it possible for clients to find solutions to their problems without going through a managed care program and having to worry about a case manager looking over our shoulder as we work."

Fourth, once you have defined your service and its features and benefits, be sure to *emphasize those benefits* in all of your marketing efforts.

"Guerrilla marketers know that every product or service has features. Automatic door locks. Insulated windows. A fur collar. Overnight delivery. They also know that no one buys features. They buy benefits. No one ever bought a drill bit. Millions of people have bought a hole."

Jay Levinson and Seth Godin (1997), *Get What You Deserve!*

PRACTICE BY DESIGN: HOW TO DESIGN A PROMOTIONAL STRATEGY

A promotional strategy is a combination of activities designed to attract people's attention and get them to call for an appointment. Your strategy must address the following issues.

1. *How will people hear about you?* Just hanging out your shingle and hoping the phone will ring is not a strategy. A strategy is a set of actions designed to accomplish a specific goal.
2. *Why will you make the promotional choices you do?* Promotions include things like advertisements, public relations, and sales promotions. When deciding whether to advertise, consider your target market and special services you've developed for them. Choose the medium your target client is most likely to notice.

In later chapters, you will learn more about the dozens of promotional choices available to you. You may decide to generate publicity by staging events, such as your own seminars and workshops, and offering to speak to community groups. You may develop a mailing list of media outlets and regularly send out press releases announcing your events and programs. An excellent resource is *Guerrilla P.R.: How You Can Wage an Effective Publicity Campaign . . . Without Going Broke,* by Michael Levine (1993).

BROWNIE MARKETING

In *Taming the Marketing Jungle: 104 Marketing Ideas When Your Motivation Is High and Your Budget Is Low,* author Silvana Clark (1994) tells the story of Rachel Glenn, an eight-year-old girl who had a small part as an extra in the movie *The Hand That Rocks the Cradle.* On the day before filming began, Rachel's manager was informed that the girl should wear clothing of earth tones to work the next day. The manager, always looking for ways to help her clients stand out, advised Rachel to wear earth tones the next day—in fact, she should wear her Brownie uniform. That's what Rachel did, and during the filming, the director twice called for Rachel to take a new speaking part. He looked at the crowd of extras and called out, "I want the Brownie to get off the bus, yelling at a friend." Later, he announced, "Get the Brownie to be in front at the school assembly scene." Because of the Brownie uniform, Rachel got herself noticed, and she ended up with a bigger part and a higher pay scale.

How might *Brownie marketing* work for you?

PRACTICE BY DESIGN: MEASURE RESULTS AND CONTINUOUSLY FINE-TUNE YOUR PROGRAM

Many businesses (not just therapists) make the mistake of putting together a campaign, often spending lots of money on it but never checking to see whether it is really effective. Think of how many times you make a first appointment with a service provider (doctor, attorney, hair stylist, etc.) or purchase an item without anyone asking you how you heard of the business. Rarely are you asked that question, which means that many businesses are spending their promotional dollars without evaluating what really works. It doesn't make much sense, but it happens more often than not.

There are four important parts of this process: evaluating the results of promotional activities, analyzing the costs and results of each activity, doing *more* of what produces results, and doing *less* of what doesn't produce results.

CASE STUDY: EVALUATING RESULTS OF PROMOTIONAL ACTIVITIES

Therapist Sheila decides to run a few ads to get her practice going. In week 1, she spends $78 to run a small but tasteful ad in the local paper. No calls. She thinks, I must need more time. So she spends another $78 on an ad during the second week. She receives one call, but no appointment was scheduled. In week 3, she decides that her ad isn't big enough. So she spends $132 for a larger ad. Again, she receives one call, but no appointment. And in week 4, she tries one more time.

STORIES FROM THE REAL WORLD

In the mental health field, advertising is like eating junk food. It tastes great going down but has little or no nutritional value and doesn't stay with you long. Well-spent marketing dollars are like a nutritious well-balanced meal. It takes more time to prepare and execute, and you reap the benefits for a lot longer.

Daniel J. Abrahamson, PhD

She just can't believe that the ads didn't produce anything. But she can't resist trying again. She thinks, maybe repetition is the key. After all, she sees so many other businesses with similar ads in the same paper, week after week. Maybe it will take a few months of advertising to make people notice me.

After 10 weeks, Sheila is out of money. What did she get for her ads? Three calls, and one scheduled consultation, and the client did not show up, by the way!

Interestingly, other therapists in town saw Sheila's ads. After a few weeks, they thought, this Sheila must be very successful if she can afford all of this advertising!

Analyze Costs and Results of Each Marketing Activity

Let's assume that Sheila did have a marketing plan. She gave herself four weeks of ads at $78 per week. She saw that for the ads to pay off, she would need to produce at least 4 × $78, or $312 worth of business to break even. If her hourly fee were $80, she would need to see about four clients.

Do More of What Produces Results

The 80/20 rule, described by Richard Koch (1998) in *The 80/20 Principle: The Secret of Achieving More with Less*, says that 80 percent of the results are produced by 20 percent of the resources. Applied to the business of psychotherapy, we can draw the following conclusions:

THE 80/20 RULE, OR PARETO'S PRINCIPLE

In 1906, Italian economist Vilfredo Pareto observed that 20 percent of the people owned 80 percent of the wealth. Later in the twentieth century, other theorists observed similar tendencies in other fields of study. Quality management guru Joseph Juran wrote of a similar phenomenon, which he called the "vital few and trivial many." The idea that 20 percent of something is always responsible for 80 percent of the results became known as Pareto's principle, or the 80/20 rule.

Source: www.about.com.

- 20 percent of the referral sources account for 80 percent of the clients.
- 20 percent of the therapists are seeing 80 percent of the clients.
- 20 percent of your marketing efforts will produce 80 percent of the results.
- Know what your top 20 percent is and spend your energy making that grow.

Do Less of What Doesn't Produces Results

If an activity is not producing results, stop doing it. Back to Sheila, we don't know enough about her ad to know why it didn't produce any clients. Perhaps the ad was the problem. Maybe the paper was the wrong place to advertise to attract the target client. Maybe Sheila never thought to target a specific type of client. But one thing is certain: If it wasn't working after the fourth week, she should have stopped what she was doing and tried something different.

How does the 80/20 rule apply to your practice? Here are some examples to get you thinking:

- 20 percent of the clients pay 80 percent of the fees. (Where did those clients come from and how can you add more of them to your practice mix?)
- 20 percent of the referral sources send you 80 percent of your clients. (Who are they and how can you get them to refer more clients? How can you find more referral sources like them?)

"You hear daily horror stories of failed businesses, and you wonder how you can succeed while others have fallen by the wayside. The way to do it is to set goals and focus on them. Here's a depressing statistic: only two percent of the population puts their goals into writing. This number certainly doesn't depress guerrillas. Instead, they are encouraged by it because it indicates the low level of competition out there. Of course businesses are going to fall on their capitalistic faces if they have no written goals."

Jay Conrad Levinson (1997), *The Way of the Guerrilla: Achieving Success and Balance as an Entrepreneur in the 21st Century.*

- 20 percent of your promotional activities produce 80 percent of the results. (What activities are the low producers, and how quickly can you eliminate them?)
- 80 percent of your referral sources produce only 20 percent of your clients. (Who are these low producers, and how quickly can you stop spending time and money on them?)

Seven Keys to Effective Marketing

Sarah Warren, a clinical, forensic, and consulting psychologist and coach who has been in practice in Chicago since 1989, offers seven keys to help make marketing a better fit (Warren 2002—reprinted here with permission). Among other interests, Warren enjoys helping clinicians find easy and effective ways to market their services. She offers individual and group coaching on practice development. Warren can be reached at 312-595-1691, by e-mail at DrWarren@multicoach.org, or via her website at www.multicoach.org.

1. *Let people know what problems you solve.* It boils down to letting people know what problems you can help them solve. As a clinician in practice, you might be able to help an anxious person become less anxious.
   - The problem is anxiety.
   - The solution is rendered through psychotherapy.
   - Your audience (the people who need to know that you offer that solution) is your potential referral source, such as colleagues and physicians.
2. *Translate clinical language.* As a clinician you are good at talking to other clinicians. To communicate to a wider audience about problems you can help them solve, you need to use nonclinical language. For instance, perhaps you have expertise from your clinical practice about angry clients, and you'd like to consult with small business owners. Here's how you might translate your clinical knowledge into a solution for small business owners.
   - The problem is managing difficult employees.
   - The solution is delivered through coaching the business owner.
   - The audience for your message is small business owners (or people who know small business owners, which is most of us.)

- Translation: "I coach small business owners to manage difficult employees."
3. *Be yourself, only bigger.* This is advice from a journalist who is
   quite introverted and often has to speak before large audiences
   and who received this useful advice from a colleague: Be yourself, only bigger. You don't have to make yourself into a different
   kind of person. You can be yourself, do what you're good at, and
   communicate that.
4. *Connect with the connectors.* Uncomfortable with the idea of broad-
   casting your services? You can get other people to do it for you.
   Form relationships with outgoing people who know lots of other
   people and love to connect people with each other.
5. *You are already marketing—take it to the next level.* Most of us are at
   least doing small things to let others know what we do. You have
   business cards, you have letterhead, and all of these count.
   Every time you tell someone what you do, you're letting him or
   her know how you can solve problems. It's not that hard to take
   the things you're already doing to the next level. What is the
   next level? More strategic thinking about what problems you
   can solve, how to communicate that, and who will help provide
   direction.
6. *The value of a plan.* When your attention is pulled in all kinds of
   directions, it's easy to get derailed from marketing your practice,
   and having a written plan with a timeline and specific steps that
   you want to take is very useful in helping achieve goals. Consider
   this in developing your business plan (see Chapter 1).
7. *Marketing can be enjoyable.* If you go with your strengths, you can
   have fun playing with different ways of marketing.

Discover and Market Your Niche

WHY IT'S IMPORTANT TO HAVE A NICHE OR SPECIALTY

Whether you choose solo practice or join a group, you should have at least one market niche — an area in which you have special expertise and interest. Having an area of specialization gives clients and referral sources a reason to choose *you* rather than the dozens of other therapists available in your area. Here are some examples of the infinite number of available niches:

- Adolescents
- Adoptive parents
- Adult children of _____
- Alcoholism recovery
- Businesspeople
- Cancer survivors
- Career refocusing
- Couples recovering from infidelity
- Divorced people
- Engaged couples
- Families of people with _____
- Grief recovery
- Immigrants from _____
- Infertile couples
- Newly retired people
- Parents of children with _____
- Parents of teens
- Parents of toddlers
- People having affairs
- People who speak a language other than English
- People with chronic illness
- People with eating disorders
- Postsurgery recovery
- Preteens
- Recovery from trauma (earthquake, tornado, etc.)
- Relocation adjustment
- Single adults in their twenties
- Stay-at-home moms

PRACTICE BY DESIGN: HOW TO FIND YOUR MARKET NICHE

When identifying your niche or specialty, the first place to look is at your own interests and life experiences. Ask yourself these questions:

- What kinds of clients do I most enjoy working with?
- What life experiences have I had that would be valuable to others?
- What training have I had that would qualify me to ethically claim that I specialize in a specific area?

You can have more than one specialty, but limiting it to a few areas is best, because you want people to think of you when they think of your specialty. Listing 8 or 10 areas of specialty in your marketing materials creates the impression that you are all over the place and don't truly specialize in anything.

Here are some examples:

- Tamara was born in Israel and speaks fluent Hebrew. She markets her counseling services to Israeli immigrants and conducts many of her sessions in Hebrew.
- Krystal spent 15 years as an executive recruiter before becoming a therapist. She specializes in career counseling and offers a support group for survivors of corporate downsizing.
- Jack is a registered dietician and licensed psychologist. He specializes in working with clients with eating disorders.
- Belinda is an adoptive parent. She runs a support group for prospective adoptive parents.

Your specialty "can't be complicated, high-minded, flowery, obtuse, or difficult to understand. It has to be a simple idea, expressed with simple words, and immediately understandable by your customers, your employees, and the media."

Al Ries (1996), *Focus: The Future of Your Company Depends On It.*

Make a list of words and phrases to help you identify one or more areas of specialty for your therapy practice. Make a list of ways in which you are unique. Write down whatever comes to mind—there are no right or wrong answers. The purpose of making this list is to help you identify areas that will help you stand out from the crowd of other practitioners in your geographic area.

Consider factors such as these:

- Where you grew up
- Where you went to school
- Places you've lived
- Special talents
- Past misfortunes
- Languages you speak fluently
- Special training
- Past careers
- Unusual skills
- Life experiences
- Things you've overcome

STORIES FROM THE REAL WORLD

When you first start your practice, you may try to be the all-purpose therapist. When clients call and ask to see you, you want to help and you want the business, so you respond to most requests. However, it is not realistic to believe that you can serve every mental health need. It is important to decide how best you can serve your clients and what type of practice will provide balance and diversity in your work life.

In addition to these basic considerations, there is the aspect of liability. If you provide treatment in areas where you are not qualified, your state licensing agency may can view it as unprofessional conduct. So decide what you want to do, where you can make the best contribution, and then get the education, training and experience to do it well. This is the best way to serve your clients, and it is best for you, too.

Susan Back, MSW

Sometimes it helps to get the opinion of a friend or colleague. Consider sharing your list with a few trusted friends and colleagues and asking them for feedback.

Examples of Therapists Targeting Niche Markets

Here are several examples of professionals who have carved out niches.

Divorce Issues. Rick Tivers, MSW, and Chet Mirman, PhD, manage the Center for Divorce Recovery. They have developed a number of practice specialties, including a therapeutic support group for women. As you probably know, support and therapy groups are often clinically relevant, cost-effective, and profitable. Tivers and Mirman train and supervise prelicensed postdoctoral staff members to lead their groups.

Prelicensed professionals may effectively lead such groups. This arrangement is legally and ethically appropriate as long as licensed professionals supervise the interns and trainees. Generally, MCOs and insurance companies do not pay nonlicensed clinicians, so these groups are offered fee-for-services at an affordable rate to draw participants. Such groups do not compete with individual clinical work.

Tivers and Mirman market the group by sending the following letter to professionals in their area:

To Whom It May Concern:

The breakup of a marriage can be an overwhelmingly stressful event, fraught with uncertainty, upheaval, and loss of control. Women going through divorce have a unique set of challenges to contend with, including financial insecurity, potentially reentering the job market, and juggling the responsibilities of children and career. The emotional toll of a divorce can be particularly difficult for women who face the challenge of integrating new and old roles as they struggle to rebuild their identity. While getting a divorce is an extremely painful experience, it can also be a time of tremendous personal growth and development.

We provide a therapeutic and supportive women's group to help women through this difficult time. Our group is a safe place for women

continues

167

(Continued)
to connect, grow, share difficult feelings, improve their sense of efficacy and self-esteem, develop tools that foster healthier intimate relationships, become more powerful, and gain greater inner strength.

We have enclosed a few flyers for you to give to your interested clients. Please consider informing your clients that this valuable resource is now available to them.

Sincerely,
Nicole R. Gerber, PsyD   Laura Harwood, PsyD

Attached to this letter is the following flyer noting aspects of the group and information about the leaders (see Chapter 12 for more information on mailers and flyers):

A Group for Women

- Connect with other women who share similar issues.
- Explore and improve your relationships with others.
- Work through feelings of sadness, fear, anger and loneliness.
- Build self-esteem and self-acceptance.
- Become more powerful and gain greater inner strength.

Call Laura or Nicole at 847-291-0468.

Dr. Laura Harwood received her doctorate in clinical psychology from the Illinois School of Professional Psychology. She currently works with individuals, couples, and groups. Her practice focuses on relationships.

Dr. Nicole Gerber received her doctorate in clinical psychology from the Illinois School of Professional Psychology. She currently works with individuals, couples, families, and groups. Her practice focuses on relationships and women's issues.

Rick Tivers, MSW, earned his MSW at the University of Illinois, Jane Addams College of Social Work. He is a group therapist who employs active process work, including psychodrama and Gestalt activities.

The preceding information is used with permission.

Services for Women with Breast Cancer. Claudette Ozoa, PhD, has developed a niche working with women who have breast cancer. It's called "One Pink Ribbon." She has developed the following tools to market to clients and referral sources in her niche:

- A website (www.OnePinkRibbon.com)
- Thematic business cards
- Professional and lay presentations
- A bimonthly newsletter called *A Common Thread*™, available in hard copy and by e-mail. It provides information on breast cancer, coping strategies, client-generated questions and answers, and a review of recent articles and research on breast cancer.

Dr. Ozoa offers the following services:

Individual coaching
- Relaxation techniques
- Communication with family and friends about breast cancer
- Self-image and sexuality
- Working with the medical system
- Becoming a proactive patient
- Developing inner strength and spirituality
- Future orientation

Group coaching
- Facilitating connection between women—developing community
- Offering group ListServ, which enables participants to connect without the constrictions of time or geography

Psychoeducational Groups. Saint Louis therapist Patricia Kyle Dennis, MSW, specializes in eating disorders and offers a 10-week psychoeducational group for adult women who struggle with overeating and weight gain. Her groups are limited to seven participants and are not intended for anyone suffering from bulimia or anorexia. The total cost of the group is $450, and follow-up groups and individual sessions are available. Dennis also offers group psychotherapy for people who have completed the 10-week psychoeducational group.

Dennis provides individual and family therapy for clients with binge eating disorder, bulimia, anorexia, and other eating disorders.

She provides a brochure called *Help for the Problems of Overeating and Weight Gain.*

She says, "I believe that strengthening private practice is an important way to preserve true psychotherapy. I am an example of someone who dropped out of managed care and survived. Not only did I survive, but I make a lot more money and have a lot more time than therapists who are chained to insurance companies." At the time of publication, Dennis is running her sixty-fifth group. The goals of the 10-week group are as follows:

OVEREATING AND WEIGHT GAIN PSYCHOTHERAPY GROUPS FOR WOMEN

- You can learn how to tune in to your natural controls over food.
- You can discover the reasons you overeat and learn alternative coping strategies.
- You can understand how weight may serve as a protection and learn other ways of protecting yourself.
- You can improve your health and self-esteem at any shape or size.

Patricia Kyle Dennis, MSW

GO WHERE OTHERS AREN'T

In *Selling the Invisible,* author Harry Beckwith (1997) describes how the success of the retail giant Wal-Mart resulted from building stores in towns where other retailers wouldn't dream of going. When founder Sam Walton died, he was the world's richest man, and Wal-Mart was the largest retailer in the United States.

The "Go where others aren't" strategy can apply to factors besides your location. It can also mean marketing your therapy services to people in special situations—especially populations that other therapists tend to avoid.

PRACTICE BY DESIGN: MAXIMIZE YOUR INCOME BY DIVERSIFYING YOUR PRACTICE

It is a challenge to make a significant income as an independent practitioner, especially in the first few years. Building related activities into the scope of your business has several benefits:

- You can earn more money when you are involved in more activities.
- You will meet more people and potential referral sources when you are involved in activities other than individual therapy.
- You avoid the problem of professional isolation when you reach out and participate in a variety of activities.

Some examples of ways to diversify your practice include the following:

- Work for a managed care company as a case manager or staff therapist.
- Do behavioral assessments for schools and companies.
- Teach classes at local schools and universities.
- Offer your services as an expert witness in areas where you have competence.
- Present seminars and workshops at local companies and organizations.
- Become a divorce mediator.

Of course, you should pursue opportunities in these areas only when you have the proper training and experience. If you are interested in learning how to do any of these jobs, start by searching the Internet using the topic of your choice as your keyword. For example, if you want to learn about divorce mediation, go to google.com, type in "divorce mediation," and follow the links. You may also find links to useful information on the websites of professional associations (APA, AAMFT, NASW, etc.) and in their member publications.

BUILD YOUR PRACTICE OUTSIDE OF MANAGED CARE

Even though you may be getting referrals from MCOs, HMOs, and insurers, you may seek to build your practice with work outside of the managed care system.

In a paper presented at the American Psychological Association's Annual Meeting in San Francisco (August 2001), Steven Walfish presented a paper outlining many practice niches that you may wish to explore. (See also the reference section at the back of this book.)

- Business psychology
- Consultation to organizations
- Fee-for-service activities
- Forensic (criminal or police) psychology
- Group therapy
- Health psychology (the relationship between mental and physical health)
- Psychoeducational services (providing education about psychological topics)
- Services to government
- Teaching and supervision

Most professional ethics (and in some cases, state laws) require that a clinician have appropriate training before independently performing any clinical or other professional service.

For a free copy of his paper, e-mail Steven Walfish at psychpubs @aol.com.

PRACTICE BY DESIGN: TEAM UP WITH PRIMARY CARE PHYSICIANS

While behavioral healthcare providers are often the most highly trained professionals in our communities, we are often isolated from the primary healthcare system. You can diminish this isolation by marketing your services to primary care physicians (PCPs).

The managed care system is placing increased pressure on PCPs to diagnose and treat a broad spectrum of emotional and behavioral problems. You can help PCPs respond to this need by offering to work with their patients. This is one way for mental health professionals (MHPs) to build their practices.

Successful collaboration with PCPs works best when it is a win-win

---

PCPs treat more than 60 percent of all mental health problems in the United States without assistance from mental health providers.

---

business relationship for everyone (the physician, the client, and the MHP). The benefits to the PCP include:

- Solving a client care problem
- Being given feedback and information about their clients' status and progress
- Receiving referrals back from you
- Reducing hassles with client care

You can provide:

- Important diagnostic information about the client
- Recommendations for additional treatment options
- Information about progress of psychotropic medications
- Increased client compliance and satisfaction

Be persistent. When you market your services to PCPs, you are competing for attention with a multitude of individuals and companies, including pharmaceutical companies, medical supply companies, and other specialists. Doctors' offices are very busy today, so you will need to be persistent, making several contacts to establish and maintain a relationship with the PCP. Plan to make regular contact; once is not enough. While it may be difficult to get your foot in the door, many PCPs invite clinicians to practice in their offices either part-time or full-time.

Communicate carefully. It is important to establish a way to communicate with the office staff, especially when a situation requires immediate action. You will need to arrange a way to quickly contact the physician's staff when you need them, and they will need a way to contact you when your services are needed. Since most PCPs take phone calls during sessions and most MHPs do not, you will need to establish clear communication procedures, especially when a situation is urgent.

Meet regularly. If possible, schedule regular meetings with the PCP to discuss mutual clients. You can meet regularly for coffee, breakfast, or lunch, or you can set up a consultation time.

Join hospital staffs. Find out how to join the staff at your local medical, surgical, and general hospitals. It can be difficult to do, but be persistent and assertive. Once you are on staff, make contact with physicians and other healthcare workers by:

- Joining their hospital staff committees
- Offering to provide continuing medical education seminars
- Offering to provide client education and/or prevention services

Look for ways to market to the entire medical community, including:

- Physician assistants
- Nurse practitioners
- Nurses
- Line staff and clerks

Provide feedback. PCPs strive to have long-term relationships with their clients and provide care that includes comprehensive, continuous services in sickness and in health. Providing feedback on client progress is essential to the PCP. Most PCPs want only a brief note (one to three paragraphs, no longer than one page) about your work with the client. They usually want a diagnosis, a brief explanation of your treatment plan, and your recommendations for improving client care.

Encourage client follow-up. It is also important to encourage the client to return to his or her PCP for follow-up visits. This is one way of continuing to market your services to the PCP.

WHERE TO FOCUS YOUR MARKETING ENERGIES

You have a variety of areas in which to focus your marketing activities. But first consider the uses of various avenues based on your goals and your practice's focus. Remember, one size fits few. Here is a quick list:

1. The power of newspapers is news. Marketing that is newsy gets noticed because news is in the forefront of readers' minds.
2. The power of magazines is credibility. Readers unconsciously attach to the advertiser the same credibility that they associate with the magazine.
3. The power of radio is intimacy. Usually radio is a one-on-one situation allowing for a close and intimate connection between listener and marketer.
4. The power of direct mail is urgency. Time-dated offers that might expire before recipients can act often motivate them to act now.

5. The power of brochures is the ability to give details. Few media avenues allow you as much time and space to expound on your benefits as a brochure.

6. The power of the Yellow Pages is in providing even more information. Here, prospects get a line on the entire competitive situation and can compare.

7. The power of the Internet is interactivity. You can flag people's attention, inform them, answer their questions, and take their orders or make appointments.

This list has been adapted from the *Guerrilla Marketing Report*, vol. 1, no. 57, June 28, 2002, written by Mitch Meyerson and Jay Conrad Levinson. They offer free marketing articles at www.gmarketingcoach .com, based on Levinson's best-selling marketing series of all time (copyright 2000, Mitch Meyerson, and reproduced with permission of the author).

PRACTICE BY DESIGN: BUILD YOUR PRACTICE BY DIRECT CONTRACTING

Direct contracting means putting together an agreement to provide clinical services to an entity such as a business, employer, association, organization, or school district. Such an arrangement eliminates the intermediate layer of managed care organizations and can be a win-win for the purchaser of the services and for the therapist.

In a direct contracting arrangement, you would discount your usual and customary clinical fees because there is no MCO taking a cut. You may be able to negotiate fees that are higher than you typically earn from MCOs. You also have the benefit of eliminating case managers or utilization reviewers.

When you are seeking to establish a direct contract, you must price your services at competitive rates. You must be able to manage the following:

- Reduced fees for service (rFFS)
- Case rates (one fee paid for an episode of care, regardless of duration of the care per client)
- Capitation (a monthly fee typically paid on a per member per month basis, regardless of the volume or cost of service utilization)

As a first step, consult with your state insurance commission to learn if is legal to direct-contract under a capitated payment system without an HMO license. It is recommended that you work with a qualified attorney or financial professional as you pursue this idea.

Following is a general overview of just one method of direct contracting. The information is not meant to be exhaustive.

Most direct contracting opportunities are best suited to group practices that can accommodate a large influx of clients. It is most likely that the contract would be with employers, since they fund employee health benefits and tend to have the authority to act without excessive bureaucracy. If you find such an employer, your group practice must be certain that you can meet their needs for mental health services. As a direct contractor, your group should be able to provide the following services:

- Individual and family therapy
- Medication consultation
- Ability to serve all age ranges
- Both general practice and specialties relevant to the employees' needs (child and family services if the employees tend to be younger, substance abuse services if there are overnight shift workers, geriatric psych services for an older population, etc.)

Many employers may be familiar (and thus more comfortable) with employee assistance programs (EAPs) or EAP-like services. Your marketing materials should emphasize the powerful role of psychotherapy in offsetting medical costs, increasing employee productivity, and so forth. You should also consider the merits and problems of providing services at the place of business as a convenience to utilization (and as a means of saving on overhead costs).

WHERE CAN I FIND DIRECT CONTRACTS?

You may be able to contract directly with businesses and organizations in your geographic area as a way to build your practice outside of managed care. Increasing dissatisfaction with MCOs and HMOs over the hassles of getting approvals for care drives many businesses and organizations to look for alternatives. Employers, who growing impatient with how MCOs and HMOs cut corners, still expect savings on the services provided. With many MHPs seeking to build practices free of managed care, there are growing opportunities for contracting directly with employers to provide psychological services.

The following organizations may offer opportunities for direct contracting:

- Businesses
- Agencies
- Organizations
- Schools, school districts, and colleges (for both employees and students)
- CEOs, benefits managers, directors of human resources, Chambers of Commerce

You will need the following set of skills to build a successful direct contracting practice:

- Strong practice management skills (see Chapters 2 through 5)
- Assessment skills (see Chapter 5)
- Treatment planning skills (see Chapter 5)
- Outcomes management skills (see Chapter 7)
- Reporting to payor (e.g., aggregated numbers of clients using services on a quarterly basis)
- Results-based findings to be used in practice management (e.g., determining mean number of sessions for which diagnoses yield certain outcomes)
- Access to legal, contractual, and financial services

Successful direct contracting typically requires the following features:

1. *Initial practice feasibility analysis.* Make sure you can deliver services at a price that works for you and your potential customers.
2. *Varied pricing structure (e.g., rFFS, case rates, capitation) capability.* You have the maximum negotiating position if you can offer your services via differing pricing models that best fit your potential customers.
3. *Outcomes management systems integrated with cost-for-care data.* Be sure to have integrated outcomes management systems in your practice so you know how extensively you can treat clients and

the costs associated with such care. That is, know the cost of your proverbial "pound of cure."

4. *Reporting protocols.* Consider what your potential customers may want in terms of reporting—typically aggregated reports of access to services utilization and the like.

5. *Strong risk management.* Ensure that crises and high-risk cases (e.g., suicidal or homicidal ideation) are handled promptly, ethically, and appropriately.

6. *Patient/employee education opportunities.* Providing such services can be more effective than providing clinical services.

7. *Good claims administration.* Make certain that billing is processed properly in order to maintain cash flow.

8. *Good utilization management.* Now it's your responsibility to make certain that each client gets the proper type and amount of services. Waste does no one any good.

9. *Integrated quality management.* Quality services are not an add-on after something has happened. Quality must be integrated into everything you do. If you don't have time to do it right the first time, how are you going to have time to do it over?

10. *Ability to manage legal and contractual issues.* Have qualified legal consultation for all contractual matters. It is a good investment.

11. *Strong contract and practice management.* Execute contracts that you know you can service, and be confident in the skills of all members of your practice—clinical and clerical.

12. *Ability to provide internal marketing and employee awareness.* Providing employee education opportunities is an effective way to get the word out to employees about your services. Involve them in educational activities before they need your clinical services.

13. *Actuarial consultation of case rate or capitated payments.* Never guess or approximate when it comes to payment rates. Obtain the advice of a qualified accountant.

14. *Prevention and wellness programming development.* Inviting employees to educational events and encouraging them to seek services sooner rather than later is more economical than waiting until they are in crisis.

15. *Agreements with hospitals.* You may need this feature if inpatient care is necessitated by a contract. Establish adjunctive, inpatient service agreements with ancillary instructions *before* you have a

client who needs such services. Otherwise you and/or your practice may be held responsible for *paying* for the inpatient care if the client is hospitalized and you have contracted to *provide all behavioral healthcare services.* The following case highlights this risk: An outpatient medical practice group contracted to provide medical services and neglected to consider that some clients may need hospitalization. When such a need arose, the medical practice group was judged to be responsible for the hospital costs as well as for the provision of their own clinical services. This was *not* what these healthcare professionals had intended. This illustrates why it is critical to establish hospital relationships before these services are needed.

Most successful and economically viable direct contracts provide quality of care and supervision. They may also keep costs down by using interns, who should be under rigorous supervision. The contracting employer and clients, of course, must understand and consent to the use of interns.

Behavioral health clinicians always exercise great caution regarding confidentiality, and it is especially important in terms of providing reports to the payor and/or employer. You must make it clear in the contract that all reports and data representation will be composed of aggregate data. They will *not* include identifying information about any individual.

Things to Consider When Developing a Direct Contracting Agreement
1. Briefer is better. Short-term therapies are the rule in this model.
2. Early identification and referral maximize the impact of your treatment and clients' gains from your program. It also generally leads to fewer sessions needed.
3. Is there a need for external referral? Consider such an option, especially if it is for services you cannot provide, such as medication evaluation if you are not an M.D.
4. Look for other ways to meet clients' needs, such as these:
   - Assess their needs to better understand what they require.
   - Find out whether they would like to have sessions on-site. These can be a convenience for the clients and reduce overhead costs for you.

- Find out whether they would like to have on-site workshops. This is a convenience for the clients and reduces overhead costs for you. It is also a way to help with prevention and early intervention.
- Find out whether they would like to have brown-bag lectures during their lunchtime on-site.

The *brown-bag lunch meeting* is a casual opportunity for you to go on-site and present talks on low-threat topics like stress management, communications, relationships, and parenting.

- Offer lots of practical tips and tools.
- Expect some participants will benefit enough that they will not need to access your services. This is good for the client and for you if you have a capitated financial arrangement.
- Expect that other participants will attend in order to size you up and determine from a safe distance whether to see you privately later.
- Early intervention is always the key, for everyone. Prevention is always the most cost-effective policy.

A typical agreement for direct contracting would include the following components:

- Three to five consultations per year per client
- A toll-free phone number with 24/7 on-call coverage
- Promotional materials provided by the group practice
- Wellness in-service presentations
- Newsletters, e-mails, and perhaps a website
- Satisfaction surveys
- Annual reports
- A process for managing referrals

See the appendix for an example of a direct contracting pricing model.

CHAPTER 10

Generate Referrals

WHAT YOU WILL LEARN:

Where Do Referrals Come From?

Practice by Design: How to Get People to Refer Clients to You

Practice by Design: Plan for Developing Referral Sources

Practice by Design: Networking 101
Networking Do's and Don'ts

Practice by Design: Your Unique Selling Point
The Elevator Introduction

Networking Groups

What to Do if You Dislike Networking

Three Referral Taboos

Management Metrics: Tracking Your Referrals
Positively Reinforce Every Referral
Referral Action Plan

Practice by Design: Beyond Networking

To succeed in private practice, whether you are in a group or on your own, you must be able to get people to refer clients to you. While a few fortunate therapists seem to have a magic touch and have a steady stream of referrals from the day they open their practice doors, the rest of us have to work at it. It may seem overwhelming, but you can learn to do it. In this chapter, you will learn where referrals come from, how you can target specific referral sources, and how to market to them.

WHERE DO REFERRALS COME FROM?

Just about anyone can refer clients to you. The following is a list of ideas to get you started thinking about the many people in your life who are potential referral sources.

- Current clients
- Former clients
- Other professionals
- People in the educational system
- Nutritionists
- Your doctor (sometimes, with a lot of hard work)
- Your next-door neighbor
- The person who installed your countertop
- Your mother-in-law
- A coworker of your spouse
- A distant relative
- The attorney who handled your divorce
- Your dentist
- Business and personal coaches
- Consumer groups
- Police departments
- Your manicurist
- Your hairstylist
- Other mental health professionals

- Attorneys
- Acupuncturists
- Chiropractors
- Massage therapists
- Ministers, priests, and rabbis
- Human resources directors
- EAP administrators
- The court system
- The probation department
- The schoolteacher of a client
- The people sitting next to you at an Amway pitch
- Sports trainers
- Personal shoppers
- The police officer giving you a ticket
- The people you meet at cocktail parties
- The cable guy
- The supermarket checker
- Social agency staff members (DCS, probation, conciliation court, etc.)

Where Do Referrals Come From?

People you meet in the following situations may also refer clients to you:

- Making presentations at professional conferences
- Conducting training at counseling centers where interns are being trained as therapists
- Offering free workshops and seminars to the public
- Participating in activities in a professional association
- Participating in Chamber of Commerce activities
- Belonging to a weekly networking group
- Regularly offering to speak to community groups and civic organizations
- Free consultations to social agencies
- Free consultations to self-help groups
- Serving on the board of directors of a social agency or nonprofit counseling center
- Giving free talks to groups at the library, schools, teacher groups, religious groups, PTA, youth groups, and so on as a public service

The following two groups offer possibilities for referrals also:

1. Doctors
   - Bariatric
   - Cardiologists
   - Dentists
   - Family physicians
   - General practitioners
   - Gerontologists
   - Internists
   - Neurologists
   - OB/GYNs
   - Pediatricians
   - Plastic surgeons
   - Psychiatrists
2. The Educational System
   - Teachers
   - Principals
   - School counselors
   - Counseling center staff

- School secretaries
- Professors
- Private learning centers
- Private tutors

"The ten best ways to build positive word of mouth are the following: keeping promises, punctuality, ethics, positive demeanor, respect, gratitude, sincerity, positive feedback, enthusiasm, and initiative."

Jay Levinson and Seth Godin (1997), *Get What You Deserve!*

PRACTICE BY DESIGN: HOW TO GET PEOPLE TO REFER CLIENTS TO YOU

Here are some suggestions for getting people and organizations to refer clients to *you* instead of to someone else.

1. Think long term. Don't give up when you hear, "I'm satisfied with the therapist I refer to now." Satisfaction may be temporary. The referrer's needs may change, or you may provide a good reason for them to refer clients to you.
2. Develop a relationship with referral sources, even if they presently refer clients to another therapist.
3. Study the needs of those who provide referrals. The key is to find a need gap and offer a solution.
4. Sell yourself. Come up with new ideas for your prospective referral sources. Show them that you are on their team, whether or not they refer to you.
5. Add value. You have to differentiate your service with added value—whatever it takes to be better than your competition.
6. Ask them to refer *just a few* people to you.
7. Be persistent. Nothing succeeds more than persistence. All things being equal, the persistent person will win the account every time. Keep in touch with prospects, think long term, be a consultant and ally, and you will plant drought-resistant seeds.

The preceding list was adapted from Tony Alessandra, PhD, Gary Couture, and Gregg Baron (1992), *The Idea-a-Day Guide to Super Selling and Customer Service: 250 Ways to Increase Your Top and Bottom Lines*.

PRACTICE BY DESIGN: PLAN FOR DEVELOPING REFERRAL SOURCES

Now it's time to get specific about how you will apply what you've learned to your own practice. Use the information on the previous pages to develop your own list of referral sources. Your list will be most useful if you make it as specific as possible, using three columns, one each for *who*, *how*, and *when* you will contact each name on the list.

PRACTICE BY DESIGN: NETWORKING 101

It should be obvious that in order for you to build your referral network, you have to network. Many therapists resist the idea of networking because it seems too much like selling, which feels intimidating and undignified. The fact is that networking is a very important part of marketing, especially marketing an intangible service like counseling.

When people decide to see a therapist, their first choice is nearly always a professional about whom they have some knowledge. The decision to look in the Yellow Pages or go through a health plan list is usually a last resort. The more people who know you, the more exposure you create for yourself, and the more potential clients will call you.

The purpose of networking is to create more referrals. Networking means going to social and business functions, talking with people, and getting to know them. It's making contact with other people so they can refer clients to you and you can refer to them.

In *Marketing Your Services: For People Who Hate to Sell*, author Rick Crandall (1996) lists four tips for smart networking:

1. *Have goals.* Know what you want to accomplish or learn when you meet people.
2. *Be prepared.* Always have business cards with you. Be sure to dress in keeping with the professional image you want to create.

3. *Make lists of contacts.* Make a list of people who can help you with information and contacts. Make a second list of people you can help. This will help prepare you for when you see them at a business or social event.

4. *Reinforce yourself.* Make notes about conversations you have after each networking event.

STORIES FROM THE REAL WORLD

Think of networking as akin to spinning a spider's web. If you weave together enough contacts and connections, something will eventually stick. Don't look for a one-to-one correspondence between your interactions in the community and referrals to your practice. Think about the big picture and the long run. Recently, I was contacted by someone looking to get into therapy who had seen me give a pro bono talk at the public library 12 years earlier.

Daniel J. Abrahamson, PhD

NETWORKING DO'S AND DON'TS

There are a few things to keep in mind while you are meeting people at business or social functions:

1. Never make fun of or bad-mouth therapy, counseling, or your profession.
2. Never make fun of "crazies" or clients.
3. Avoid shoptalk with other therapists when you are interacting with people of other professions.
4. Never practice "therapy" at parties or business functions.
5. Pay attention to the questions people ask you. Sometimes you are being interviewed as a potential therapist.
6. Be aware of friends and acquaintances of your clients who may be attending the same gathering you are. Always keep your confidentiality monitor turned on high.

An important networking skill is to introduce yourself in an interesting way. In *Marketing Your Services,* author Crandall advises that you avoid the "prisoner of war" introduction—simply stating your name, rank, and serial number. He suggests that you remember to speak with enthusiasm, humor, and to include something personal about yourself. You should also mention your areas of specialty.

PRACTICE BY DESIGN: YOUR UNIQUE SELLING POINT

Many businesspeople call their special introduction their unique selling point (USP). According to Jacci Howard Bear in her article "Develop Your USP" on www.about.com:

> USP is your *unique selling point*. It is what sets you and your business—or you as an individual—apart from your competition. It can be an actual fact or a perceived difference or specialty. Every business needs one.
>
> Your USP may be expressed as a summary of what you do and how you do it better or differently than others. Often, a USP can be summed up in just a few words that become something of an advertising jingle or catch-phrase. No matter how you express it, your USP should focus on how it benefits the customer.

THE ELEVATOR INTRODUCTION

Lynn Grodzki (2000) describes the same idea in *Building Your Ideal Private Practice: A Guide for Therapists and Other Healing Professionals*. Grodzki calls it the *elevator introduction*. She says that when you are doing any type of marketing, you need to make your message concise. She advises that you learn to communicate what you do in the amount of time it would take for a short elevator ride. This sounds easy, but it can be difficult to do unless you practice beforehand.

Grodzki suggests these guidelines for designing your elevator introduction:

- Limit your description to just two or three brief sentences.
- Avoid using technical terms.
- Speak in a positive way.
- Focus on just one aspect of your work (keep it simple).
- Practice until you can say it without hesitation.

Here are a couple of ideas to help you put together your introduction:

"Hello, I'm _____. I've been a licensed counselor for _____ years. I work with both individuals and couples, and I am specially trained to help adolescents and their families. I seem to have a special talent for helping families thrive during the adolescent years."

"My name is _____. I'm a licensed marriage and family therapist here in Springfield. I help couples put the spark back into their relationships."

Networking Groups

There are business networking groups in almost every city and town across the United States. You can find one by contacting your Chamber of Commerce and asking local business people. Here are some suggestions for getting the most from such groups:

1. It's best to visit each one once and then choose one or two to join. You won't get the maximum benefit by just visiting one time, since that doesn't enable you to develop a relationship with anyone.
2. Attend regularly and participate actively in the discussions. Look for ways to contribute, and give as much time and effort as you can. It will come back to you. It may take a year or more, but your efforts will not be wasted. Think of your time as an investment in your business.
3. If there aren't any groups in your area, start your own. Go through the telephone book or the Chamber of Commerce mem-

---

"There may be very little difference between your product and your competitors'—but if you can't find a way to communicate uniqueness and connect it to a need of your target, you might as well quit fighting your competition and sell out to them."

www.BusinessTown.com

"Networking is a lifestyle of sharing resources, information, and ideas. Networking requires work—time, effort, and energy."

Susan Roane (1993), *The Secrets of Savvy Networking: How to Make the Best Connections for Business and Personal Success.*

bership list and call people. There are always others out there who want to develop their business relationships.

In *Getting Business to Come to You: Everything You Need to Know to Do Your Own Advertising, Public Relations, Direct Mail, and Sales Promotion, and Attract All the Business You Can Handle,* authors Paul and Sarah Edwards (1991) provide the following tips for making your networking efforts productive:

1. Arrive at any networking event at least 15 minutes early.
2. Don't wait for something to happen to you. Take matters into your own hands. The authors suggest that you view every networking event as if you were the host instead of a guest. Walk up to other guests, smile, and hold out your hand.
3. Prepare a dynamic introduction and use it. They call this a "16-second sizzler."
4. Always bring plenty of your business cards.
5. Ask every person you meet for a business card.
6. Make notes on the business cards you collect.
7. Print your name on your name tag in large letters. Wear it on your right side so people can see it easily.

STORIES FROM THE REAL WORLD

Professional societies such as your state psychological association can provide you with more networking and marketing benefit per dollar spent than just about anything else you do. Think of your dues as a small investment in your practice. If you don't pay your rent, you won't have an office. If you don't pay your professional dues, you won't have a profession.

Daniel J. Abrahamson, PhD

8. Focus on one person at a time. Take your time and avoid rushing.

9. When a conversation slows down, politely wrap it up. Excuse yourself and move on to a new person.

10. Stay at least 15 minutes after the event. Take your time and don't rush away.

11. Place a follow-up phone call to people with business-related potential within a few days after the event. Arrange meetings with them to get to know each other better. Keep the focus on how you can help each other get more business.

12. Add the names of everyone you meet to your mailing list.

13. Send a thank-you note or place a thank-you telephone call to anyone who sends you a referral.

14. Keep your networking activity to a manageable level. Attending too many events will leave you feeling burned out.

WHAT TO DO IF YOU DISLIKE NETWORKING

Plenty of people say they dislike the idea of networking. The idea of going to a new place, walking in alone, and making small talk with a bunch of new people is pretty frightening to most of us. If networking intimidates you, here are two ways you can make it easier on yourself:

1. *Identify the best networker you know.* Think of three or four people who network especially well. Ask them to help you learn to network. People love being asked for advice and guidance.

2. *Don't go alone.* Ask a friend to join you. Explain ahead of time that social gatherings intimidate you and ask your friend if you can lean on him or her. Then make conversation with your friend and others. Here are some things to talk about at business and social functions:
   - The facility
   - The food
   - The organization
   - The traffic and parking dilemma
   - The guest of honor
   - The charity or community that will benefit from the event

THREE REFERRAL TABOOS

When you are talking with a referral source, be sure to avoid the following:

1. Never talk about how you need business. Concentrate on how you can help others.
2. Never give referral sources a lot of promotional materials. Do not mail or e-mail or stop by with a stack of your cards, newsletters, or brochures—unless the person has asked for them.
3. Never say anything negative about any client, another therapist, or competing counseling practice.

This advice is from Paul and Sarah Edwards (1991), *Getting Business to Come to You: Everything You Need to Know to Do Your Own Advertising, Public Relations, Direct Mail, and Sales Promotion, and Attract All the Business You Can Handle* (p. 414).

MANAGEMENT METRICS: TRACKING YOUR REFERRALS

Always ask new clients how they heard about you. Have a place to keep track of this information. It will help you identify:

- Which 20 percent of your referral sources are referring 80 percent of your clients
- Which 20 percent of your marketing efforts are producing 80 percent of your clients

POSITIVELY REINFORCE EVERY REFERRAL

Remember the principles of positive reinforcement as you build your practice. *Always* send a thank-you note or call anyone who refers a client

---

"Go for upbeat, unusual observations that will pique people's interest."

Susan Roane (1988), *How to Work a Room: A Guide to Successfully Managing the Mingling.*

---

to you. Keep in mind confidentiality guidelines and simply say, "thank you for the client referral."

REFERRAL ACTION PLAN

See Table 10.1 for a plan-of-action example.

TABLE 10.1   Referral Action Plan

I want to have _____ weekly clients by _____. My average hourly fee will be $_____. I will get there by selling, hustling, giving, sharing, talking, teaching, loving, wanting, showing, doing, _____, , _____, _____, _____, _____, and with the following four groups of people:

A. Professionals	B. Local Businesspeople	C. Friends and Acquaintances	D. Others
_____	_____	_____	_____
_____	_____	_____	_____
_____	_____	_____	_____
_____	_____	_____	_____
_____	_____	_____	_____
_____	_____	_____	_____
_____	_____	_____	_____

I will make myself known to Groups A, B, C, and D in the following ways (use the accompanying bulleted list for inspiration):

A. _____   _____   _____
B. _____   _____   _____
C. _____   _____   _____
D. _____   _____   _____

- Advertisements
- Brochures
- Business directories
- Card decks
- Classes
- Community contacts
- Media contacts
- Networking
- Newsletters

- People from the past
- Personal contacts
- Posting flyers
- Press releases
- Sending flyers
- Speaking engagements
- Volunteer assignments
- Workshops
- Writing articles

PRACTICE BY DESIGN: BEYOND NETWORKING

In *Nichecraft: Using Your Specialness to Focus Your Business, Corner Your Market and Make Customers Seek You Out,* author Lynda Falkenstein (2000) describes the importance of going beyond networking to build relationships. She says that it is critical to actually schedule time for developing and maintaining relationships with business and professional friends and colleagues. Exchanging business cards is just the beginning—if your goal is to build a relationship of trust and mutual respect, you will have to take the time to earn it.

Start at the beginning, when you attend a gathering where you know you will be meeting someone you want to get to know better. Take the time to learn a few things about several of the people you are likely to meet, and don't be afraid to mention it when you are talking with them. Use your therapist skills to ask good questions and listen carefully. Just as you connect with clients and build on the connection, use the same skills and natural abilities to connect with new business associates. You know what to do: Ask the open-ended questions you know so well how to ask, and sit back and be yourself.

Visit www.falkenstein.com for information about Falkenstein's excellent books and products.

CHAPTER 11

Attract Media Attention

WHAT YOU WILL LEARN:

Why Publicity Is an Essential Part of Marketing

Practice by Design: Learn about the Local Media
    Know the Key Players at Newspapers and Television Stations

Practice by Design: Send Your Materials to the Right People
    Where Should You Target Your Publicity?

Practice by Design: Tips to Help You Establish Your Publicity Strategy

Practice by Design: Start Locally, Go Global Later
    Choosing a Spokesperson for Your Group
    Tips for Working with Representatives of the Media

Practice by Design: How to Write Press (Media) Releases
    How to Make Your Press Release Stand Out
    Sample Media Release

Practice by Design: Public Service Announcements (PSAs)
    Sample PSA

Practice by Design: Tips for Writing Broadcast Media Releases
  and Scripts

Practice by Design: Attract Attention by Writing a Feature Story

Practice by Design: Make the Most of Your Timing
    Should You Follow Up?

Practice by Design: Make Rain with a Media Promotional Kit

Practice by Design: Your Publicity Action Plan

Why Publicity Is an Essential Part of Marketing

Publicity means gaining media coverage for your practice. A strong publicity campaign should be an essential part of your marketing program for the following reasons:

1. Unlike advertising, publicity doesn't cost any money.
2. Favorable publicity (being mentioned in a newspaper article or on a television news program) means increased credibility for your practice.
3. Positive media exposure often results in referrals.
4. Being mentioned in the media often results in being invited to speak to groups. This leads to further positive exposure.
5. Favorable publicity can be used in brochures and other marketing literature.

It takes a bit of work and lots of creativity, but a strong public relations campaign can result in many referrals. In this chapter we will look at how to create such a campaign.

Practice by Design: Learn about the Local Media

When you begin to develop your publicity campaign, you should create two lists: print and broadcast media outlets. Consult the Yellow Pages and newspapers to find contact information about the following.

Print Media
- Daily newspapers
- Suburban and local weekly newspapers
- Regional and national magazines
- Shoppers (small advertising circulars)
- Company publications
- Utility company newsletters
- Shopping center and other public bulletin boards
- School, PTA, and board of education newspapers
- Homeowner association newsletters

Broadcast Media
- Television stations (local, network, and cable)
- AM and FM radio stations
- College television and radio stations

KNOW THE KEY PLAYERS AT NEWSPAPERS AND TELEVISION STATIONS

It helps to know the staff positions and their functions:

Print
- Managing editor: Responsible for the overall functioning of the paper.
- City editor: Responsible for news story assignments.
- Editor: Separates material, determines what to print; assigns stories. Each department may have its own editor.
- Reporter: Gathers material and prepares stories for editing.

Broadcast
- Assignment editor: Appoints reporters to cover news stories.
- Program director: In charge of the entire program offering at a station.
- Producer: Responsible for the programming of an individual show.
- Public affairs director: Supervises public service messages and the use of public-service airtime.
- Reporter: Gathers material and prepares a story for editing

The organization of a newspaper or television station depends on its size. Smaller operations combine many of the job responsibilities into one or two positions.

Staff members may specialize in particular subject areas such as:

- Book reviews
- Business/finance
- Civic affairs
- Consumerism
- Education
- Ecology
- Gardening
- Health and medicine
- Interior decorating
- Lifestyles
- Science
- Social events

- Entertainment
- Fashion
- Food
- Travel
- Women's interests
- Sports

In general, newspaper reporters specialize more than television and radio reporters. However, television and radio programs more often concentrate on particular areas of interest, such as financial news, women's interests, and current events.

PRACTICE BY DESIGN: SEND YOUR MATERIALS TO THE RIGHT PEOPLE

You will increase your chances of getting your information printed or broadcast if you direct your publicity material to the correct person. If possible, find out the name of the person currently assigned to a specific subject or type of program related to your material. Decide where to send your story.

When you are deciding which media to target, the most important thing is not the size of the circulation or the listening/viewing audience. Focus instead on the proportion of that audience that comprises your target market.

In addition, the following characteristics will help you decide which medium would be best for your story.

Best for Print Media
- Detailed information such as statistics, formulas, and lists
- Resource material to be saved for future reference

Best for Broadcast Media
- Having a wide appeal (television/radio require material of widest interest because airtime is more limited than newspaper space)
- Entertaining (humorous, light, dramatic)
- Visually appealing for television (demonstrations, sample products, etc.)

You must decide which newspaper section or television/radio program best fits your story. Then relate the subject matter to the appropriate section of the medium you've chosen. For example:

Subject: How to put the spark back in your marriage
Print: Lifestyles, family, women's interest
Broadcast: Women's interest show, consumer interest segment of a general show, or public service spots

WHERE SHOULD YOU TARGET YOUR PUBLICITY?

Think of who your target audience is. Make a list of the publications they read and the television and radio programs they are likely to tune in. Then select the most appropriate staff members within the publications and broadcast stations you select. These are the people to whom you will send your press releases and public service announcements.

For example, if your target client is in the business community, you might send publicity materials to the editor of the financial page of the local daily newspaper, the editor of a local weekly business newsletter, and the producer of the business report for the nightly television news.

PRACTICE BY DESIGN: TIPS TO HELP YOU ESTABLISH YOUR PUBLICITY STRATEGY

Think about which would present your material most favorably:

- A news release for an editor to print or a script for an announcer to read
- A newsletter or fact sheet for an editor or announcer to use as background information
- A representative or spokesperson from your practice appearing in person for an interview or demonstration

Your publicity effort might include one, two, or all three of these ideas.

If you choose a written message, enhance your chances of success by doing the following:

- Deliver the material by hand to meet the media representative in person.
- Call in advance to schedule an appointment. Be sensitive to deadlines.

- Be prepared with complete written information about you and your group.
- Make the visit brief.

PRACTICE BY DESIGN: START LOCALLY, GO GLOBAL LATER

News or information that concerns the residents of a limited geographic area is considered local. The area in question may range from the city or town to the county, district, state, or region. Material that is localized is more attractive to the media serving a particular geographic area. This is true for the following reasons:

- The local media can't compete against national magazines and network television, so they concentrate on local material.
- Large metropolitan daily newspapers publish special editions for various segments of their readership area. This enables them to compete with small-town and suburban weekly papers.
- The local media are generally understaffed. They need public relations people to help them gather news.

The readership and viewing audiences in any geographic area want to know what *local* people and groups are doing. They also enjoy hearing about their neighbors and people they know personally. You will in-

---

SEVEN WAYS TO GET PUBLICITY

1. Do something bold.
2. Have your event photographed.
3. Write a controversial letter to the editor.
4. Sponsor an event, such as a seminar or class.
5. Tie into holidays.
6. Create your own news—publish a newsletter or how-to booklet relating to a current event.
7. Donate a gift certificate for your services.

Rick Crandall (1996), *Marketing Your Services: For People Who Hate to Sell.*

---

crease the chances of your news (whether it's about a workshop, event, or your practice specialty) being picked up if you emphasize its local quality. The following suggestions will help you give your material even more local appeal:

- Include names of local people wherever possible.
- Mention the person's name, background, and alma mater.
- Disperse this information throughout the release to discourage the editor from deleting it.

The best way to submit your publicity is in person. However, if you are unable or unwilling to personally deliver your materials, try these ideas:

- Send it with a short cover letter introducing yourself, your organization (if you are representing a group), and the enclosed publicity material.
- Telephone the contact person and introduce yourself and your organization. Follow up by sending the material you have discussed. Most newspapers and broadcast stations will not accept information over the telephone.

CHOOSING A SPOKESPERSON FOR YOUR GROUP

If you are part of a group and wish to select a spokesperson, choose the most suitable member based on:

- Knowledge of and experience in the subject being discussed
- A professional appearance
- The ability to respond quickly and thoroughly to interview questions
- The ability to express ideas and opinions well
- An outgoing personality

Prepare the following background information for the spokesperson:

- Biographical information (two or three paragraphs) emphasizing credentials for speaking (academic degrees, work experience, other background information). If possible, include a black-and-white head shot taken by a professional photographer.

- If the person's name is difficult to pronounce, include a phonetic spelling.

If your goal is to arrange an on-air interview of your spokesperson, follow these guidelines:

- Compose a pitch letter briefly explaining the presentation, why it is noteworthy, and several points that can be covered on the air.
- This letter should be easy to read and written with an enthusiastic tone. It should include just enough information to pique the reader's interest without giving the entire presentation.
- Mention types of visuals to be used (film footage, slides, charts, demonstrations).
- Six to eight weeks before the target date of the interview, send the pitch letter, bio, and photo to the station contact.
- Follow up by phone with the station contact a few days after you expect him or her to receive the information.
- If the station is interested in your interview proposal, it will schedule the interview. Always confirm this information in writing.

TIPS FOR WORKING WITH REPRESENTATIVES OF THE MEDIA

1. Use the proper format (news release, script, etc.) for any material you submit.
2. Be aware of deadlines. Submit material well in advance to allow enough time for rewriting, fact-checking, and so on. Ten days' lead time is a minimum.
3. Editors and commentators have the final say on copy. When you submit material, do not ask to review the final article or script.
4. Your material should stand on its own merit. Do not ask for special favors.
5. Double-check all information. Inaccurate material creates a bad impression and may hinder future placements.
6. Never use business or advertising department contacts to place your material.
7. Don't expect your media contacts to promise to use your material or to give it a certain amount of space or time. They can't. Accept the fact that some of your news releases will get airtime or print space and some won't.

8. If your material is not used, do not call and ask why. This sounds as though you are questioning your contact's judgment. Your story was most likely not picked up because:
   - It was not newsworthy.
   - It was not accurate.
   - Other news was more important.
   - The presentation of your material was not up to par and would have required too much rewrite time.

9. Know the needs of the station or paper. Ask your contact or request a copy of the in-house stylebook. Many media outlets post their stylebooks and submission guidelines on their websites. It helps to know the following information:
   - Deadlines
   - Copy style
   - Photograph policy (whether the organization takes its own, would accept yours, doesn't use them at all; whether a television station uses still photos)
   - Grace period (the time between submission of material and when it is printed or broadcast; where you may add last-minute facts or correct errors)
   - Program themes (women's interest, legislation, etc.)
   - Program format (interview, demonstration, etc.)

10. Stay in touch with your contacts even when you are not submitting material. Keep your lists updated as staff changes and new policies develop.

11. Expect your media contacts to ask controversial questions. They anticipate what their readers and listeners are thinking and would want to know. However, keep in mind that you don't have to answer everything.

12. Be candid about exclusivity. If you have submitted the same material to another source, say so. If your contact demands exclusive material, the next time you may wish to reserve it for his or her consideration before sending it to others. If he or she chooses not to use your information, you are then free to send it to other media outlets.

13. Inform your media contacts immediately if an event is canceled or a situation changes. This enables them to cancel the story or interview.

14. Media representatives appreciate consideration. Maintain rapport by sending thank-you notes when your material is used.

PRACTICE BY DESIGN: HOW TO WRITE PRESS (MEDIA) RELEASES

A press release is a short, factual description of an event or issue. It is prepared for the media. It is also referred to as a *media release* or a *news release*.

A *release to print media* (newspapers, magazines, etc.) is written for the eye rather than the ear. Limit it to one page to lessen the chances of its being edited.

A *release to the broadcast media* should be written in the form of a script. The purpose of a media release is to attract attention and create interest for the event.

You will find a few examples later in this chapter. Here are a few guidelines:

1. A press release answers five key questions: who, what, when, where, and why. Include every necessary detail, but omit everything else.
2. Think of a press release as a pyramid, with the most important points at the top and the less important at the bottom.
3. Media releases should be typed and double-spaced.
4. Include your name, address, and business telephone number at the top.
5. Write in a simple, clear style.
6. State the purpose of the event and why it is important. Include both facts and relevant quotes.
7. If there is to be a speaker at the event, mention the speaker's name and credentials.
8. State why the information is of interest to local readers.
9. Mention whether the event is open to the public.
10. If your event requires a registration fee or deadline, include the telephone number (with area code) where readers may call for information.
11. If your release is informing readers of an event that has already

taken place, be sure it is significant and interesting enough to warrant publication.

12. If the release is longer than one page, type the word *more* at the bottom of each page. Indicate the end of the release by typing "# # # #" at the bottom center.

13. Ask about the publication's photograph policy. You may be able to include a photo with your release or request that the publication send a staff photographer to take pictures of your event.

A well-written release and the resulting publicity may be more valuable to your practice or your organization than the workshop or meeting itself. If you decide to write and send media releases, it is imperative to take the time to write them well and send them in a timely manner to the right people. This is especially true if you live in a major metropolitan area, where your release is competing with hundreds of others for just a few spaces in the newspaper or a short spot on the radio.

HOW TO MAKE YOUR PRESS RELEASE STAND OUT

In *Marketing Your Services for People Who Hate to Sell,* author Rick Crandall (1996) says that it's important to make your press release stand out from the crowd. He writes, "45% of editors said that they get more than 30 press releases a day. About 20% said they read more than 50% of the releases, and a third said they scan them all. In other words, they actually do look at them. However, 42% said only 10% or less were actually useful. Remember, editors are looking for something very early on that shows that it's appropriate for their audience."

Crandall tells about one publicist who printed her press releases on purple paper. When she makes follow-up calls to editors to see whether they got her release, she tells them, "It's the one on the purple paper."

Another of Crandall's examples is the suggestion of the late Stanley Marcus, former CEO of Neiman Marcus. He said that one way to gain the attention of almost anyone is to send a box via UPS. While promoting a book, Marcus once sent someone a large box with 14 boxes of chocolate chip cookies inside. Do you think he got some attention for his book?

Here are a few more ideas to help you and your event stand out:

1. Send a glossy photo of yourself (or whoever is the center of your event). An editor looking for an interesting story will be more drawn to the one with the picture.
2. Two alternatives to sending your attention-getting release in a box are to send it via FedEx (again, to make it stand out) or in an envelope of unusual size and/or color. How do these ideas relate to your practice?

SAMPLE MEDIA RELEASE

Media Release

Susan Forth
233 Taylor St.
Willowdale, NY 10278
555/555-0405

CONTACT: Heidi Royale

Marriage & Family Therapist Offers Free Parenting Classes

Willowdale, NY—August 31, 2005—Susan Forth, MS, is presenting a four-week Parenting Skills Class for parents in the greater Willowdale area. The series of seminars will meet on Saturday mornings from 9 to 11 A.M. starting on September 17. All four sessions will be held at the Willowdale Methodist Church on Phillips Avenue. The sessions are limited to 20 participants, and are being presented as a public service.

"Children are our most important responsibility," says Ms. Forth. "Unfortunately, they don't come with a training manual, and many parents are at a loss when it comes to discipline and guidance. This series of classes helps parents of children from 2 to 12 find constructive and positive ways to parent." Ms. Forth offers the class twice each year and has trained hundreds of parents.

Ms. Forth has been a Licensed Marriage and Family Therapist in New York and Georgia since 1989. To make a reservation or for more information, call the Willowdale Methodist Church at (555) 555-0405.

# # # #

PRACTICE BY DESIGN: PUBLIC SERVICE ANNOUNCEMENTS (PSAS)

Radio and television stations set aside time to announce events of community interest. These events are announced for free through public service announcements, community calendars, and public affairs programs.

Contact your local television and radio stations to learn about their policies on giving free airtime to community groups and individuals. Their media kits will specify the types of publicity available, deadlines, and guidelines for submitting information. In order to qualify, your event most likely should be a genuine community service.

You will need to plan far ahead if you want your event to be publicized on a community calendar or public affairs program. Most stations require at least four or five weeks' lead time.

A media release for radio or television is usually written in the form of a script. You submit it in written form, and an announcer or commentator reads it on the air. To enhance your chances of having your event announced, submit your release in varying lengths to fit a few different time slots, from 10 to 60 seconds. The following guidelines will help you write your releases:

10 seconds — 25 words
20 seconds — 40 words
30 seconds — 80 words
60 seconds — 160 words

If you decide to submit different versions of your announcement, type each one on a separate page.

Some radio and television stations may accept broadcast-quality audio- or videotaped announcements. Either you or your group's spokesperson could read these. Many stations will even allow you to record your message at their facilities.

SAMPLE PSA

February 6, 2004
Mark Lefkowitz, MSW
1312 Alegria Street, Suite 13
New Albany, PA 19191
(555) 333-9899

30-Second Message

Children don't come with operating instructions, but now you can learn how to be a great parent. Join the next "Parenting 101" workshop scheduled to begin at Hall Elementary School on Saturday, March 19. This workshop series will meet for four consecutive Saturdays and is open to all parents of children from 2 to 12. The cost of the series is just $75—and the first five parents to sign up get a free stuffed animal. Call Hall School for more information at 555-7575.

If you are publicizing an event for your private practice, it is important to remember to emphasize the *community service* aspect of your event. If you are presenting the event for a school or church, the public service aspect is more obvious than if you are presenting your workshop as part of your business.

When you are writing for broadcast, it is even more important to keep it simple. Limit yourself to the basic facts. Use words that are easy to pronounce and understand.

Think about the different ways your material could be used:

- In a straight newscast?
- As a public service announcement?
- On a talk show?

PRACTICE BY DESIGN: TIPS FOR WRITING BROADCAST MEDIA RELEASES AND SCRIPTS

In addition to the guidelines on the previous pages, the following points apply to writing for the broadcast media.

1. As you write, keep in mind that you are writing your material for the ear, not the eye, (i.e., how it sounds, not how it reads).
2. Broadcast copy is less formal than printed copy.
   - Think about how you speak: You use fewer full words and you use contractions. For example, you would say *don't* instead of *do not.*
   - Follow normal conversational guidelines for sentence structure, vocabulary, and so forth.
   - Use simple, descriptive words that create pictures in the listener's mind. Pay attention to descriptions of size and color.
   - Avoid tongue-twisting phrases or complicated sentences.
   - Keep verbs in the present tense.
3. When you are writing a *television* script, synchronize the copy with slides, demonstrations, or other visuals.
   - The slides or pictures should flow smoothly at an interesting pace.
   - Demonstrations should be lively to keep the viewer's attention.
4. Most broadcast stations have guidelines for submitting copy. Here are some general guidelines, but every station is unique. Be sure to obtain the specific guidelines for each of your local stations.
   - Type all copy on 8½- by 11-inch paper.
   - Triple-space the copy on one side of the paper only.
   - Begin your message one-third of the way down the first page.
   - Leave large margins.
   - Type your name, affiliation, and address in the upper right corner.
   - Type the date in the upper left corner.
   - Indicate the exact timing on the front of the release. For example, "For use Monday, July 11, through Friday, July 15, 2005."
   - If the timing is not crucial, type "For Immediate Release."
   - Don't write, "For Use Monday through Friday."
   - Time the script and count the number of words. Position this information on the front page.
   - Spell out all abbreviations, titles, and names.
   - Include in parentheses the phonetic spellings of difficult names and words.

- If your release is more than one page long, type the word *more* at the bottom of each page.
- Type # # # # at the bottom center of the last page to indicate the end of the release.

Division 42 (Independent Practice) of the American Psychological Association provides press releases, PSAs, and pitch letters for the use of its members. If you are a member of APA, you can visit its website (www.APA.org) and download these documents. You can use them as a model and adapt them to suit your needs.

PRACTICE BY DESIGN: ATTRACT ATTENTION BY WRITING A FEATURE STORY

A feature story is different from a news release in both purpose and intent. While a news release reports an event, a feature story adds an interpretation of the event. It adds depth and color to the bare news facts, and it may also instruct or entertain.

Feature stories tell the unique, dramatic, or unusual. Their goal is to help, inspire, encourage, or entertain. They provide more information than a basic news item and are designed to create understanding.

A feature story should have a friendly and informative tone. Unlike a news story, it may include an opinion or point of view. It's meant to be interesting and quick to read.

When writing a feature story, put your personality into the article by using the first person (*I* and *we*). Attract the reader's attention by opening your story with an interesting lead. Hold the reader's attention by keeping him or her entertained throughout the article. Finish the story by leaving the reader something significant to remember.

Types of Feature Stories
How-to articles feature a step-by-step process of doing something. For example, you might write an article on how a man stopped smoking after three sessions of hypnosis.

News features combine a news event with human interest details. A weekend retreat for women at midlife, for example, would be a good subject for a feature story.

Personality articles describe people in the community. For example, you could write about members of your organization, their concerns, and their community contributions.

Experience features describe another person's experience. For example, you could describe how a woman in your Assertiveness Training Workshop succeeded in getting a promotion at work two weeks after she attended your seminar.

When you are writing feature articles, keep in mind that people are interested in other people. They want to hear about their successes, failures, problems, and what they did to improve themselves.

Volunteer Your Services and Get Free Publicity

- Offer to write a regular column for the local paper. Focus on behavioral health issues, but don't call them that. These issues have strong reader appeal, especially articles about parenting, stress, relationships, and the like.
- Write an occasional article on a topic that you specialize in. Be careful to use lay language and avoid sounding self-serving. Your insights will be excellent publicity for your practice.
- Offer to write a regular column for the newsletter of a company or association outside the mental health field, such as the state bar association.

STORIES FROM THE REAL WORLD

Whether it is a scholarly article in a well-respected journal or a brief how-to piece in the campus newspaper at the local community college, publish something. If you do not have something to say that is worth publishing and the ability to get it published somewhere, then you know where you should be focusing your energy. Publish.

Daniel J. Abrahamson, PhD

PRACTICE BY DESIGN: MAKE THE MOST OF YOUR TIMING

Consider synchronizing your promotional plans with the release of a new book or an upcoming speech. You can also write articles and offer presentations that fit the calendar. Table 11.1 shows some examples of topics that are appropriate to various times of the year.

SHOULD YOU FOLLOW UP?

There are opinions on both sides of the fence when it comes to following up after you have sent out a press release or article in search of publicity.

In *Marketing Your Consulting and Professional Services,* authors Richard Connor Jr. and Jeffrey Davidson (1985) write, "It is not recommended

TABLE 11.1 Seasonal Topics for Promotional Materials

Month	Event	Related Topics
January	New Year's Day	Goals planning, growth, renewal, substance use
February	Valentine's Day	Love, relationships, sexuality
March	Ides of March	Anger management, dealing with betrayal
April	National Secretaries Day	Getting along with a difficult boss
May	National Anxiety Screening Day	Anxiety and related spectrum disorders
June	Marriage	Love, relationships, family, sexuality
July/August	Vacations, back to school	Time management, parenting, school and education issues
September	Grandparents Day, 9/11	Family, recovery, resiliency
October	Breast Cancer Awareness Month and Mental Health Awareness Week	Importance of support, stigma
November	Thanksgiving	Families, managing expectations, overeating
December	Christmas, Hanukkah, Kwanzaa	Families, managing expectations, overeating

that you call the editor, ask for clippings, or seek a publication date. Your release, if used, is printed based on the newspaper's needs, availability of space, prominence of you and your firm, and a host of other factors already at play. Any contact that you attempt to make after submitting a release is usually perceived as an irritation to the editor. So write'm, send'm, and relax!"

You may also wish to consider the opinion of Paul and Sarah Edwards (1991), who write in *Getting Business to Come to You,* "All media materials should be followed up within a week by a telephone call. Even if your materials were hand delivered, they may just have been placed on the top of the pile, and there is no guarantee they will be read or considered. . . . We continue to be amazed at how many media packages we throw away only to have someone call later and provide us with the information that convinces us to do an interview."

PRACTICE BY DESIGN: MAKE RAIN WITH A MEDIA PROMOTIONAL KIT

One of the authors (Chris Stout) has been on a number of television programs (*Oprah,* CNN, and others) as well as a number of radio shows. Most of these opportunities resulted from sending a press release and later sending a promotional kit to a producer. The kit was a key tool in increasing the likelihood of being invited for an interview. The information in the promotional kit makes the interviewer's job easier and makes it more likely that you will be chosen over someone else.

You can assemble your kit advance or you can keep the materials on file and then assemble your kits as you need them. This allows you to keep the kit updated and to tailor each kit to the specific need or topic. You may also consider doing the same thing with electronic documents in order to send information via e-mail or post it on your website.

Your kit should include the following components:

- An 8½- by 11-inch two-pocket folder in a color that suits the nature of your practice
- Your name or your practice's name on the cover (perhaps custom-printed to make it look even more professional)
- One of your business cards or a preprinted Rolodex card in the slotted spot in the folder's pocket

Additional items should be kept on file to include in your kit as needed:

1. Keep a single-page prose bio. If your budget allows, include head-shot photo in your bio. One of the authors (Chris Stout) paid a nominal fee to an artist to sketch his photo. This makes it easy to photocopy and fax the bio without it turning black, as a photograph would. Keep in mind that you are sending your bio and photo to the media and they want to see how you look.
2. Keep copies of your formal vita or resume.
3. Keep a list of references that may include past interviews (print, radio, web, cable, broadcast television).
4. Keep a list of the names of the publications where your work has been published. Include only the names of the publications, not the titles and not in reference format. For example, *Journal of Consulting and Clinical Psychology, Psychological Bulletin, Psychiatric Services,* and so on.
5. List the titles of books you may have written and the publisher of each. You may include thumbnails of the covers on this page if you have more than two books. You can copy these from Amazon.com or from your publisher's website. You may also include full-page color copies of each book's cover if there are just one or two.
6. File copies of popular press articles by or about you.
7. Retain dubs of videos (VHS or DVD) or audiotapes (cassette or CD) of speeches or interviews you have done (or other coverage of you).
8. Keep a notation of your website's URL and perhaps a hard copy of your home page.
9. File 10 questions that the interviewer could ask you.
10. Keep copies of 10 talking points that convey that your topic(s) would be interesting or important to others. Think of the general population and current events.
11. File a copy of your most current press release.

Send a press release every time you do something notable, such as starting a new group, winning an award, publishing your work, and so on.

PRACTICE BY DESIGN: YOUR PUBLICITY ACTION PLAN

Now it's time to get specific about how you will apply the ideas in this chapter to your own practice. Use the information on the previous pages to develop your own list of publicity ideas. Your list will be most useful if you make it as specific as possible: who, how, and when you plan to contact each name on the list.

Media Outlet (newspaper, television station, etc.)	Reasons to Contact (event)	Deadline
1. _____	_____	_____
2. _____	_____	_____
3. _____	_____	_____
4. _____	_____	_____
5. _____	_____	_____
6. _____	_____	_____
7. _____	_____	_____
8. _____	_____	_____

Publicity Idea	Ways to Make My Work Stand Out	What I Need to Do to Make It Happen
1. _____	_____	_____
2. _____	_____	_____
3. _____	_____	_____
4. _____	_____	_____
5. _____	_____	_____
6. _____	_____	_____
7. _____	_____	_____
8. _____	_____	_____

CHAPTER 12

Advertise Your Practice

WHAT YOU WILL LEARN:

Whatto Expect from Advertising

Practice by Design: How to Write an Effective Ad

Types of Advertisements
    Newspaper Ads
    Yellow Pages Ads
    Magazine Ads
    Broadcast Advertising
    Websites

Practice by Design: How to Build Your Website

Other Sources of Promotional Material

Management Metrics: How to Evaluate the Results of an Ad

Flyers, Mailers, and Newsletters
    Direct Mail

Practice by Design: Design Principles
    Other Sources of Promotional Material

Practice by Design: What to Do with Your Flyers
    Postcards
    Newsletters

Practice by Design: Apply This to Your Practice

Stationery and Brochures
    Why Your Stationery Is Important

Practice by Design: Guidelines for Designing Stationery That Expresses
  Your Personality
    What about New-Practice Announcements?
    Do You Need a Brochure for Your Practice?

Practice by Design: Information to Include in Your Practice Brochure
    Research the Competition
    A Different Kind of Brochure

What to Expect from Advertising

Advertising can be a very effective way of bringing clients to your practice. It also helps establish your image and presence in your community so that when people seek counseling services, they think of you. In addition, advertising is a way to announce new services, such as workshops and classes. Being in the newspaper on a regular basis and having a display ad in the Yellow Pages may influence people in your town to choose you when they are looking for a special speaker for their group.

Figuring out what makes an ad effective and productive can be a confusing and expensive experience, however. Every market is unique; an ad that brings in 10 clients in Los Angeles may be completely ignored in Skokie. Every community has a unique personality. The opportunities for exposure vary greatly, too. Some areas have just one major publication, while others have small, affordable local newspapers that make it possible for you to experiment.

Creating and running a series of ads in your local newspaper is a commitment that most likely will not pay off right away. You have to be patient and remind yourself that you are running the ads to establish your presence in your community. Running the same ad every week or two for a year is expensive, but it is one effective way to demonstrate consistency and create the impression that you are an established business.

Assuming your ad is well designed and is placed in a publication targeted to the clients you seek to attract, it should eventually produce results. Unfortunately, however, there are no guarantees—and no refunds.

Practice by Design: How to Write an Effective Ad

Most bookstores devote entire sections to books about the business of advertising. Most advertising how-to books, however, are written for businesspeople who have tangible products to sell, not those of us who have a service to sell.

In *The Guerrilla Marketing Handbook,* authors Jay Levinson and Seth Godin (1994) list several basic rules to follow for successfully advertising in newspapers:

1. Have a strong headline. It has to communicate a benefit or intrigue the reader.
2. Include a picture of your product or service. Translated to the mental health business, that means you should consider having a warm, smiling picture of yourself in your ad. Unless you are quite unattractive, this is critical. Have it taken professionally, and order a supply of black-and-white glossies in various sizes.
3. Potential clients will feel more secure about choosing you if they have an idea of what you look like. Seeing your friendly, open face will cause more clients to choose you over the therapist down the street if the other ad lacks the photo.
4. As you write your ad, speak to an individual reader, not to a group. Remember that you are speaking to one person at a time. Your headline should be personal. Use the word *you.*
5. In your ad copy, emphasize outcomes and state what makes you unique.
6. Avoid cluttering your ad with too much information.
7. Offer something for free or a test. In the mental health business, a free consultation gives potential clients a no-risk way to meet you.
8. If you can afford it, hire a professional to write your ad. If that's not possible, write your ad yourself. If you need help in the beginning, study a few of those books from Amazon.com and ask a friend or colleague for help. Don't let newspaper people write it for you, or your ad will look like everyone else's in the paper.
9. Run as big an ad as you can afford.
10. The most important element of advertising is repetition. According to Levinson and Godin (1994), the average consumer ignores two out of three ads. They say that the consumer must see an ad at least nine times before he or she remembers it.

How to Get Started Developing Your Ad

1. Define your target client, as outlined in Chapter 9.
2. Choose newspapers and magazines targeted at the same client.
3. Request a media kit from each newspaper and magazine. This will give you their rates.
4. If you can afford it, find a graphic designer who can create your ads for you. Unless you have a design background or are highly skilled in desktop publishing, you are probably going to need some design help.

Types of Advertisements

The main kinds of advertisements include the following:

- Newspaper
- Magazine
- Yellow Pages
- Websites

- Television
- Newsletters
- Card decks
- Direct mail

There are many types of ads, but these are the most common.

Newspaper Ads

Placing ads in local newspapers can be an effective way of bringing new clients into your practice. As was mentioned earlier, though, newspaper advertising requires a long-range emotional and financial commitment. The advantages of newspaper advertising are as follows:

1. Newspapers are disposable. They have a short shelf life. The challenge is to catch the reader's attention and stand out from the hundreds of other ads, mostly for retail businesses.
2. If your phone doesn't start ringing right away after running a newspaper ad, it may not mean the ad isn't effective. When the product is a service like psychotherapy, people who are just starting to think about seeing a counselor may notice your ad the first week, read it the second week, and tear it out the third week. Then they will carry it around with them for a month or two (or six), finally calling you for the first time seven or eight months after you ran your ad.
3. Even though newspaper advertising is less expensive than television or magazines, it is still expensive. To make an impact on the reader, you will need to buy the largest ad you can afford and run it as often as possible.
4. Smaller, local newspapers are less expensive than the local editions of larger papers like the *Los Angeles Times* and the *Chicago Tribune*. Before you do anything, call all of your local newspapers and ask for a media kit with a rate card. Be prepared to have flashbacks to your graduate school statistics class (or whatever class you found most confusing).

5. Some therapists advertise in the classifieds section of local weekly publications. The rates may be more affordable, and they may seem like a bargain compared to the large metropolitan daily paper. Just be sure that any publication you choose reaches your target client.

Some weekly publications, especially the alternative types, are a bad idea because your ad will be placed next to ads for massage parlors and telephone sex outlets. No matter what the price, such an ad is never a bargain.

YELLOW PAGES ADS

Opinions are mixed about whether you should have a Yellow Pages display ad. In some areas, therapists will tell you that such ads are essential. In other areas, most therapists say that it is a waste of money. One way to find out is to look at the previous three years of your local Yellow Pages to see whether the same therapists are repeating their ads. If not, these ads are probably not effective.

When you begin advertising, place your ad in the main Yellow Pages book. It's probably a good idea to delay spending money on the minor and specialty Yellow Pages books until you have established your practice and have enough cash flow to test the effectiveness of other books. Your first priority should be to design a productive ad for your main Yellow Pages.

THREE REASONS WHY MARKETERS FAIL

1. *Lack of commitment.* If you don't believe in your product, or if you're not consistent and regular in the way you promote it, the odds of succeeding go way down.
2. *Lack of a clear benefit.* Customers don't care about your skills or inventory. They want to know what's in it for them.
3. *Poor positioning.* Sometimes there is no position available in a crowded or depressed market. But markets where there are no positions available are few and far between.

Jay Levinson and Seth Godin (1994), *The Guerrilla Marketing Handbook*

In *Marketing Your Services: For People Who Hate to Sell,* author Rick Crandall (1996) provides the following list to guide you in writing your Yellow Pages ad:

1. Include as many facts about yourself as you can without the ad looking too crammed with information.
2. Give your ad a classy look. Study ads in upscale magazines, newspapers, and the Yellow Pages. Notice which ones look tacky and which look classy. Use an upscale font for your headline, such as Bookman. If you are going to use a photo (which is highly recommended), use only one taken by a quality photographer.
3. Make your ad sound as personal as possible. Remember that you are speaking to one reader at a time.
4. If you accept credit cards, Crandall recommends that you say so in your ad. Others might disagree for the counseling profession. While it is a great idea to accept credit cards for payment of services, some say that it is tacky to include this in your ad.
5. Attract attention with a strong headline.
6. State the reasons why people should buy from you.
7. Design your ad yourself or with professional help. Don't let the Yellow Pages people do it for you.

We can help you put the balance back in your life.

Many families today are feeling the stress of having too much to do. It can come from one or both parents having demanding jobs or when the kids are involved in too many activities. If you feel like this is a problem in your family, we can help you find the best balance for you.

We specialize in Solution Focused Brief Counseling and may be able to help you in only a few sessions.

Judith Jacobs and Associates   (888) 555-1234
877 Montclair Ave.   Specializing in Family Wellness
Life is meant to be enjoyed

---

8. If you can't make yourself stand out from your competition, don't advertise. People usually respond to three kinds of ads: the first ones in a category, the biggest ads, or the ads that grab their attention. If your ad is half the size of the largest one in your category (usually counseling, marriage and family counseling, psychologists, or social workers), you can make it productive if you have a strong headline and offer.
9. Include a photo or graphic to catch the reader's eye. It also conveys part of your message by communicating that you are approachable and trustworthy.

For more examples of ads and other marketing materials, see *The Therapist's Advertising and Marketing Kit* by Laurie Cope Grand (Wiley, 2002), which includes samples of all types of ads, flyers, brochures, postcards, press releases, stationery, and web pages.

MAGAZINE ADS

Much of what has been said so far in this section applies to magazine advertising. Beyond that, the advantages and disadvantages of magazine advertising are:

1. It enables you to target a very specific audience. For example, advertising in *Divorce* magazine might be a good idea for a marriage and family therapist who specializes in divorce mediation.
2. Advertising in a magazine creates a feeling of prestige for your practice. This could be important if you have targeted an upscale client.
3. Magazines have a longer shelf life than newspapers. People keep them around longer and may look at them more than once.

AN IMPORTANT NOTE

Many states have specific rules about advertising by professionals. Make certain that your advertising, business cards, and brochures comply with your state's regulations.

---

4. Magazines may be passed along from one person to another, giving your ad even more exposure.
5. Magazine advertising is extremely expensive. To justify the expense, an ad will need to produce enough clients to pay for itself.

BROADCAST ADVERTISING

Both radio and television advertising are expensive — beyond the means of most mental health professionals in private or even group practice. Here are some pointers.

1. As always, if you decide to pursue broadcast advertising, be sure the radio or television station you are considering reaches your target clients.
2. Radio and television ads are sold based on the following factors:
   * How long your spot is (usually 15, 30, or 60 seconds)
   * How many times per day your ad airs
   * The time of day your ads run (morning or evening drive time, midday, evening, or late night)
3. If you are investigating television advertising, cable is by far the more affordable option, especially in off-hours. Cable also targets a more specific audience and may make more sense for that reason. For example, if your target audience consists of clients suffering from depression or posttraumatic stress disorder (PTSD), who often have difficulty sleeping, they may be more likely to see your spots.

WEBSITES

Many businesses are setting up websites these days. A site on the Internet can be a low-cost way for you to make your presence known to the world.

Do You Need a Website?   While it's possible to establish your presence on the Internet, it is uncertain whether the payback would be worth the cost in time or effort. Depending on the nature of your practice and clientele, consider whether someone would look for you online. If you coach, treat children, work with technology-minded folks, or consult for businesses, having a website may be a good idea. Others may not look for mental health services via the web.

It could also vary by the degree to which your community is technology-savvy. It's likely that everyone in Silicon Valley would look to the web for information and referrals, regardless of the needed clinical specialty. On the other hand, impoverished community mental health center clientele may be less likely to use the web.

The best reason to have a web page is that it enables a therapist to make volumes of information available to the public. You can publicize details about your practice such as the following:

- Therapeutic approach
- Types of services offered
- A photo (taken by a professional)
- Training and credentials
- Benefits of your services
- Articles you've written
- Future public appearances (e.g., workshops you'll be leading)
- Hours of availability
- Office location, including a map

What to Do with Your Web Address. List your web page address on all of your communications, including:

- Your advertisements
- Your business card and letterhead
- At the end of any article or newsletter you publish

PRACTICE BY DESIGN: HOW TO BUILD YOUR WEBSITE

If you decide to publish a website, where you start will depend on your level of computer and Internet expertise. The following steps will help.

1. Surf the Internet looking for sites of other therapists and counseling centers. Look for sites that are interesting and gather ideas from them.
2. If you're not sure where to start, go to a search engine such as Google or Yahoo and type in keywords such as *therapist, counseling,* and *counseling center.*
3. Many websites have links, or connections, to other sites. Click on any links that interest you.

4. It is often possible to print pages of websites. If you find a page or site you like, print it out. When you get ready to design your own page, use the pages you've collected for ideas.

5. If you have the expertise, time, and desire, you may wish to develop your own web page. Depending on how fancy you want to get, you can design simple pages with Microsoft Word and Microsoft Publisher. Microsoft Front Page is a bit more advanced.

6. If you don't have the skills or the time to design your web page yourself, you may wish to hire someone to design your site for you. If you can afford this option, you can find a designer in one of several places, including:
   • Local Yellow Pages
   • Local ads, especially in business publications
   • Ads in computer and Internet magazines

At the end of many web pages, there are links to the person or company who designed the web page. Find one you like and contact the designer directly.

Websites can be fairly inexpensive, depending on what you want them to do. Both authors of this book have websites. One of us (Chris Stout) has a no-frills site run by Register.com and uses the site as an electronic brochure of work, current projects, and biographical information (see stoutventures.com). Register.com allows you to register a unique domain name and receive e-mail. It offers construction tools that are template-driven and very easy to use.

There are many professional web designers who can build your site for you. The cost for your site can range between $500 and $2,500 or more, depending on your needs and how elaborate you want the site to be.

OTHER SOURCES OF PROMOTIONAL MATERIAL

Your Chamber of Commerce may be able to help you promote your practice. For example, the Chicagoland Chamber of Commerce has developed some effective promotional pieces on workplace drug and alcohol problems. These flyers and ads are simple and powerful. If you can get involved in a project like this one, it can add some credibility and provide you with some visibility in your community. In Chicago, the ads ran in various business trade magazines.

Learn how to manage your drug problem.
Come to the Chicagoland Chamber of Commerce Drug-Free
Workplace Program free roundtable discussion
8-9am, Wednesday, April 15th
"How to Manage Your Drug-Free Workplace Program"

You're a business owner, line manager or HR manager responsible for your organization's drug-free workplace program. You've developed a policy or are in the process of getting one up. You know what pieces comprise a comprehensive drug-free workplace program—drug/alcohol testing supervisor and employee training & EAPs, treatment programs. And now you want to pull them all together into a well-managed program.

Come to this free discussion and talk with our experts about the "nuts and bolts" of managing and administering your program on a day-to-day basis, whether you have 12 employees or 12,000. Bring your questions and be prepared for a frank (and no doubt, lively) discussion of the issues with two seasoned veterans from the drug-free workplace program trenches.

CHICAGOLAND CHAMBER OF COMMERCE
Our business is keeping drugs *out of yours.*
www.chicagolandchamber.org

"None of my employees abuse alcohol."
[This is the first sign of a drug problem.]

Denial. It's the first sign of a problem at work. Fact is, one in every five employees abuses drugs or alcohol. And when you think of how much that cuts into productivity (by 74% to be exact) it's enough to put you right out of business.

That's why the Chicagoland Chamber of Commerce Drug-Free Workplace Program and the Worksite Wellness Council of Illinois are sponsoring this seminar. We'll help you identify the signs, solve the problems and make your business a *certified* drug-free workplace. Then you and your employees can get back to work. Enclosed are your complimentary ticket to the Expo and a registration form for the seminar. Contact (312) 494-6730 for more info.

CHICAGOLAND
CHAMBER OF COMMERCE
Our business is keeping drugs *out of yours.*

MANAGEMENT METRICS: HOW TO EVALUATE THE RESULTS OF AN AD

If you are going to spend the time and money to advertise, you should also plan to take the time to track the results of your efforts. The following steps will help you organize your evaluation efforts.

1. When a new client calls and requests an initial appointment, always take a moment at the end of the first phone call to ask how the client heard about you. Record this information on a separate tracking sheet like the one shown at the end of this chapter.
2. Determine whether your ad is effective. If you are spending a lot of money and getting less return (in terms of client fees resulting directly from the ad) than the amount you spend, you should do something different. This could mean changing the ad, changing where or when you are advertising, or changing something else.
3. Correct your mistakes and move on. Unfortunately, the only accurate way to find out what works is to change something about your ad and test the results.
4. Place your ad in a different paper, advertise on a different day, or change something about the ad.
   - Perhaps your ad is too small or in the wrong section of the paper.
   - Maybe its design prevents it from standing out from the crowd of ads in the paper.
   - Perhaps it lacks one of the key elements of an effective ad, such as a strong headline.
   - Maybe adding your photo would increase the response.
5. Keep tweaking your ad and its placement until the results show that you are on the right track.

Design a form like the one shown in Table 12.1 to keep track of new clients and where they heard about you.

FLYERS, MAILERS, AND NEWSLETTERS

Flyers, postcards, and newsletters are an important part of any practice's marketing program. After you have planned your marketing activities

TABLE 12.1 Client Tracking Record

Date	Name	Source	Comments
6/5/05	Sandy S.	*Courier-Review* ad	Mentioned free consultation
6/7/05	Jack W.	Yellow Pages ad	Said I looked friendly
6/8/05	Lana B.	Friend of Allen E.	Covered by insurance plan
6/12/05	Suzanne F.	*Courier-Review* ad	Close to home
6/14/05	Penny Z.	Yellow Pages ad	Friendly face

for a 6- or 12-month period, you should develop a plan for publicizing each activity. In addition to sending press releases and running ads, you may also decide to distribute flyers and postcards to individuals and groups in your area. This chapter provides guidelines and ideas for producing pieces that will attract clients to your practice.

DIRECT MAIL

Entire books have been written about how to use direct mail to reach new clients. Here are the key points to know about it.

1. *Skills needed.* It takes a lot of skill to develop a mailing piece that will catch recipients' eyes and get them to open and read. It's probably better not to spend the money unless you have a fairly good idea about how to do it properly.
2. *Costs.* Direct mail is expensive when it is well executed. Costs include:
   - Having your piece designed
   - Purchasing good-quality paper
   - Purchasing or developing a targeted mailing list
   - Mailing costs
3. *Where to send your direct mail piece.* If you are thinking about sending a flyer, newsletter, or postcard to residents of your area, you will need a mailing list. You can get these names from the following sources:

- If you want to send a flyer to local organizations, you can get an updated list from your local Chamber of Commerce.
- If you want to send a publication to individuals, you can purchase a mailing list from a mailing list house. You can find these in the Yellow Pages under *Mailing lists.* You can specify the criteria for the households where you will send your mailing. For example, you may want to send it to households in zip code 87654 with annual incomes $150,000 and higher, and who subscribe to the *Wall Street Journal.* The cost depends on how many names you want and the criteria you specify.

PRACTICE BY DESIGN: DESIGN PRINCIPLES

In *Looking Good in Print: A Guide to Basic Design for Desktop Publishing,* author Roger Parker (1993) says that the design process involves the following steps:

1. Describe whom your piece (flyer, newsletter, etc.) is directed to.
2. Outline your basic message—who, what, when, where, and why.
3. Choose a format to convey your message: newsletter, mailer, postcard, book, website, PowerPoint presentation.
4. Experiment with solutions. Parker recommends that you turn off your computer and sit down with a pencil and pad of paper. Sketch layout ideas on paper. Don't be concerned about details. Just let your ideas flow.
5. In your daily life, look for ideas that appeal to you. Pay attention to direct mail pieces you receive and tune in to what impresses you as effective and ineffective design. If you come across something that seems confusing or too busy, analyze what turns you off.
6. Keep a file of designs that you really like. Use them for inspiration.
7. Every element of your design should relate to your piece. Form follows function.
8. Always be concerned about clarity, organization, and simplicity. If you are using desktop publishing software, don't get carried

away by it. Resist the temptation to do something just because you can.

9. Remember that your message is the heart of your document.
10. Make the most important ideas visually more prominent than secondary ideas.
11. Well-designed documents are consistent. They have consistent margins, typeface, and graphic elements.
12. Contrast creates impact.
13. Keep it simple. Restraint will help you create a better design.
14. Headlines help readers decide whether to read your document. Keep your headline short and concise.
15. Make your headline stand out from the rest of your document by making it larger and using a different font.
    - If the body of the document is in a serif font (such as Times Roman), use a sans serif font (such as Arial) for the headline. Serif means that each character has a small stroke at the end of it. (*Sans* is French for "without.")
    - Serif fonts are easier to read, which is why most newspapers and magazines use them in their body text.
16. Use bullets to add emphasis to a list.
17. Use type size that matches the importance of the message.
18. Draw attention to headlines and subheadings with screens.
19. Leave plenty of white space to rest your readers' eyes.
20. Experiment with a border to draw attention to your text or artwork.
21. Build your message around your logo and address rather than treating them as an afterthought.
22. Keep the number of fonts you use to a minimum. Roger Parker says using too many fonts is "the ransom note school of typography," which "makes your pages look amateurish and confusing."

For more examples of ads and other marketing materials, see *The Therapist's Advertising and Marketing Kit*, by Laurie Cope Grand (Wiley, 2002), which includes samples of all types of ads, flyers, brochures, postcards, press releases, stationery, and web pages.

UNDERLINING

"Try to use bold or italic type instead of underlining. More than a few underlined words cause visual clutter and confusion."

Roger Parker, *Looking Good in Print.*

PRACTICE BY DESIGN: WHAT TO DO WITH YOUR FLYERS

You can increase your visibility by distributing your flyers to a multitude of places.

1. Send them to former clients who may be interested in the event mentioned in the flyer (if you know it's okay to send them mail at home).
2. Send flyers publicizing workshops or seminars to churches, synagogues, civic organizations, and schools.
3. Take your flyers to the library and local places of business. Ask for permission to post a flyer and leave a stack for people to pick up.
4. Send your flyer to other therapists and counseling centers in your town. Ask them to post it or leave a stack in their waiting room.
5. Send your flyer to your friends. Attach a note saying, "Thought you'd like to know what I've been up to. Would you like to come and bring a friend?"
6. Send it to everyone in your networking group, Rolodex, and Chamber of Commerce membership roster.
7. Send it to every teacher at your child's school with a note inviting them to attend.
8. Some might find this one a little over the top, but you decide: Go to the library and find the section of books that relate to the topic of your flyer. Place your folded flyers inside each of those books.

POSTCARDS

You can send postcards to prospective clients and referral sources for two reasons:

- To announce an event or special offer
- As a follow-up to a flyer

Sending two mailings to your list of names is a very effective way of getting people to come to your seminar or workshop. You can send the first flyer or postcard three weeks before the event, followed by a postcard (a miniversion of the flyer) one week before.

Postcards are an effective way to reach potential clients and referral sources because they are less expensive to produce and send. They also have a better chance of being read than a flyer sent in an envelope, since they don't have to be opened.

Following is an example of a postcard announcing a therapist's workshop.

Mothers & Daughters Together: Can't We All Just Get Along?

A workshop with Dr. Angela Leff
Saturday, October 4th · 9 a.m. to noon
New Bedford High School Conference Room
$45 for each mom/daughter pair—includes snack & workbook

Call (888) 555-1234 to reserve a space for both of you.
Workshop fees will be donated to New Bedford Youth Services.

Angela Leff, Ph.D.
98 E. Bedford Blvd., Suite 7
New Bedford, IN 76589

These are a few of the things you will learn at Mothers & Daughters Together:

- The five most common sources of mother-daughter conflict
- Ten easy communication skills that will help you get along

Place Stamp Here

To:

NEWSLETTERS

The purpose of sending a newsletter is the same as running an ad or creating other kinds of publicity—to bring clients into your practice. Newsletters are a selling vehicle that should be designed to reflect your personality and professionalism.

Newsletters don't have to be elaborate to be effective. A two-sided communication every quarter is perfectly fine. It doesn't have to be fancy—in fact, today's desktop publishing software and even the word processing applications (like Microsoft Publisher and Microsoft Word) have newsletter templates. These make it very easy to produce a decent publication.

As you think about what it would take to produce a newsletter that people would actually read, here are a few things to consider:

1. What would be the purpose of your newsletter?
2. Who is your target audience? Do you have names and addresses in your database, or would you need to purchase a mailing list?
3. Can you afford to write, print, and send enough copies of this newsletter for it to be worth the time spent writing it?
4. Are you computer-literate? Do you have access to desktop publishing or word processing software?
5. Are you willing to spend from four to eight hours every quarter gathering information to include in your newsletter? Would you commit to this every single quarter for the next year?
6. What would you call your newsletter?
7. What would you include in it? What would you *not* include?

For more information about writing and sending newsletters, see *The Therapist's Newsletter Kit* by Laurie Cope Grand (Wiley, 2002). It includes over 50 complete newsletters that you can edit and customize to use for marketing your practice.

PRACTICE BY DESIGN: APPLY THIS TO YOUR PRACTICE

How will you apply what you've learned to your own practice? As always, your list will be most useful if you make it as specific as possible.

1. Who are your target clients?
2. What special services do you plan to offer these clients? Think workshops, groups, practice specialization.
3. How does this translate into a newsletter, flyer, or postcard?

STATIONERY AND BROCHURES

WHY YOUR STATIONERY IS IMPORTANT

Your business stationery is part of your professional image and your marketing campaign. You use it to communicate with clients, potential clients, colleagues, workshop guests, and referral sources. You need business stationery to keep in touch with former clients, to acknowledge referrals, and to send thank-you notes.

PRACTICE BY DESIGN: GUIDELINES FOR DESIGNING STATIONERY THAT EXPRESSES YOUR PERSONALITY

Your stationery and business cards convey a message about your business and tell something about the work you do. They also make a statement about your personality.

Always keep in mind that if you want to be noticed, you have to stand out. Your business cards and stationery are an opportunity to do that in a professional way. When you design your stationery, you can do what everyone else does, and your stationery will look like everyone else's, or you can use this occasion to design something that people will really notice.

Basic Information for Your Stationery. Your business stationery (card and letterhead) should include:

- Your name, degree, and license number (required in some states)
- Your telephone number and address
- Your e-mail address and website URL

You may also wish to include the following (if allowed in your state):

- Your full title (e.g., Licensed Clinical Professional Counselor)
- Your area of specialization
- Whom you work with most often (individuals, families, couples, groups)
- On the back, perhaps your services or your philosophy of serving clients
- A folded card, which is like a miniature brochure

A horizontal card is easier to read than one printed vertically.

Printing Options. Business cards used to be fairly unimaginative and most of them looked alike. But these days, it is common for people to be more self-expressive and creative. Remember, the idea is to stand out. The following are four alternatives for having your stationery printed:

1. Visit www.vistaprint.com and design your stationery using hundreds of templates online. Vistaprint products are printed on quality paper and the prices are reasonable. Its process is easy to use and the company delivers quickly.
2. Design your own on your computer and print your stationery yourself. You can order a wide variety of styles from catalogs such as PaperDirect, which even offers next-day delivery. Call 1-800-A-PAPERS to request a free catalog, or visit www.paperdirect.com.
3. You can have your cards and stationery designed by a graphic designer. This can be expensive, but you will get the most customized look this way.
4. Visit a print shop such as Kinko's and look through its catalogs of samples.

WHAT ABOUT NEW-PRACTICE ANNOUNCEMENTS?

Many therapists send out announcements when they open a new office. You may choose to do this, but don't expect to get any business from it. Unfortunately, announcements like these usually go in the trash.

A more productive suggestion might be to put together a package of presentations and offer to speak as a public service. (See Chapter 13 for information about how to do this.) Send your package to every civic, social, and religious organization within a 10-mile radius, and send another package again three months later. You've announced your presence in the community and offered to give something to people. This will bring clients into your practice if you keep at it.

Do You Need a Brochure for Your Practice?

Ask five marketing people whether you should have a brochure, and you'll get five different opinions. To help you decide whether the investment of designing, printing, and distributing a brochure is the right move for you, first ask yourself two questions:

1. Why do I want a brochure?
2. What will I do with it?

If your answers make you think that you will add clients to your practice as a result of your brochure, then move on to the next set of questions. In *Marketing Your Services: For People Who Hate to Sell*, Rick Crandall (1996) lists five considerations:

1. Who is your target audience?
2. What do you stand for?
3. What is your image?
4. How are you different from other therapists?
5. Why should people come to you?

Your professional association may offer brochure help. Many professional associations make brochures available to their members. Some may be customized to your practice. The American Psychological Association's Division of Independent Practice (#42) offers brochures on many topics. Some examples include Shyness, Psychotherapy with Children and Adolescents, Separation and Divorce, Aging, ADHD, Heart Disease, Serious Medical Illness, Choosing a Psychologist, and Breast Cancer.

Brochures on many topics are available from American Association for Marriage and Family Therapy (AAMFT). Examples of the many topics include Adolescent Behavior Disorders, Adoption Today, Alcohol Use Disorders, Bereavement and Loss, Caregiving for the Elderly, Children and Divorce, Domestic Violence, Female Sexual Problems, Infertility, Infidelity, Male Sexual Problems, Marriage Preparation, Postpartum Depression, and Suicidal Ideation and Behavior.

PRACTICE BY DESIGN: INFORMATION TO INCLUDE IN YOUR PRACTICE BROCHURE

In addition to your name, address, telephone number, and e-mail address, you can include the following kinds of information in your brochure:

- Introduction and overview of your practice
- Your education, credentials, and special training
- Your areas of specialization
- Features and benefits of your services, emphasizing how you are different from other therapists (how you can help clients and why it matters to them)
- Your practice location (cross streets or a map)
- Your website address (URL), if you have one (e.g., www.Your-PracticeName.com)

You may also wish to include your photo or other graphics. One panel could also be a coupon (perhaps good for a free consultation) or reply card.

When you begin to design your brochure, start with an 8½- by 11-inch piece of paper. Fold it in thirds and give each of the six panels a number. Identify which information will go on each of the panels.

Figure 12.1 shows a sample layout for a practice brochure.

Place additional information about your practice on the *inside* of the brochure.

For designing and printing your brochure, you have the same four alternatives as you did for your business card:

1. Visit www.vistaprint.com (or a similar website) and design your brochure online.
2. Design your own brochure on your computer and print your own copies on paper from PaperDirect (or similar products).

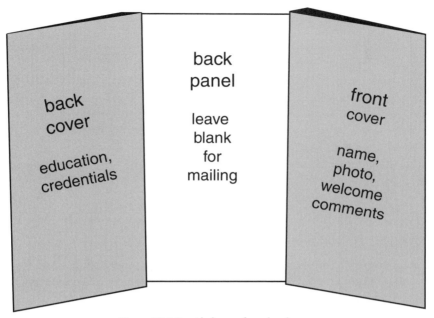

Figure 12.1 Outside layout for a brochure.

3. Have your brochure designed by a graphic designer.
4. Visit a print shop such as Kinko's and look through catalogs of sample brochures.

RESEARCH THE COMPETITION

An important step in planning your brochure is to find out what your competition is doing. In *Marketing Your Consulting and Professional Services*, authors Richard Connor Jr. and Jeffrey Davidson (1985) recommend contacting other therapists and counseling centers to request copies of their brochures. You don't have to identify yourself as a fellow therapist. If you are concerned about obtaining such information from your competitors, you can always contact therapists outside your market area.

Connor and Davidson suggest that you collect at least 10 brochures and look them over carefully. Analyze the features that appeal to you. Consider the following factors:

- Details such as flaps, pockets, and fold-overs
- Size and dimension
- Paper quality and weight
- Pictures and graphics
- How professionals are described; how credentials and affiliations are mentioned
- Whether there's any mention of clients or testimonials
- Number of pages or panels
- How color is used
- Interesting formatting (bullets, captions, shaded boxes, photos of people doing their jobs)
- What fonts are used and what impact they make

A DIFFERENT KIND OF BROCHURE

The purpose of a brochure is to create interest in your services and bring clients to your practice. Here are two alternative ways to accomplish the same thing without developing a traditional brochure.

1. Develop a brochure, but focus on your *services* rather than on *you*. Let's say, for example, that you have decided to promote your practice by offering to make free presentations to local clubs and organizations as a community service. You design a brochure on your computer with a simple desktop publishing program. Your brochure details 6 to 10 workshops that you are offering to present to groups such as the Chamber of Commerce, local churches and synagogues, and the Rotary Club. The brochure focuses on the workshops, listing a few key points for each one.

2. Instead of a traditional brochure, you can present the same information discussed in item 1 (6 to 10 seminars), but in a different format. Such a format helps you stand out from the crowd and increases the chances that your promotional material won't be thrown away. Instead of a brochure, design a set of 3 by 5 cards. Each card contains information about one of the presentations, including the main points, how long it is, how to contact you, and so on. Package your cards in a colorful envelope and hand-address 30 or 40 to local groups. (See Figure 12.2.)

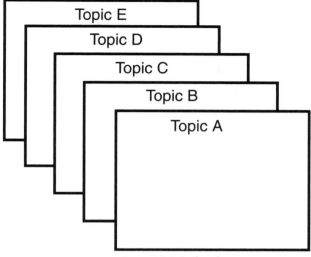

Figure 12.2 Card pack.

You may also adapt the card pack to include information about each of your services. For example, you could have one card for each type of service you offer. Each card includes brief bulleted items that describe the service. Examples of services include:

- Individual counseling
- Relationship counseling
- Couples group therapy
- Grief recovery group
- Other support groups
- Community presentations and workshops

Presentations, Speeches, and Workshops

WHY PUBLIC SPEAKING IS AN EFFECTIVE PRACTICE BUILDER

The counseling profession is unique in several ways. When you think about what we therapists do all day—listen to people tell us their deepest secrets and feelings—it's a pretty amazing thing. How do our clients choose us? They are looking for someone who is competent and trustworthy, which is difficult to judge from an ad or even based on the word of a friend.

This means that one of our challenges in our efforts to help more clients find and choose us is to look for more ways to showcase our personalities, our talents, and our trustworthiness. The more visible we are, the easier we make it for potential clients to *choose us*. This is why presenting seminars and workshops is an ideal marketing activity. What better way to place ourselves on display in a nonthreatening way (nonthreatening to our audiences, that is) so that potential clients can see who we are?

Making presentations to groups provides these benefits:

- Increased visibility in your community
- Exposure as an expert on your subject
- The opportunity to cultivate referrals and build your referral base
- The opportunity to sell additional products (your books, tapes, CD-ROMs, etc., which is known as *back-of-the-room sales*)
- The opportunity to increase your professional income by earning speaker fees
- The chance to network with other professionals and businesspeople

---

"Being successful and invisible are contradictions of terms . . . no one can ever commit to your product or service unless they have at least established some awareness of your existence. Hence, you must create systems that take your niche product into your potential clients' lives at their every turn. . . . The niche message must be totally clear. Whatever vehicle you use for telling people about your seminar, be certain it clearly expresses the specialness of your product."

Lynda Falkenstein (2000), *Nichecraft.*

PRACTICE BY DESIGN: HOW TO GET SPEAKING INVITATIONS

There is no magic when it comes to being invited to speak to groups. The best thing you can do is offer. Offer your services to as many groups as you can think of, and do it regularly.

Put together a set of workshop topics and develop a brief outline for each. Put them together in a nice package with a cover letter in which you offer to speak as a public service. Create a mailing list of clubs, organizations within a 10- or 15-mile radius of your office. Send your package to every organization on the list every six months. Make it a little different each time. Before long, you will have your first invitation.

WHAT SHOULD YOU SPEAK ABOUT?

You understand that it's important to get your name in front of the public and that offering to do presentations and workshops is an excellent way to do it. But what can you talk about? For some therapists, it's easy to sit down and make a list of topics that they would feel comfortable presenting. Others need a bit of inspiration. Consider the following when you make your list:

- The topic should be one that you are qualified to talk about.
- It should be one that your target clients are interested in.
- It should be important and relevant.
- It should be broad enough to fill the time you have available.

If you decide to develop your presentations yourself, follow these steps:

1. Research the topic at the library and on the Internet. If you have very little information to begin with, the easiest place to start is with a search engine like Google. Go to www.google.com, type in your topic, and see what comes up. Search through the sites until you find what you are looking for.
2. Develop an outline.
3. Fill in the outline with information you find in your research.
4. Write a script for your presentation.
5. Include as much audience participation as you can, depending on the amount of time available. The shorter the presentation, the more you must rely on lecture.

6. Design visual aids, such as transparencies, slides, or posters.
7. Develop handouts to be given to participants.
8. Be very careful to credit all of your sources.

Ideas for Presentation Topics.   The following topics are included in the three books listed in the box, "Presentation Guides." Use these lists to generate your own ideas for topics.

- Visit Google or Yahoo and type in phrases such as *women's issues* or *career issues* or *marriage and family;* follow the links.
- Look at the covers and tables of contents of current magazines to see what is on people's minds.
- Ask colleagues, friends, and business associates for ideas.

General Life Topics
- I have everything I've ever dreamed of. Why aren't I happy?
- Midlife checkup.
- Understanding depression.
- How to increase your self-confidence.
- How to recover from loss.
- Dealing with guilt and regret.
- Managing anger.

PRESENTATION GUIDES

If you don't have the time or inclination to develop your own presentations, see these three books on presentations available from John Wiley & Sons (*The Life Skills Presentation Guide, The Marriage & Family Presentation Guide,* and *The Workplace Skills Presentation Guide*) by Laurie Cope Grand (Wiley, 2000). Each book offers complete presentation outlines on 10 different topics. Each presentation topic includes a leader's guide, handouts, sample press releases, and other items to help you market your practice with professional presentations. You can use them directly from the book or adapt them to fit your practice philosophy and audience needs.

- Understanding personality types with the Myers-Briggs Type Indicator®.
- Raise your emotional intelligence quotient.
- How people change.

Marriage, Family, and Relationship Topics
- Before the wedding: skills for marriage success.
- The good marriage: skills for making your marriage thrive.
- The marriage checkup.
- Recovering from infidelity.
- Survival skills for single parents.
- How to minimize the emotional toll of divorce.
- How to avoid emotional disasters: just for teens.
- Managing conflict creatively.
- Managing the emotional challenges of caregiving.
- Parenting your teen.

Workplace Topics
- Emotional intelligence in the workplace.
- Balancing work and family.
- How to give effective performance feedback.
- Career crash.
- Does your company need family therapy?
- Take charge of your life: Plan your best year yet.
- Manage your stress.
- How to create a positive work environment.
- Managing conflict at work.
- The art of effective communication.

SHOULD YOU SPEAK FOR FREE?

Many groups will ask you to speak at their meetings or conferences during the course of your career. Some groups will offer to pay you, and others will ask you to speak pro bono (for free). Pro bono speaking is a way for you to satisfy the ethical guideline of most professional organizations that recommend that a portion of your services be provided without charge. Three other benefits of speaking for free are:

- It enhances your visibility in your community.
- It enables you to refine your presentations; you will learn something new each time you give your talk.
- The more often you speak, the less anxiety you are likely to feel about speaking to a group.

When you are being paid to speak, there are a few things to ask about beforehand. Be sure to clarify these details and eliminate the risk of misunderstanding.

- Is the group paying for travel expenses?
- Which expenses are covered (e.g., air, hotel, airport transportation, meals)?
- If you are speaking at a convention, is the group paying your registration fee?

Expenses can quickly add up when you travel to a speaking engagement. When they are added to your lost practice income, these costs can be greater than your speaking fee.

It can be difficult to ask these questions when you have been invited to speak to a group. The Professional Speaking Agreement (see the appendix) will help you clarify these details and formalize your agreement.

PRACTICE BY DESIGN: HOW TO GET REFERRALS WHEN YOU SPEAK TO GROUPS

Here are some ways to get client referrals by making presentations.
Speak as often as possible to any group you can think of.

- Community, social, and religious groups
- Business networking groups
- Charitable organizations
- Local schools (elementary, middle and high schools, community colleges and universities)
- In classes as a guest speaker
- PTAs
- Parks and recreation departments
- YMCA, YWCA
- Department stores and shopping malls

Be exceptionally well prepared.

- Be confident, but not overly so.
- Be relaxed and personable.
- Be rested; eat lightly beforehand.
- Use brief notes.
- Maintain eye contact with your audience.
- Self-disclose.
- Vary your voice tone.
- Be enthusiastic.
- Use vivid stories and visual aids (prepare them beforehand).
- Dress professionally. Wear your favorite clothing.
- Avoid using professional jargon.
- Build in group participation. Ask the group for examples of points.
- Keep within the time limits you agreed on.

Know something about who is in the audience, and use this information in your presentation.

- Anticipate participants' questions.
- Give examples that relate to their interests.
- Ask for examples based on their life experiences.

Share your personality and life experiences with the group. Illustrate your points with your own experiences as a therapist. Of course, you must keep all details general and protect confidentiality.
Give examples of situations where people become your clients.
Prepare a folder of handouts for each participant.

- Remember that your handouts are actually marketing materials, so make them beautiful.
- In each packet, include a business card and coupon for a free consultation.

BE PREPARED TO ANSWER SOME TYPICAL QUESTIONS

Regardless of what topic you are speaking on, people are curious about what it's like to be a counselor and what happens in therapy. The fol-

> "Give serious advance thinking concerning the results you want from the seminar. What, do you want to have happen as a result of the event? What do you want attendees to do? How you answer these questions will strongly influence what you put into the program."
>
> Lynda Falkenstein (2000), *Nichecraft.*

lowing questions are typical of those you might expect. Some questions may be a bit challenging, but just answer them honestly and from your own experience.

1. What is therapy? How does it work?
2. What is the difference between a psychologist, a counselor, and a social worker?
3. How does someone know when he or she should see a counselor?
4. How can I know whether counseling will help me?
5. How much do therapists charge?
6. Do you guarantee that your clients will get better?
7. I saw a counselor once, but it didn't help. How do I know you could help me?
8. Do people sometimes get better on their own, without help?
9. I can't imagine what could be worth $125 an hour.

HOW TO MANAGE YOUR ANXIETY WHEN GIVING A PRESENTATION

You've most likely heard that public speaking is the number one fear among humans. If the idea of standing up in front of a group makes you nervous, you are not alone. But that doesn't mean that you should not give it a try. Here are 10 ways to stack the deck in your favor when you speak before a group.

1. If you are reluctant to make a presentation on your own, team up with a trusted colleague and offer yourselves as a package deal. It can be much more fun and less intimidating to have a coleader. A team presentation may also make you more attractive to an organization.

2. Preparation is the key to success on the rubber-chicken circuit. When you are 100 percent prepared, you have much more confidence than when you are winging it. Preparation includes things like these:
   - Write a complete outline of your talk. Commit every single point to paper.
   - Prepare twice as much material as you think you'll need. Then you won't have to worry about running out of things to say with 30 minutes left on the clock.
   - Practice more than you think you need to.
   - Practice in front of at least one person. If you can put together a group of three or five, so much the better.
   - Videotape yourself and watch the tapes. Do it over and tape yourself again. Notice the improvement.
   - Audiotape yourself giving your talk. Listen to the tape in your car whenever you run errands.
   - Prepare visual aids and rely on them. List the key points of your presentation on transparencies, easel pages, or slides. You can talk from these and you won't have to worry about forgetting anything. If you are going to speak from your visuals, practice doing so beforehand.
3. Keep your message simple.
4. Prepare plenty of handouts for the participants. You won't have to worry about remembering the information that's on them.
5. Never read your presentation from a script.
6. Use humor only if you are absolutely certain it will be effective and if it fits the topic. Humor is difficult for most speakers to pull off.
7. Give plenty of examples and anecdotes that illustrate your points.
8. Include practice exercises, case studies, and other opportunities for participant involvement. It's more interesting for the participants if they can interact with the material and not have to listen to you lecturing every minute. In addition, you will have some time to regroup when they are engaged with an exercise.
9. Since you are a therapist, you know about visualizing a successful performance. Do it. It works.
10. As a therapist, you also know about relaxation exercises. Do them. They work.

IDEAS FOR CREATING SUCCESSFUL PRESENTATIONS

1. Always confirm your plans two or three days in advance. At the very least, leave a voice mail for your contact person confirming that you will be there on the agreed-upon day and time. Misunderstandings happen, and this is one way to avoid them.

2. At least one day before your presentation, if possible, arrange to visit the room where you will be speaking. Seeing it beforehand gives you a chance to learn about potential problems while you still have a chance to solve them. It also enables you to visualize yourself giving your presentation, which lowers your anxiety. Here are some things to look for:
   - Is the room large enough? Too large?
   - Will you be able to rearrange the chairs and/or tables before your presentation if you want to?

STORIES FROM THE REAL WORLD

I was giving a free presentation titled "Are You Co-Dependent and What Can You Do About It," a hot topic in the early 1990s. I arrived early at the shopping center in Azusa with my handouts and flip chart and practice literature. It took me about 20 minutes to find the meeting room, which was hidden away on the second floor. It was very long and narrow and was a jumble of plastic folding chairs. I did my best to arrange it in a way that created a welcoming feeling, but no matter how I moved things around, the room looked like the inside of a train car. I laid out my handouts and waited for the audience to find me.

I should have been glad that the room filled up, but the faces that evening were particularly grim. This was not a group who wanted to interact with each other or with me. No matter what I did, they barely looked at me. The room arrangement didn't help at all—I had no choice but to stand at one end of the room and shout to make sure everyone all the way in the back could hear me.

If I had only taken the time to see the room before the night of my presentation, I could have asked to move to a different location. That would have made all the difference.

Laurie Cope Grand, M.S.

Tips for Successful Presentations

- Be personal; come across as though you were speaking to individuals rather than to a group.
- Use audio or visual aids.
- Take no more than 70 percent of your allotted time to present your information.
- After the applause dies down, leave some time for interaction with the audience (e.g., questions and answers).

C. Browning and B. Browning (1986), *Private Practice Handbook* (3rd ed.). Los Alamitos, CA: Duncliffs International.

- Is the audiovisual equipment you've requested available? Does it work? Will you have a chance to check it before showtime?
- Is the temperature comfortable? Can it be adjusted?
- Is the lighting adequate?
- Will people be in the adjacent rooms while you are giving your presentation? Is this likely to present a problem?

3. Plan to arrive in your meeting room at least 45 minutes in advance of your presentation. Arrange the room to suit the activities you have planned. Having the right seating arrangement can make a great difference in the effectiveness of your presentation. See sample seating arrangements in the appendix.

4. Make certain that each piece of audiovisual equipment works properly. Never make the mistake of assuming you'll know how to work the VCR. You will certainly get the one with the weird buttons. Try it beforehand to make sure you can operate it.

5. If time allows, plan some kind of warm-up exercise. It doesn't have to be elaborate, but it sets a nice tone and places the audience at ease.

6. Bring at least 20 percent more handouts than you think you'll need. Then you won't need to worry about running out of them.

7. Include relevant article reprints with your handouts. Be sure your name and telephone number appear on all handouts.

8. Bring breath mints and have a glass of water next to you at the front of the room.
9. Be sure to look at the faces of the participants as you begin your presentation. Remember to smile. Introduce yourself slowly and tell the audience how glad you are to be there.
10. If possible, arrange to tape your presentation. You will be able to review your performance afterward. You may be so impressed that you'll decide to sell the tape or include it in some other kind of promotional package to market your practice. You can also use the tape to get other speaking engagements.
11. Send a thank-you note to your contact person in the organization, saying you hope you'll be invited back again.

THINGS TO FIND OUT ABOUT YOUR AUDIENCE

In *Marketing Your Services: For People Who Hate to Sell,* author Rick Crandall (1996) stresses the importance of building a relationship with your audience. He outlines eight pieces of information to find out about participants before you make a presentation:

1. Where are they from?
2. What do they like about their careers (or their lives)?
3. What do they dislike?
4. Are their spouses at the meeting?
5. What types of jobs do audience members do?
6. Whom do they admire?
7. What competitive issues do they face?
8. What other groups are they members of?

"If you're not comfortable presenting solo, or you're simply too early in your career to pass as an expert, then assemble a panel discussion and bring in the heaviest hitters you know. Your role as moderator and producer of the event will give you a boost."

Sarah White (1997), *Marketing Basics.*

Practice by Design: Your Presentation Planner

Answer the following questions to begin planning presentations for your own practice. You will find a blank copy of a presentation planner in the appendix.

1. What are five topic ideas for presentations you could make within the next six months?
2. Which of your colleagues could you ask to copresent with you? They don't necessarily have to be therapists. For example, if you present a workshop for people who have been downsized, your copresenter could be a management recruiter. You could focus on maintaining self-esteem, and the recruiter could focus on interviewing skills.
3. List 10 organizations you can approach about making a presentation.

Present Your Own Workshop or Conference

At some point, you may want to present your own conference or workshop. This can be an effective marketing tool and may also generate some income. If you enjoy doing presentations, you might want to think about presenting a half- or full-day workshop.

If your audience is likely to be made up of professionals who need continuing education units (CEUs), consider getting approval to provide them. Offering CEUs can make a world of difference in the attendance rate at your seminar or conference. Check the website of your professional organization to find out how to apply to become a CEU provider.

A related strategy is to learn when clinical professionals' licenses are coming due for renewal. If you offer your workshop or conference (with CEUs) a few months before that time, you are more likely to attract participants who need credits for license renewal. *Timing can be everything.*

Clayson (1990) offers the following keys to maximizing attendance at your workshop:

- Be familiar with hotels or resorts in the area you wish to hold your conference or workshop.
- Find out which venues have adequate facilities for a presentation like yours.
- Find out which venues are the most participant-friendly (easy to get to, abundant free parking, safe, handicapped-accessible, adequate rooms, amenities like pools, exercise facilities, restaurants, shopping, entertainment, etc., not too expensive, family-friendly, etc.).
- When you have chosen a date for your event, make certain that you will not be competing with the National Association of Percussionists' annual meeting across the hall from your workshop.

Do the Math: Estimating Costs and Speaker's Fees

The rule of thumb of the ratio of expenses to registration fee is 75 percent just to break even. For example, if you think 150 people will register, set the registration fee to cover all the expenses if only 75 percent of that number register (113 people). You will also need to adjust the numbers if you offer discounts for spouses, early preregistration, and so on. In order to make a profit, adjust the fee upward.

The National Speakers Association (602) 969-2552 or www.nsaspeaker .org) is a great resource for its journal and its audiotapes, which are filled with practical advice and tips. You can also purchase a listing in its national guide.

Practice by Design: Conference Organization and Planning Checklist

Planning and timing are critical to the success of any conference or seminar. Consider the timeline shown in Table 13.1 (Clayson, 1990).

TABLE 13.1   Presentation Timeline

How Long Before the Event	Task to Complete
18 months	Ensure proper time for license renewals for CEUs. Select a site. Select a date. Set planning budget. Reserve meeting room.
10–12 months	Select a theme or topic.
3–6 months	Formalize specifics (block of rooms, meals, audiovisual needs, etc.). Sign contract and pay deposits. Contract staff to manage registration. Purchase appropriate mailing lists. Investigate possibilities of Internet ListServs for getting the word out, but first be sure such promotions are permissible.
60–90 days	Develop marketing materials. Arrange professional printing and bulk mailing. Advertise in appropriate publications.
30 days	Confirm all preparations. Print registration packets, CEU certificates, and handouts. Send out press releases on the conference to everyone under the sun, *but* make them relevant to those receiving them, not just self-serving.
10 days	Preregistration deadline arrives. Verify meal counts, room counts, and so on. Assemble registration packets. Get petty cash and credit card materials for on-site registrants.
On the day of the event	Troubleshoot all problems. Obtain attendee evaluations of the conference. Distribute CEU certificates.

Source: D. Clayson (1990). "Teaching," in E. A. Margenau (Ed.). *The Encyclopedic Handbook of Private Practice.* New York: Gardner Press, Inc.

Customer Service Skills for Therapists

While running a counseling practice is different from operating a retail store or restaurant, you can borrow some principles from any well-managed service business and apply them to managing your practice. Trying some of these ideas can help you go beyond surviving to thriving, especially as managed care increasingly raises the stakes.

PRACTICE BY DESIGN: STRATEGIES FOR ATTRACTING AND KEEPING CLIENTS

In this section, we look at ways that therapists can market more of their services to clients and referral sources.

Stay humble. It's important to come across as competent, professional, and confident, but watch out for being perceived as perfect or a know-it-all. In *Selling the Invisible: A Field Guide to Modern Marketing,* Harry Beckwith (1997) says, "Prospects do not buy how good you are at what you do. They buy how good you are at *who you are.*"

Respect your right to charge money for your services. If you think your price is too high, you'll find a way to undercut yourself. Make a list of 10

PROFIT AND SERVICE

"To be a therapist in private practice, you need to decide to really be in business. This starts by finding a way to reconcile two seemingly opposite concepts, profit and service. Here's a simple definition of both:

- Profit = financial gain, an advantage, moneymaking
- Service = assistance, helping others, benefiting the public

"A business is an enterprise that makes a profit through financial gain. Yet as a therapist, your focus is on service and helping others. You need to resolve these concepts for yourself or you will falter when it comes to making the necessary, sometimes hard business decisions that will keep your practice financially healthy."

Lynn Grodzki, *Building Your Ideal Private Practice.*
New York: W.W. Norton & Co., 2000, p. 154.

---

reasons why your price is fair. Learn to market your service with confidence because you believe it has value.

Learn to speak with confidence. Hesitating, mumbling, and fidgeting as you talk with your clients and referral sources creates an impression of weakness. Do whatever it takes to learn to speak with confidence. If you need to, use audio- or videotape, take a class, or hire a coach.

Ask the right questions. Always ask clients what their goals are and how they want their lives to be different. This is why they come to you and spend their precious money. They want you to keep them focused on this. Amazingly, many therapists never ask. As a corollary, *ask lots of questions* to understand the client's needs before you say what you think.

Explain how you can help. Most clients want to know your plan.

Be prepared to respond to objections. Make a list of the most common reasons a client might decide not to go ahead with a block of sessions after the first consultation. Be prepared to respond to those objections.

Follow up. Call back when you say you will. If you tell the client, "Let's have three sessions and then assess how you feel," be sure to bring it up at the end of the third session.

Take responsibility for how your practice is doing. Building a business can feel like the impossible dream, and it's understandable to feel discouraged when the phone isn't ringing. But don't let yourself fall into the trap of blaming managed care or kicking yourself for not having a PhD. Instead, make a list of 10 things you can do right now to jump-start your business.

State your bottom line. In your marketing communications, tell people why they should use your counseling services rather than those of someone else.

Make your service easy to buy. Look for ways to make it convenient and effortless for clients to see you. Here are some places to look for opportunities:

- How quickly do you return calls when prospective clients make their first contact with you?
- How quickly do you schedule new clients for the first time?
- How flexible are you about seeing clients when they are available?

261

- How much information about your practice is available to clients before they meet you?

Focus on the positive. Beckwith (1997) tells a story you may have heard before. " 'In the factories we make perfume,' Revlon founder Charles Revson once said. 'But in the stores we sell hope.' So do we all. Everywhere, people are buying happiness, or the hope of it. People want to smile. And will pay handsomely for it." Beckwith advises you to eliminate anything in your marketing and advertising that doesn't focus on the positive result every client is seeking:

- Avoid designing ads and flyers with messages like, "Do you sabotage yourself?"
- Revise tired old forms that focus mainly on symptoms and problems.
- Replace brochures that show sad faces rather than faces with positive expressions.

Study Your Points of Contact

If Nordstrom opened a counseling practice, what would it be like? If this seems like an odd question, stay with it for a minute. If you intend to build a successful therapy practice in today's competitive marketplace, you must be willing to look at things from new perspectives. In a world where managed care dictates where clients go for counseling and pays mental health professionals minimal fees, it is difficult for many therapists to survive, let alone thrive. You will survive *and* thrive — and have fun doing it — if you are bold enough to ask yourself questions like this one.

Beckwith (1997) advises, "Study every point at which your company makes contact with a prospect. Your business card. Your building. Your office. Your public appearances. Just a few points of contact decide whether or not you get the business. Then ask, "What are we doing to make a phenomenal impression at every point? Does the client feel respected, amazed, impressed, delighted?"

Like Nordstrom, your goal should be to make a positive impact on your clients at every point of contact. For example:

1. *Pay attention to the details.* Invite a friend or two to visit your office. Choose people who (1) understand what counseling is and (2) like you enough to be candid with you. Ask them to tell

you their honest impressions about the experience of coming to your office.

- What mood does it create?
- What do they see?
- Do they feel safe?
- Is it relaxing?
- Does any detail seem not to fit?

A therapist invited a friend who was in the home furnishings business to visit her new office and give her some feedback. He sat in each chair and looked around at the office from each vantage point. He noticed that he felt least comfortable when he sat facing a blank wall and suggested she fill the space with a picture of a restful scene. She placed a print of a sleeping dog there. When clients enter her office for the first time, they nearly always remark on how warm and inviting it is. Even the UPS delivery person looked around and said, "Wow! This is nice!"

2. *Think of ways to add value to your service.* You appreciate the small touches at a fine restaurant or special store. Why should your counseling service be any different? For example, when you give a presentation, pay attention to the details. Your handouts are very important—they send a message to your participants about

---

YOU CAN TRANSLATE THIS TO THE THERAPY BUSINESS

"Design your business to operate for the convenience of your customers, and make it very easy to do business with you.

- Enable prospects to make purchases from you seven days a week.
- Accept as many credit cards as you can.
- Offer the convenience of a toll-free number.
- Publish a brochure so that customers have easy access to data about your products.
- Examine all aspects of your business, and although they should be geared to quality and profitability, be sure they are also oriented to speed."

Jay Conrad Levinson (1993), *Guerrilla Marketing Excellence: The Fifty Golden Rules for Small Business Success.*

---

you and your practice. Put some imagination into the package you put together. Do something unexpected and different from the other therapists in your town.

3. *Maintain your competence.* Seek supervision on a regular basis to make certain that you are doing good work. Attend workshops and conferences regularly to learn new skills and meet new colleagues. Stores like Nordstrom take pride in having the newest items for sale. Why should your practice be any different?

4. *Make certain that your policies are up-to-date and client-friendly.* For example:
   - What do you do if a client cancels at the last minute?
   - What if a client doesn't show up?
   - Separate yourself from the mental health field for a moment. *What would Nordstrom do?*

PRACTICE BY DESIGN: CAN I GET A LITTLE SERVICE, PLEASE?

The following exercise is adapted from Tony Alessandra, PhD, Gary Couture, and Gregg Baron (1992), *The Idea-a-Day Guide to Super Selling and Customer Service: 250 Ways to Increase Your Top and Bottom Lines.*

List five ways you can do a more effective job of marketing your services to both clients and referral sources.

1. _____

2. _____

3. _____

4. _____

5. _____

List five ways you can make your counseling services more client-friendly. Consider your office, your actual services, your policies, and your marketing materials.

1. _____

2. _____

3. _____

4. _____

5. _____

More Great Clients
List five clients with whom you have had a *successful* therapy experience.

1. _____

2. _____

3. _____

4. _____

5. _____

List the characteristics of these clients. _____

_____

_____

List five clients with whom you have had an *unsuccessful* therapy experience.

1. _____

2. _____

3. _____

4. _____

5. _____

List the characteristics of these unsuccessful clients. _____

_____

How can you find *more* of the first group of clients? _____

_____

_____

MANAGEMENT METRICS: YOU CAN MEASURE MANY ASPECTS OF YOUR SERVICE

Many aspects of our work as therapists are difficult to measure. However, several points of your service can be measured, evaluated, and perhaps modified. These include the following:

- Your office location
- The length of your sessions
- Your fees for various services
- Insurance reimbursement and participation in managed care programs
- How much information you provide your clients
- What services you offer in addition to counseling
- What kinds of clients and issues you work well with
- Your availability and office hours

You have made decisions about each of these aspects of your service. It is important to evaluate whether your decisions match what your clients value. Let's take a look at a few examples.

In *Building Your Ideal Private Practice* (2000), Lynn Grodzki recommends that therapists package their services in a variety of ways, offering clients choices. She suggests that you "create a menu of options for clients. Choice is a strong business selling point, and one that is severely underutilized by therapists. To offer more choice, list the services you currently offer in menu form. Then find the best combination of services for each person" (p. 119).

OFFICE LOCATION FACTORS

This is a very important aspect of your service. As you evaluate your office setting, consider the following:

- How easy is it to find your office?
- Is there plenty of free parking?
- Does it feel safe in the daytime and at night?
- Is it accessible to people with disabilities?
- Is it clean?

- Is it comfortable and friendly?
- Does it have a professional feeling?

You have made decisions about each of these aspects of your service. It is important to evaluate whether your decisions match what your clients value.

TIME FACTORS

Time is an important part of your service. Consider the following, and add your own items to the list.

1. *How long are your sessions?* Have you started seeing clients for less time at the same fee? How do you think the clients feel about this? What would happen if you did the opposite, perhaps offering 90-minute sessions? Remember, those who give the client more than he or she expects will be the winners in this competitive climate.

2. *Are you rigidly seeing clients once each week, or are you willing to be flexible and try new arrangements?* What about seeing them every other week and touching base with a 10-minute telephone call in between? It would mean one less trip to your office for your busy clients. Many of them might appreciate it.

THE BRAND CALLED "YOU"

"It's a new brand world. What makes You different? What's the pitch for You? What's the real power of You? What's loyalty to You? What's the future of You?

"The good news—and it is largely good news—is that everyone has a chance to stand out. Everyone has a chance to learn, improve, and build up their skills. Everyone has a chance to be a brand worthy of remark."

Tom Peters, "The Brand Called *You*" in *Fast Company* magazine, August/September 1997. To view the entire article, visit www.fastcompany.com/magazine/10/brandyou.html.

---

3. *How quickly do you work with clients?* Are you willing to embrace the current methods of doing therapy by spending less time with each client? Have you asked your clients what they prefer?

CONVENIENCE FACTORS

Consider how easy you make it for your clients to get what they need and want from you. Can you think of any unnecessary barriers that may have gone unnoticed and that could be eliminated?

For example, therapist Gilda's only available hours are on Tuesdays and Saturdays. She works for a large group practice and is one of about 20 therapists on the staff. The only way for clients to reach her is through the practice, and they must always leave a voice-mail message.

Gilda's lack of availability creates significant frustration. It also creates significant opportunities for her competition!

What are your own examples of how you could create more value for your clients and stand out from other therapists in your area?

Self-Care for Therapists

The Pitfalls of Making Your Practice Too Private

When you first thought of becoming a therapist, part of your dream probably had something to do with being your own boss. Many therapists had one or two careers before becoming a counselor, and part of the appeal was the idea of working independently.

Once you are out on your own for a while, however, you may discover the downside of independence: feelings of isolation and loneliness. This drawback doesn't have to drive you back to a group work setting, though. It can be managed by looking for ways to connect with other business and professional people. The following suggestions may help you deal with this challenge.

Practice by Design: Ten Ways to Stay Connected to Colleagues and Business Associates

1. Resolve to have lunch or coffee with at least one therapist each week.
2. Join a case-conferencing group that meets regularly. If you can't find a group to join, form one yourself.
3. Join the Chamber of Commerce in your town. Attend at least one function each month.
4. Join a business networking group. These groups typically meet weekly and the members get to know one another quite well. It can be an excellent support system; the fact that the other members are not therapists helps you create some variety for your work life.
5. Attend at least one professional conference every year. It doesn't matter whether it's your national professional association conference or one at the state or city level. Just get out and mix with other therapists every year. It can be a very refreshing experience.
6. You may feel isolated if you have an office all by yourself in an office building. One solution is to move to an executive suites office when it's time for a new lease. Executive suites are a group of offices that share secretarial services. Each executive has a separate private office, but there is a shared space with a receptionist, conference rooms, kitchen, eating room, and so forth.

The advantage here is that you will have much more exposure to the other executives and many more opportunities to meet some new professional friends. Having other people nearby makes you feel less isolated.

7. Remind yourself about why you dreamed of going out on your own. Reread your journal entries (if you still have them) from the days when you felt trapped in an organization and longed to get out and be your own boss. Remember that boss from hell who made you resolve never to work for someone else again?

8. Write an article for a business or professional publication that requires you to interview other people. Interview as many of these people as you can in person rather than over the phone. This will get you out of your office and mixing with other people.

9. Become a supervisor of interns. This will take you regularly into a counseling center setting and give you a chance to become part of a group, but on a limited basis.

10. If all else fails, join or create a group practice.

WORKING IN A GROUP PRACTICE: SPECIAL CONSIDERATIONS

Many group practices are very successful, but others encounter serious problems and the group disbands. It is ironic that the professionals trained to be expert communicators, compromisers, and collaborators can become remarkably possessive, competitive, and almost paranoid when working in a group. Sharing data, referral sources, income levels, and other information can be difficult, especially after being in solo practice where such information was kept private. If you decide to form a group, expect it take a considerable amount of time to start and maintain it.

The primary issue is control. Who is in charge and who is the boss? Sometimes groups never get beyond this issue.

Many practitioners who have been running a successful practice for years have a hard time believing that they may have a peer, let alone a possible superior, when it comes to practice management. It is difficult for many groups to discuss these issues in a forthright manner. Sometimes it helps to vote on who should be in charge, but votes may be cast based on a candidate's charisma rather than on true management performance capability and real leadership skills.

A similar control issue is that of reporting relationships, chain of command, and organizational hierarchy. Who gets to tell whom what to do? This becomes a problem because most group members tend to be independent and it's difficult to get used to reporting to another clinician.

It can take hours to resolve simple issues such as whose answering service the group will use or whether to use voice mail instead. Arguments may rage over whether to use Mac or Windows, Word or WordPerfect, Quattro Pro or Excel, Palm or Windows CE. Members will be upset after discussions about who gets a pager, whose cell phone is paid for by the practice, or who gets a company notebook computer.

When clinicians in separate practices join to form a larger practice, the issue of consolidation and eliminating duplication may be a challenge. Some staff members may have to be let go, and this is difficult to do. Discord may arise because each practice wants to lay off staff from the other, not its own.

PRACTICE BY DESIGN: A ROAD MAP AROUND SOME OF THE PITFALLS

If you are looking to collaborate with other therapists, don't let the possible pitfalls keep you from giving it a try. However, you increase your chances for success if you are alert to possible obstacles from the beginning. Discuss the following issues with other group members as you are forming your team:

1. What is the group's philosophy and mission statement?
2. How will the group be structured? Who will be responsible for what?
3. What is the group's policy on sharing referral sources, and how will you deal with members who don't comply?
4. How will you deal with disciplinary concerns? Does your group have a procedure for handling conflicts between supervisor and supervisee and between peers? If so, what does it say? Is it binding? Is there an appeal process when you disagree with a supervisor's opinion on a clinical directive?
5. How will cases be peer-reviewed? For example, are they blind reviews in which the reviewer does not know whose records he or she is reviewing? How may biases based on different clinical approaches be reconciled when reviewing one's treatment?

6. How will your different clinical orientations get along? What are the potential difficulties?

7. When there is an impasse about an issue, what will the process be for breaking the tie?

8. What risk management system will the group use? Are regular chart reviews conducted? If so, do they simply query whether the records are current, or do they also look for quality of the content? Are protocols in place and staff clear regarding confidentiality laws and exceptions, how to handle clinical emergencies, how to manage therapeutic noncompliance or potentially violent clients, and similar issues?

9. How will you get to know one another well enough to feel comfortable with triage, referral, case management, and shared liability risk?

10. What will happen if a principal owner or de facto leader becomes disabled, dies, or leaves the practice for any reason?

11. Does everyone share a common view of business operations? How do you know?

12. How will you deal with group members whose personalities and styles conflict?

13. What are your contingency plans when Murphy's Law takes effect? Do members of the group seek to help in taking care of one another? Can staff request and get episodic stress breaks following some particularly challenging cases or times? Are retreats championed? Do members of the group support healthy lifestyles of all members and practice what they preach?

14. How will the group reconcile the risk takers and those who are more conservative?

15. What is the process for bringing new members into the practice (interviewing, checking credentials, orientation, etc.)?

If you find partners with whom you mutually wish to affiliate and have reconciled the group's office and clinical operations, you will need to revisit your market. Consider the following issues:

1. Should you develop or join an integrated delivery system?

2. Do you want relationships with hospitals and/or residential programs?

3. Have you developed direct contracts with employers or employer groups?
4. Are you now an anchor group with major payor organizations?
5. How would you evaluate your seamless outcome management systems?
   - Are they in place?
   - Are they fully automated and cost-efficient?
   - Are they integrated with treatment planning as well as accounting?
6. Are you ready to bid for capitated contracts?
7. Do you know your costs?
8. Do you know your profit margin?
9. Should you consider developing an alliance with a not-for-profit agency or a community mental health center? What could you offer them and what could they offer you?
10. Have you established targets and goals of market share, payor mix, clinical quality and performance, and staff development retention?

PRACTICE BY DESIGN: SKILLS FOR BEING A PRODUCTIVE TEAM PLAYER

If you decide to join or form a team practice, everyone in the group should work on developing the following skills:

1. Listen carefully to your fellow team members.
2. Respect and appreciate differences.
3. Show empathy for others on the team.
4. Admit your mistakes.
5. Communicate assertively.
6. Stay in control of your behavior. Exercise patience and restraint.
7. Develop strong negotiation skills.
8. Look for ways to lessen stress.
9. Celebrate everyone's successes.

Developing these skills will help you create a work environment where people feel free to participate fully and contribute their ideas, which results in a highly productive work team.

"When you're out on your own, no one owes you anything, no matter how nice you are or how good you are at what you do. No one is there to rescue you. Whereas a boss might take pity on you, customers won't. People don't buy products or services from a sense of pity or guilt, or even fairness. They buy based on competence and the results they receive. Your raise becomes effective when you do."

Paul and Sarah Edwards (1991), *Making It On Your Own: Surviving & Thriving on the Ups and Downs of Being Your Own Boss.*

MAINTAINING MOMENTUM

Staying motivated can be a challenge when you are working solo in a business where success sometimes seems elusive. In *The Way of the Guerrilla: Achieving Success and Balance as an Entrepreneur in the 21st Century,* Jay Conrad Levinson (1997) has a few suggestions for staying motivated. He writes, "The guerrilla entrepreneur knows that the journey is the goal. He also realizes that he is in control of his enterprise, not the other way around, and that if he is dissatisfied with his journey, he is missing the point of the journey itself."

Conrad adds these suggestions:

1. *Strive to stay in balance.* Make sure your work schedule includes free time.
2. *Don't expect success to happen overnight.* Expect it to take time and don't ever rush yourself.
3. *Don't expect to feel stressed.* If you do, take it as a sign that you are doing something wrong.
4. *If you aren't excited about your work, something is wrong.* Stop and pay attention to your feelings and figure out what it is.
5. *Compensate for your weaknesses by surrounding yourself with people who make up for them.* Entrepreneurs of the past valued their independence and avoided relying on anyone else. Today's entrepreneurs value their teammates.
6. *Look for ways to collaborate with another entrepreneur.* You'll both get more out of it.
7. *Continually evaluate how you are doing.* Look at the results you are producing and don't fool yourself.

8. *Focus on what you are doing today.* Don't spend too much time thinking about the past, and don't get ahead of yourself, either. You should aim to be someplace between out-of-date and on the cutting edge.

9. *Be efficient, but don't let it interfere with your effectiveness.* Value time above all else—yours and others'.

10. *Always have a road map for your business.* Reevaluate your plan regularly and change it if you need to.

11. *Stay flexible.* You risk a breakdown if you refuse to compromise.

12. *Keep your focus on results.* While growing your business is gratifying, it is not as important as doing your work efficiently and well.

13. *Allow yourself to depend on others.* You will not be successful without the help of friends, family, and colleagues.

14. *Always seek to learn new things.*

15. *Stay passionate about your work.* Your enthusiasm will have an impact on others.

16. *Always keep your goals at the top of your mind.* Don't allow distractions to throw you off track.

17. *Manage your time well.*

18. *Keep a positive attitude.* Problems will arise and you will not always feel as though you are making progress. Don't let glitches stop you from moving in the direction of your goals.

STORIES FROM THE REAL WORLD

Getting my practice started took about two years. I committed to one marketing activity a day (a phone call, designing a flyer, placing an ad, going to a lunch, etc.). That is a lot of contact in one year. By planting seeds in lots of different places, I eventually formed a solid network of referrals. To this day, I often have people telling me, "I've heard of you" from something I did maybe three years ago. Or I've gotten referrals from people I do not know because they got my name from one of my original contacts. This has been very gratifying. Today I'm up to 30 clients and a waiting list. My hard work has definitely paid off. Some days it's hard for me to believe I'm here . . . but I have to say that some of the reason for my success in building my practice is because I focused time and energy on it.

Susan Papalia, MA

PRACTICE BY DESIGN: WHAT TO DO WHEN YOU FEEL LIKE GIVING UP

Many times, staying with your dream of a successful private practice requires managing anxiety. When things look discouraging, you may need to create a process for yourself that's reminiscent of a cognitive therapy session. Even if you don't practice cognitive therapy, you may recall some of the ideas:

- Your feelings are the product of your thoughts.
- If you want to change how you feel, you have to identify your cognitive distortions.
- Once you see where your thinking is twisted, replace your distorted thoughts with more rational ways of thinking.

The following 12 kinds of cognitive distortion are outlined in David Burns's (1998) popular book on mood disorders, *Feeling Good: The New Mood Therapy.* See how they apply to you when you are feeling discouraged about building your practice.

All-or-nothing thinking. Seeing things in black-or-white categories. If a situation falls short of perfect, you consider it a total failure. Example: "I was mortified when that video wouldn't work during my presentation. It ruined the whole thing."

Overgeneralization. Interpreting a single negative event to mean that bad things will always happen or that good things will never happen. Example: "He no-showed last time. I don't know how I can ever depend on him again."

Mental filter. Zeroing in on a single negative aspect of a situation and blocking out everything else. Example: "It's nice that I found this nice office. But I wish I weren't on the second floor."

Discounting the positive. Ignoring all positive events, telling yourself that they don't count. This takes the joy out of life and leaves you feeling inadequate. Example: "I can't believe I blew the whole meeting by forgetting to bring that list with me. All that preparation for nothing."

Jumping to conclusions. Placing a negative interpretation on an event, even though there are no facts to support your conclusion. Example: "They never called me back from that networking group. They probably don't want another therapist."

Mind reading. Assuming that someone is thinking bad thoughts about you. Example: "She didn't say a word to me. She must hate me."

Fortune-telling. Predicting that something will turn out badly. Example: "Why should I agree to do this presentation? Five people will probably show up."

Magnification. Seeing problems and setbacks in exaggerated terms — or minimizing good things. Example: "So what if three new clients called. They probably won't even show up."

Emotional reasoning. Assuming that your negative emotions reflect the way things really are. Example: "I hate going to these meetings. I shouldn't feel this way. I'm just not cut out for all of this marketing stuff."

Should *statements.* Saying that things should be the way you thought they would be. Example: "I should have at least 15 clients by now. I must be a complete loser."

Labeling. Attaching a negative label to yourself rather than describing what happened. Example: "I can't believe I forgot to call her back. I am such an idiot."

Personalization and blame. Holding yourself personally responsible for something that isn't completely under your control. Example: "My client is still so depressed. I'm just not a very good therapist."

Now that you have a way to catch yourself engaging in twisted thinking, what can you do about it? First, stop yourself and acknowledge what you are doing. Second, replace your irrational thoughts with rational ones. Here are some examples.

Instead of: "They never called me back from that networking group. They probably don't want another therapist."

How about this: "I really liked that networking group and I think it would help me get more visibility. I think I'll call them and follow up on whether I can join."

Instead of: "I was mortified when that video wouldn't work during my presentation. It ruined the whole thing."

How about this: "I sure learned a lesson about being prepared. Next time, I'll have a plan for what to do if the equipment breaks down."

Instead of: "My client is still so depressed. I'm just not a very good therapist."

How about this: "My client is still very depressed. It's a good thing he decided to seek help."

PRACTICE BY DESIGN: CRASH PREVENTION

Michael Yapko (1998) offered advice on managing mood disorders in his book *Breaking the Patterns of Depression* that is appropriate for the entrepreneurial therapist who wants to manage his or her anxiety and frustration. Let's look at how you could adapt Yapko's suggestions for preventing discouragement from overtaking you:

Build your life around things you can control. There will be days when all of your clients cancel, your MasterCard bill arrives, and the air-conditioning doesn't work in your car. You can't allow yourself to get lost in such a string of events and use them as evidence of failure.

Learn self-acceptance. Being an entrepreneur is an art. You were probably not taught the skills for successful small business management when you were a child or when you were in graduate school. You will have to make up your rules as you go along and accept that not everything will work. Just learn from it.

Become aware of selective perception. Watch out for the tendency to focus on the failures and ignore the successes. You have to be a good boss to yourself and pat yourself on the back.

Shift your locus of control. Put your energy into things you can control. Don't waste your time worrying about things you can't.

Focus on the future, not the past. If something didn't work, learn from it and move on.

Develop a sense of purpose. This is your life. This could be great. You can make it whatever you want.

Strengthen boundaries and set limits. You know what this means — you're a therapist. And it applies to you, too.

Build positive and healthy relationships. You will need a strong support system. You will have to build it yourself. It won't come looking for you. Make it a priority.

Avoid isolation. Talk to people about what's going on with you.

Change your ways of thinking. Don't defeat yourself with twisted thinking or by doing things the ways they've always been done. Be on the lookout for new ways of being a therapist. The rules are being rewritten.

> "The key word is flexibility, the ability to adapt constantly. Darwin said it clearly. People thought that he mainly talked about survival of the fittest. What he said was that the species that survive are usually not the smartest or the strongest, but the ones most responsive to change. So being attentive to customers and potential partners is my best advice—after, of course, perseverance and patience."
>
> Philippe Kahn, in *301 Do-It-Yourself Marketing Ideas* (Sam Decker, editor, 1997).

KEEP YOUR EYE ON YOUR MARKET

The last chapter of Sarah White's (1997) *Marketing Basics* is titled, "Marketing Is Like Doing Dishes: It's Never Done." She writes, "The environment changes, or you change, and new responses have to emerge. That means you have to keep revisiting what you've done and exploring new ways to do it better."

It's true that the environment is changing. The city I (Laurie Grand) knew when I moved to Los Angeles in 1976 was a very different place when I moved away 20 years later. The 1984 Olympics, the 1992 riots, the 1994 Northridge earthquake, and the O. J. Simpson debacle had left their mark.

While your town or city may not experience such radical changes, your market is what White calls "a moving target." Regardless of where you live, managed care has come to your town and is causing you to make decisions that therapists never had to face 10 or 20 years ago. These kinds of changes will continue to have their impact in ways we can't even imagine today. The baby boomer generation continues to have enormous influence on the way we live and do business in America. Generation X follows right behind it, making its own waves.

What can you do about it? Educate yourself, by reading books such as *Rocking the Ages*, *The Age Wave*, and *The Popcorn Report*. Read the *Wall Street Journal* and the *New York Times;* tune in to MSNBC and CNN. Surf the Internet a few times a week. Pay attention. Think about how all of these changes might affect the services people need and want as well as how you will deliver those services in the future. Be open to trying new things.

> "Your life will be filled with antacids and anxiety if you expect your marketing, brilliant or otherwise, to produce superb results immediately. But if you give your marketing program—and having a program is paramount—the time to penetrate and motivate, to persuade and create desire, you will discover that it always works and that age-old techniques are the secret to success."
>
> Jay Conrad Levinson (1993), *Guerrilla Marketing Excellence: The 50 Golden Rules for Small-Business Success.*

AVOID THE TRAP OF LOSING YOUR FOCUS

Building a successful practice takes a few years. Some experts say that it takes at least three years to establish a small business. When results are lacking, it is tempting to blame your marketing campaign and think about trying something different. If your program is based on a well-thought-out analysis, however, changing tracks may be the wrong move. It will certainly be confusing to your colleagues and referral sources. Try the following instead:

1. Talk it over with someone who can advise you.
2. Consider making minor adjustments to your plan before you make any radical changes.
3. Ask a few trusted friends or colleagues to help you brainstorm ways to get your business moving.

PRACTICE BY DESIGN: USE YOUR IMAGINATION TO BUILD YOUR BRAND

Most marketing writers agree that it is important to build a brand for your business so that when people think of psychotherapy or counseling, they think of you. In *Success* magazine, author Michael McKenzie (1998) outlined five ways to build your brand and build your business. These are the secrets of one of the best-known athletes of all time — Muhammad Ali.

McKenzie writes, "When someone refers to 'the greatest athlete of all time,' only one person's name comes to mind. Not Michael Jordan. Not Tiger Woods. Not Babe Ruth. Only Muhammad. How did he become

'The Greatest'? Let's put aside his awesome athletic skills for a moment. This guy could just be one of the most talented brand builders ever." After interviewing Ali and his wife Lonnie, McKenzie summarized the brand-building lessons he learned in five key points. How will you apply them to building your practice?

1. *Be more outrageous than anyone around you.* Even though we learned modesty from the time we were children, you need to learn to "trumpet your skills unabashedly."
2. *Get a great team.* Find trusted associates to whom you can turn for advice. McKenzie says, "You simply won't get anywhere if you insist on going it alone."
3. *Create a loyal following.* You will create loyalty by listening to the people around you and allowing them to do what they do best.
4. *Set realistic goals.* At one time, Ali's fee for a public appearance was just $5,000—not what you would expect "The Greatest" to get. Today, he is paid six figures for appearances. He got there by setting concrete, measurable goals to grow his business. The numbers grew in stages, not all at once.
5. *Walk away from bad deals.* Ali says, "If you want to succeed in business, you have to be true to yourself, not compromise your values—and leave the rest alone." Know what you want and stay away from the kind of work you don't want, even if it means losing a business opportunity.

FINAL THOUGHTS

If you had unlimited resources and could design a counseling practice just the way you want it, what would it look like?

How would your clients experience your practice? Trace the client's experience from the first moment he or she hears about you.

What would your practice look like physically?

How would it work operationally?

What special touches would there be?

How would your practice stand out from those of other therapists in your area?

If you designed a package for your practice, what would it look like?

What are you waiting for?

Good luck. You can do it!

Sample Forms

CHAPTER 3: CREATE A BUSINESS PLAN
SWOT Analysis

Strengths: What makes your practice effective, different, or special?

1. _____
2. _____
3. _____
4. _____
5. _____

Weaknesses: In what areas does your practice need to improve?

1. _____
2. _____
3. _____
4. _____
5. _____

Opportunities: Where are there opportunities for you to enhance your practice and improve your chances of achieving your goals?

1. _____
2. _____
3. _____
4. _____
5. _____

Threats: Aside from internal weaknesses listed in this worksheet, what are real threats to the success of your practice?

1. _____
2. _____
3. _____
4. _____
5. _____

Model Business Plan

The following sample business plan (Irwin 1995) is modified for a behavioral healthcare practice with the fictional name Clinical Concepts. Your business plan may be longer or shorter, depending on your plans for your practice. The size is relatively unimportant as long as you include all relevant details. You can tailor this model to your specific needs and goals. This model plan is offered to help you get started, but it is not a substitute for professional assistance. Substitute your own information for blank lines and italicized or bracketed text. All names and numbers in this sample plan are fictional and are used to make the sample plan easy to read and understand.

Business Plan for *Clinical Concepts*
Table of Contents

Executive Summary

Clinical Concepts was formed as a proprietorship/partnership/corporation/ limited liability corporation in November 1995 in Chicago, Illinois, by John Doe, PhD, a licensed clinical psychologist, in response to the following market conditions: Start-up/growth opportunities exist in _____. There's a need for efficient clinical methods in these overlooked markets. I/we have several MCOs/clients/ businesses/hospitals/HMOs/PPOs who are willing to engage large contracts within the next three months.

Several other prospective clients have expressed serious interest in doing business within six months.

I/we previously operated a private practice in the behavioral health-care industry. Over the past few years, I/we spent much time studying ways to improve overall quality, clinical performance, and efficacy and increase profits. This plan is a result of that study. The basic components of this plan are:

1. Sign contracts.
2. Increase advertising.
3. Increase office staff.

To this end, I/we need investment from private individuals and/or companies. A total of $*XXX* is being raised, which will be used to finance working capital, office, equipment, and so on. The company will be incorporated and common stock issued to investors. The company will be run as a proprietorship/partnership/corporation/LLC.

Financial Goals

	Year 1 ($ millions)	Year 2 ($ millions)	Year 3 ($ millions)
Sales	650	3,880.00	16.649
Net income	99.03	1,120.83	16.649
EPS	$0.25	$2.80	$9.58

The Management

President	John Q. Doe, PhD, Chief Executive Officer and Clinical Director
Chief Financial Officer	Sally Smith, MBA, Chief Financial Officer, Treasurer, and Fiscal Director
Vice President	Larry Black, MSW, Secretary, Executive Vice President, and Operations Director
Vice President	Linda Long, BA, Director of Marketing

Responsibilities

John Q. Doe, PhD, Chief Executive Officer, is responsible for the entire operation. Oversees management function and all other executives. Salary $60,000.

Sally Smith, MBA, Chief Financial Officer, is responsible for financial operations, accounts payable, accounts receivable, interaction with auditors, investor relations. Salary $40,000.

Larry Black, MSW, Executive Vice President, is responsible for clinical operations. Salary $35,000.

Linda Long, BA, Director of Marketing, is responsible for marketing, human resources, and training. Salary $30,000.

Total Executive Compensation $165,000

Company History

Clinical Concepts was recently conceived and is still in the beginning stages. Up to this point, the following has been accomplished:

1. A team consisting of [list names and primary responsibilities (e.g., Linda Long, Marketing)] has been formed.
2. A prospective customer/client list has been drawn up.
3. Strategy meetings are being held every Monday, Wednesday, and Friday evening.
4. This business plan has been drawn up.

[Link the past to the future—why a former company will lead into this one or how your present company and history will lead into any future plans. A short paragraph should suffice.]

We are now able to adequately address the markets we have targeted. We have adjusted our staff, redirected our marketing efforts, and added the services necessary to meet the needs and expectations of our customers.

Service Description

Clinical Concepts intends to offer [service(s)]. This service offers our clients the best possible solution as it:

1. Provides a service that is not presently available in this area.
2. Is strengthened by a team with combined experience of *XX* years.

3. Is of high quality.
4. Provides an alternative, cost-effective way for them to receive care.

[If a general service to be offered is not obvious, explain what the service is. Then give a detailed description of your particular service and its uniqueness.]

Short Examples:

Our _____ is state of the art.
Our consulting practice will address these specialized areas [list]:
Even though at this time our expertise is unique in the marketplace, we expect advances to be made and competitors to arise and offer similar services. We will meet this challenge by:

1. Hiring staff specialized in these new areas.
2. Increasing our continuing education and training expense.
3. Adding complementary services.
4. Making regular investments in new equipment.

Objectives

Long-Term Objectives

Clinical Concepts believes very strongly in clinical, technical, financial, ethical, business, and moral excellence. To secure a stable future for all those connected with Clinical Concepts, we have set the following long-term goals:

Present market is estimated at $*XXX*. Our goal for market share is *XX* percent.
We want to be considered by our peers to be the market leader as evidenced by:
- Trade industry awards
- High end of scale in financial ratios
- Major market share
- Technical excellence (awards, honors, etc.)
- Community involvement (Rotary, United Way, etc.)

Short-Term Objectives

1. Market share goals:
   First year   *XX*%
   Second year   *XX*%
   Third year   *XX*%
   Fourth year   *XX*%
2. Decrease and maintain costs through acquisition of new sites and equipment.
3. Increase productivity by investing in staff training and education.
   - Budget for complete computer training for appropriate applications.
   - Set up and maintain employee benefit program for continuing education.
   - Budget for necessary seminars and/or continuing job-specific education.
4. Maintain state-of-the-art accounting system for careful tracking.
5. Generate monthly reports on financial status vis-à-vis the industry.
6. Aggressively recruit the best clinical staff in the industry.
7. Support company involvement in various local and national charity events.

Competitors

Competitor 1
Name
Address
City, State
Strengths:
- Location—Adjacent to medical center, on major transportation artery, close to city.
- Pricing—Known for aggressive pricing policy.
- Service—All Purdue University graduates.
- Management—Everyone has an MBA from the University of Chicago.

Weaknesses:
- Delivery—Only one outpatient office location.
- Dedication—If it's sunny, they're on the golf course.

- Machinery—Running Windows 3.1.
- Overhead—Spend lavishly on corporate dining room, limousines, and champagne.

Our Competitive Advantages

The distinctive competitive advantages that Clinical Concepts brings to this market are:

1. Experience in this market. I/we have *XX* years of hands-on experience in this industry.
2. Sophistication in management and finance. We are able to run an efficient and lean structure, yet still provide quality service to our clients and customers.
3. Because of the nature of this industry, we will be able to rent office space in more moderately priced buildings.
4. As a unique service company, we will be able to keep our margins high, allowing us to provide internal financing for growth possibilities.
5. A level and policy of that will allow us to fully address the respective markets with comprehensive marketing plans.
6. By keeping overhead low, I/we will be able to funnel profits back into operations, thus avoiding high debt ratios or lost income opportunities.
7. Innovation. I/we have a history of innovative ideas. [List your most meaningful ideas and any new ideas you have for the future.]

Summary
Through my/our leadership, I/we will be able to reduce overhead as a percentage of clinical productivity, thereby increasing the amount of profit to be retained in the business. We propose to use good solid business sense, economies of scale, and efficient financial techniques. This will allow us the following options:

- Increase client services.
- Increase marketing expenditures.
- Increase profits.
- Increase selection of services offered.

This plan will give us tremendous flexibility to use any of these options or a mix of them to effectively attack our target markets and meet our long-term goals. This combination of experience, sophistication, capitalization, and innovation will assist Clinical Concepts as it strives to reach its productivity, profit, and return objectives.

Pricing

Before I/we set the price for our service, I/we forecast what our fixed monthly costs were going to be. I/we then determined what the market rate for comparable services was. At this rate, it was determined that for all but the lowest billing projections, this service would turn a profit at this rate.

Specific Markets

Market 1

General History

Mid-cap companies have found that carving out behavioral healthcare services has, over time, resulted in increased costs in medical healthcare via increases in attrition, workers' compensation, and so on. In our proposed market area, there are 15 mid-cap companies with whom we could directly contract.

Entry Strategy

Our computerized office allows us to track our clients' needs and schedule services on one hour's notice.
We intend to attack this market aggressively through the use of:

1. _____
2. _____
3. _____
4. _____
5. _____

Since we are offering a unique service, it is of utmost importance that we inform nearby corporations of our capabilities.

Growth Strategy

After having successfully completed this entry phase into this market in the geographical area, we will then expand our market by doing the following:

1. _____
2. _____
3. _____
4. _____
5. _____

Market Size and Share

The current market for _____ is estimated at $_____ annual revenue based on data furnished by XYZ Survey. We estimate that we can achieve *XX* percent market share within *YY* years.

We are in the process of collecting marketing data for other markets.

Other Markets

[Use the same format for additional markets.]

Targeting New Markets

To continue our growth, we will be using the following methods to expand our markets and to increase our new areas of doing business:

1. Make contact with individuals in corporations and learn what their needs are.
2. Obtain corporate referrals.
3. Add complementary services.
4. Perform online computer prospecting and qualifications (DIALOG, D&B, etc.).
5. Conduct market surveys.
6. Do research and development.

Locations

[Discuss your locations and why they are prime and well suited for accomplishing your objectives.]

Research and Development

We have already spent a considerable amount of time researching and developing our _____. We have thus far been able to _____ and discover several cost-cutting methods. The largest achievement to date is _____.

Our research is currently supervised by our Clinical Director, John Q. Doe, PhD. He will continue in this capacity. Having been the researcher involved with all our activities to this point, as well as CEO, he is well qualified to continue our research efforts.

Our next research project will center around _____.

Up to this point, our research has paid for itself as _____. However, now that we are becoming more experimental in our research efforts, such a continued success ratio may not be maintained.

We have been investigating several potential government (both state and federal) funding sources. Our present program of joint outcome research with the local university has proven very beneficial.

Historical Financial Data

[This discussion could include all facts pertaining to your financial statements.]

Income Statement [Discuss both positive and negative aspects of your income statements.]

Balance Sheet [Discuss both positive and negative aspects of your balance sheet.]

Asset Worksheet [Discuss both positive and negative aspects of your assets.]

Pro Forma Financial Data

Pro Forma Cash Flow Analysis
  Assumptions

Cash receipts	Percentages as indicated
Rent	Building rental at $12 per square foot
Utilities	Water, gas, sewer, trash, electric

Telephone	Local, long-distance, cellular
Salaries	Executives
Payroll	Hourly, nonexecutive
Withholding	Figured at XX percent
Inventory	
Office supplies	
Postage	
Advertising	Trade, magazine, etc.
Professionals	
Commissions	Figured at 10 percent
Insurance	
Travel and Entertainment	
Research	[Explanation]
Miscellaneous	
State Taxes	XX percent
Federal Taxes	XX percent
Terms from suppliers	Suppliers offer 3 percent cash discount

Sales Forecast

Sales have been forecast at the following growth rates:

	Year 2	Year 3
Service 1	XX%	XX%
Service 2	XX%	XX%

Cash Flow Variables

We project that we will be able to generate sufficient capital from operations to meet our initial needs after the infusion of $200,000. However, our projections are with companies that have never been fully addressed and are based on present real buying conditions and our own experience. Should productivity not meet projections, adjustments will be made in operations and long-term commitments will be decreased or postponed.

Statement Assumptions

Discounts	We are offering a range of discounts that mimic MCOS. Average is estimated to be 20 percent.
Expenses	Total from cash flow analysis spreadsheets.

Risks and Variables

Our books will initially be maintained manually. In the future, we plan to convert to a computerized accounting system to monitor our financial performance. This information will be compiled at the end of each month for preparation of financial statements. These statements will be reviewed monthly against our pro forma statements and appropriate action taken to adjust costs or budget. If we find that we are continually over budget, our first step will be to reevaluate our markup on services and then to recheck our costs to make certain that we are operating within optimal ranges.

Breakeven Point

The following chart shows our breakeven point.

Profit	Revenue	Fixed Costs	Variable Costs
$0	$20,000	$3,900	$16,100

It is intended that Clinical Concepts will be profitable in the nth Quarter, 200X.

Effects of Loan or Investment

The money invested in Clinical Concepts will be used for the following purposes:

- Working capital ($50,000)
- Leasehold improvements (est. $15,000)
- Start-up costs—legal fees, filing fees
- Inventory—raw materials ($25,000)
- Computer equipment
- Office equipment and supplies
- Initial office expenses, lease deposits, phone equipment, office furniture, and so on

These outlays will enable us to operate at a level that will allow us to meet our conservative sales goals for the first year. This will also allow us to purchase these items outright rather than finance or lease them.

Adapted from Irwin, R. D. (1995). Sample Business Plan. *Multimedia MBA* (CD-ROM). Burr Ridge, IL: Compact Publishing.

Chapter 5: Set Up Shop and Measure Results

The following is made available from Eric Harris, JD, EdD, and Bruce E. Bennett, PhD, of the American Psychological Association Insurance Trust (APAIT), 750 First Street NE, Suite 605, Washington, DC 20002-4242. Telephone (800) 477-1200; fax (800) 477-1268. While it was originated for psychologists, the form is applicable to most behavioral healthcare providers.

You may adapt the text of the document for your practice or agency. Sections of the draft where you should insert numbers are designated *XX*, and sections you may want to add or specially modify are [bracketed].

Psychotherapist-Client Contract
[Print on your letterhead]

Outpatient Services Contract

Welcome to my practice. This document contains important information about my professional services and business policies. Please read it carefully and jot down any questions you might have so that we can discuss them at our next meeting. When you sign this document, it will represent an agreement between us.

Psychological Services

Psychotherapy is not easily described in general statements. It varies depending on the personalities of the psychologist and client and the particular problems you bring forward. There are many different methods I may use to deal with the problems that you hope to address. Psychotherapy is not like a medical doctor visit. Instead, it calls for a very active effort on your part. In order for the therapy to be most successful, you will have to work on things we talk about both during our sessions and at home.

Psychotherapy can have benefits and risks. Since therapy often involves discussing unpleasant aspects of your life, you may experience uncomfortable feelings like sadness, guilt, anger, frustration, loneliness, and helplessness. On the other hand, psychotherapy has also been shown to have benefits for people who go through it. Therapy often leads to better relationships, solutions to specific problems, and significant reductions in feelings of distress. But there are no guarantees of what you will experience.

Our first few sessions will involve an evaluation of your needs. By the end of the evaluation, I will be able to offer you some first impressions of what our work will include and a treatment plan to follow, if you decide to continue with therapy. You should evaluate this information along with your own opinions of whether you feel comfortable working with me. Therapy involves a large commitment of time, money, and energy, so you should be very careful about the therapist you select. If you have questions about my procedures, we should discuss them whenever they arise. If your doubts persist, I will be happy to help you set up a meeting with another mental health professional for a second opinion.

Meetings

I normally conduct an evaluation that will last from 2 to 4 sessions. During this time, we can both decide whether I am the best person to provide the services you need in order to meet your treatment goals. If psychotherapy is begun, I will usually schedule one 50-minute session (one appointment hour of 50 minutes duration) per week at a time we agree on, although some sessions may be longer or more frequent. Once an appointment hour is scheduled, you will be expected to pay for it unless you provide XX hours [days] advance notice of cancellation [unless we both agree that you were unable to attend due to circumstances beyond your control]. [If it is possible, I will try to find another time to reschedule the appointment.]

Professional Fees

My hourly fee is $XXX. In addition to weekly appointments, I charge this amount for other professional services you may need, though I will break down the hourly cost if I work for periods of less than one hour. Other services include report writing, telephone conversations lasting longer than XX minutes, attendance at meetings with other professionals you have authorized, preparation of records or treatment summaries, and the time spent performing any other service you may request of me. If you become involved in legal proceedings that require my participation, you will be expected to pay for my professional time even if I am called to testify by another party. [Because of the difficulty of legal involvement, I charge $XXX per hour for preparation and attendance at any legal proceeding.]

Billing and Payments

You will be expected to pay for each session at the time it is held, unless we agree otherwise or unless you have insurance coverage that requires another arrangement. Payment schedules for other professional services will be agreed to when they are requested. [In circumstances of unusual financial hardship, I may be willing to negotiate a fee adjustment or payment installment plan.]

If your account has not been paid for more than 60 days and arrangements for payment have not been agreed upon, I have the option of using legal means to secure the payment. This may involve hiring a collection agency or going through small claims court. If such legal action is necessary, its costs will be included in the claim. In most collection situations, the only information I release regarding a client's treatment is his/her name, the nature of services provided, and the amount due.

Insurance Reimbursement

In order for us to set realistic treatment goals and priorities, it is important to evaluate what resources you have available to pay for your treatment. If you have a health insurance policy, it will usually provide some coverage for mental health treatment. I will fill out forms and provide you with whatever assistance I can in helping you receive the benefits to which you are entitled; however, you (not your insurance company) are responsible for full payment of my fees. It is very important that you find out exactly what mental health services your insurance policy covers.

You should carefully read the section in your insurance coverage booklet that describes mental health services. If you have questions about the coverage, call your plan administrator. I will provide you with whatever information I can based on my experience and will be happy to help you in understanding the information you receive from your insurance company. If it is necessary to clear confusion, I will be willing to call the company on your behalf

Due to the rising costs of health care, insurance benefits have increasingly become more complex. It is sometimes difficult to determine exactly how much mental health coverage is available. Managed health care plans such as HMOs and PPOs often require authorization before they provide reimbursement for mental health services. These plans are often limited to short-term treatment approaches designed to work out specific problems that interfere with a person's usual level of functioning. It may be necessary to seek approval for more therapy after a certain number of sessions. While a lot can be accomplished in short-term therapy, some clients feel that they need more services after insurance benefits end. [Some managed care plans will not allow me to provide services to you once your benefits end. If this is the case, I will do my best to find another provider who will help you continue your psychotherapy.]

You should also be aware that most insurance companies require you to authorize me to provide them with a clinical diagnosis. Sometimes I have to provide additional clinical information such as treatment plans or summaries, or copies of the entire record (in rare cases). This information will become part of the insurance company files and will probably be stored in a computer. Though all insurance companies claim to keep such information confidential, I have no control over what they do with it once it is in their hands. In some cases, they may share the information with a national medical information databank. I will provide you with a copy of any report I submit if you request it.

Once we have all of the information about your insurance coverage, we will discuss what we can expect to accomplish with the benefits that are available and what will happen if they run out before you feel ready to end our sessions. It is important to remember that you always have the right to pay for my services yourself to avoid the problems described above [unless prohibited by contract].

Contacting Me

I am often not immediately available by telephone. While I am usually in my office between 9 A.M. and 5 P.M., I probably will not answer the phone when I am with a client. I do have call-in hours at *XXX*. When I am unavailable, my telephone is answered by an answering service [machine, voice mail, or by my secretary] [that I monitor frequently or who knows where to reach me]. I will make every effort to return your call on the same day you make it, with the exception of weekends and holidays. If you are difficult to reach, please inform me of times when you will be available. [In emergencies, you can try me at my home number.] If you are unable to reach me and feel that you can't wait for me to return your call, contact your family physician or the nearest emergency room and ask for the clinician/psychologist/psychiatrist on call. If I will be unavailable for an extended time, I will provide you with the name of a colleague to contact, if necessary.

Professional Records

The laws and standards of my profession require that I keep treatment records. You are entitled to receive a copy of your records, or I can prepare a summary for you instead. Because these are professional records, they can be misinterpreted by and/or upsetting to untrained readers. If you wish to see your records, I recommend that you review them in my presence so that we can discuss the contents. [I am sometimes willing to conduct a review meeting without charge.] Clients will be charged an appropriate fee for any professional time spent in responding to information requests.

[For therapists who practice in states that require client access to records, use the following language, unless doing so would cause emotional damage, upset, etc.]

The laws and standards of my profession require that I keep treatment records. You are entitled to receive a copy of the records unless I believe that seeing them would be emotionally damaging, in which case I will be happy to send them to a mental health professional of your choice. Because these are professional records, they can be misinterpreted and/or upsetting to untrained readers. I recommend that you review them in my presence so that we can discuss the contents. [I am sometimes willing to conduct a review meeting without charge.] Clients will be charged an appropriate fee for any time spent in preparing information requests.

[For therapists who practice in states that do not require client access to records, use the following language.]

As I am sure you are aware, I am required to keep records of the professional services I provide (your treatment, or our work together). Because these records contain information that can be misunderstood by someone who is not a mental health professional, it is my general policy that clients may not review them; however, I will provide at your request a treatment summary unless I believe that to do so would be emotionally damaging. If that is the case, I will be happy to send the summary to another mental health professional who is working with you. [This service will be provided without any additional charge.] [You should be aware that this will be treated in the same manner as any other professional (clinical) service and you will be billed accordingly.] [There will be an additional charge for this service.]

Minors

If you are under 18 years of age, please be aware that the law may provide your parents the right to examine your treatment records. It is my policy to request an agreement from parents that they agree to give up access to your records. If they agree, I will provide them only with general information about our work together, unless I feel there is a high risk that you will seriously harm yourself or someone else. In this case, I will notify them of my concern. I will also provide them with a summary of your treatment when it is complete. Before giving them any information, I will discuss the matter with you, if possible, and do my best to handle any objections you may have about what I am prepared to discuss. [At the end of your treatment, I will prepare a summary of our work together for your parents, and we will discuss it before I send it to them.]

Confidentiality

In general, the law protects the privacy of all communications between a client and a psychologist, and I can release information about our work to others only with your written permission. But there are a few exceptions.

In most legal proceedings, you have the right to prevent me from providing any information about your treatment. In some proceedings involving child custody and those in which your emotional condition is an important issue, a judge may order my testimony if he or she determines that the issues demand it.

There are some situations in which I am legally obligated to take action to protect others from harm, even if I have to reveal some information about a client's treatment. For example, if I believe that a child [elderly person, disabled person] is being abused, I must [may be required to] file a report with the appropriate state agency.

If I believe that a client is threatening serious bodily harm to another, I am [may be] required to take protective actions. These actions may include notifying the potential victim, contacting the police, or seeking hospitalization for the client. If the client threatens to harm himself or herself, I may be obligated to seek hospitalization for him or her or to contact family members or others who can help provide protection.

These situations have rarely occurred in my practice. If a similar situation occurs, I will make every effort to fully discuss it with you before taking any action. I may occasionally find it helpful to consult other professionals about a case. During a consultation, I make every effort to avoid revealing the identity of my client. The consultant is also legally bound to keep the information confidential. If you don't object, I will not tell you about these consultations unless I feel that it is important to our work together.

While this written summary of exceptions to confidentiality should prove helpful in informing you about potential problems, it is important that we discuss any questions or concerns that you may have at our next meeting. I will be happy to discuss these issues with you if you need specific advice, but formal legal advice may be needed because the laws governing confidentiality are quite complex, and I am not an attorney. [If you request, I will provide you with relevant portions or summaries of the state laws regarding these issues.]

Your signature below indicates that you have read the information in this document and agree to abide by its terms during our professional relationship.

Signature: _____

Name (printed): _____

Date: _____

Initial Treatment Plan
[Print on your letterhead]

Name _____   Date of referral ____/____/____

Date of birth ____/____/____   Date first seen ____/____/____

Diagnosis: DSM-IV

Axis I: _____   Axis II: _____   Axis III: _____

Axis IV: Psychosocial and Environmental Problems (check and specify):

_____ Problems with primary support group _____

_____ Problems related to social environment _____

_____ Educational problems _____

_____ Occupational problems _____

_____ Housing problems _____

_____ Economic problems _____

_____ Problems with access to health care _____

_____ Problems related to legal system/crime _____

_____ Other psychosocial/environmental problems _____

Axis V: Current GAF: ____ Highest GAF past year: ____ GARF: ____
SOFAS: ____

Initial reason for seeking treatment (include brief history) and description of symptoms:

_____

_____

_____

_____

_____

Initial Treatment Plan—page 2

Other relevant history (personal, family, legal, developmental, etc.):

_____

_____

_____

_____

Prior treatment efforts (psychiatric, alcohol, drug): _____

_____

_____

Current medications and medical history: _____

_____

_____

Mental Status Exam (check all that apply)

Appearance

1. Dress: Unusual_____ Unclean_____ Unkempt_____
   Normal_____ Other_____
2. Hygiene: Poor_____ Fair_____ Normal_____ Other_____
3. Exceptional Physical Characteristics: _____

Orientation: Person_____ Place_____ Time_____

Sensorium

1. Vision: Intact_____ Impaired_____ Corrected_____
2. Hearing: Intact_____ Impaired_____ Corrected_____

Mood

1. Depressed_____ Blunted_____ Manic_____
   Angry_____ Anxious_____ Frightened_____
   Labile_____ Other_____
2. Appropriate_____ Inappropriate_____

Perception: Hallucinations: Visual_____ Auditory_____
Other_____ None_____

Thought processes

1. **Form:** Logical_____ Loose_____ Tangential_____
   Rigid_____ Flight of ideas_____ Scattered_____
   Other_____
2. **Content:** Delusional_____ (Type)_____
   Obsessional_____ Phobic_____ Ambivalent_____
   Hopeless_____
   Narcissistic_____ Persecutory_____ Other_____

Insight: Poor_____ Fair_____ Good_____

Judgment: Poor_____ Fair_____ Good_____

Suicidality/homicidality risk: Minimal_____ Low_____
Moderate_____ High_____

Attitude: Cooperative_____ Welcoming_____
Hostile_____ Suspicious_____ Manipulative_____
Apprehensive_____ Other_____

Motor behavior: Slowed_____ Hyperactive_____
Normal_____ Other_____

Speech: Quiet_____ Pressured_____ Affected_____
Normal_____ Other_____

Intellectual functioning: Low_____ Average_____
High_____

Memory: Immediate_____ Recent_____ Remote_____

Client Risk Profile

Client name: _____ ID# _____

Date: ____/____/____ Client's GAF:_____/_____

Y N 1. Symptoms of psychosis: hallucination, delusions, thought disorder, impaired reality testing, etc., with acute onset.

Y N 2. Withdrawal from alcohol or drugs leading to severe withdrawal symptoms (abnormal vital signs, convulsions, etc.).

Y N 3. Dangerous or impulsive behavior placing self/others at risk.

Y N 4. GAF score of 40 or less with acute onset.

Y N 5. Symptoms of organic brain syndrome: memory loss confusion, decreased intellectual capacity, etc., that places a person who is without supervision at risk.

Y N 6. Symptoms of moderate to severe affective disorder: depression, psychomotor retardation, mania, hypomania, blunted affect, sleeplessness, weight loss, loss of appetite, etc.

Y N 7. Anorexia with a weight loss of greater than 25 percent of body weight, signs of malnutrition or with psychosis.

Y N 8. Symptoms of severe anxiety disorder leading to functional impairment: panic disorder, obsessive compulsive disorder, etc.

Y N 9. Active substance abuse or dependence resulting in significant functional impairment or clinical instability.

Y N 10. Dual diagnosis, including both a mental disorder and a comorbid medical condition that may complicate treatment.

Y N 11. Intractable chronic pain.

Y N 12. Probable abuse of minor or vulnerable adult requiring report to protective services.

Y N 13. Baseline GAF of under 50 or SSI/SDI status for mental illness.

Y N 14. A history (past two years) of hospitalization for detox or mental illness.

Y N 15. Client, provider, or facility requests a psychiatric consult (if yes, document referral).

Y N 16. Current/recent use of a mood stabilizer or antipsychotic medication.

Client referred to: _____

Risk assessment (circle): Minimal Low Moderate High

Therapist's signature: _____

Therapist's name printed: _____

(If applicable): Case manager: _____

Clinical director/supervisor: _____

Progress Notes

Client name: _____

ID#: _____ Visit number: _____

Session length: _____ minutes   Session type: Ind. _____
Fam. _____ Grp. _____

Date: ____/____/____

Diagnosis: Axis I: _____ Axis II: _____ Axis III: _____

Problem(s): _____

_____

_____

_____

Goal(s): _____

_____

_____

_____

Intervention and progress toward goal(s): _____

_____

_____

_____

Risk assessment (circle):   Minimal   Low   Moderate   High

Description of risk: _____

_____

Plan: _____

_____

_____

_____

_____

Signature: _____

Client Receipt
[Print on your letterhead]

Date: _____ Client: _____

Office Service   **Fee**

90801: Diagnostic Interview

90808: Office Psychotherapy: 75 Minutes

90806: Office Psychotherapy: 50 Minutes

90804: Office Psychotherapy: 25 Minutes

90847: Family Therapy

90853: Group Therapy

96100: Psychological Testing

Results Interpretation

Preparation of Report

99223 Inpatient Admission

90816: Inpatient Psychotherapy: 25 minutes

99239: Discharge Hospital Management

Diagnosis: Axis I: _____ Axis II: _____

Treatment services provided by: _____

                    Your name and degree   Title

License number: 1234567   Tax ID: 12-345678

Authorization to release information: I hereby authorize the release of
any information necessary to process this insurance claim.

Client's signature: _____

Total fee: $_____   Payment: $_____   Check number _____

Balance due on _____ $_____

    (Date)

Next appointment: _____ at _____

                M T W Th F Sat   A.M./P.M.

Treatment Update

Client name: _____ ID#: _____ Visit number: _____

_____ Progress note and treatment update

_____ Treatment update only

_____ Close case

Session length: _____ Minutes   Session type: Ind. _____
Fam. _____ Grp. _____

Date: ____/____/_____

Diagnosis — Axis I: _____ Axis II: _____ Axis III: _____

Problem(s): _____

_____

Goal(s): _____

_____

Progress to date

Intervention(s):

_____

_____

_____

Risk Assessment (circle):   Minimal   Low   Moderate   High

Description of risk: _____

Plan

Justification for additional sessions (check all that apply):

For continued visit certification, cases *must* meet guidelines A and B and either C or D.

_____ A. Client is generally motivated and participating actively in the therapy process.

_____ B. Symptoms, behaviors, or problems still require ongoing treatment.

_____ C. There appears to be progress with the treatment where progress could be reasonably expected.

_____ D. Little or no progress but outpatient visits stabilize the client enough to prevent hospital admission.

Signature: _____

_____ Visits certified until: ____/____/_____

_____ Arrange for case conference; case manager: _____

Date contacted: ____/____/_____

Closing Summary

Client name: _____ ID#: _____ Visit number: _____

Date of closing: ____/____/_____

Extent of contact: _____

Client seen from ____/____/____ until ____/____/____

Total number appointments: _____

Number of missed appointments: ____ Number of cancellations: ____

Reason(s) for closing (check all that apply):

____ Treatment goals achieved

____ Therapist transferred client to a different therapist: _____

____ No longer eligible for services

____ Client referred elsewhere: _____

____ Client moved away

____ Client dropped out

Additional comments: _____

_____

_____

_____

Termination letter sent on: ____/____/_____

Diagnosis at end of treatment

Axis I: _____ Axis II: _____ Axis III: _____

Prognosis: _____ Axis V: GAF at closing: _____

Recommendation for further treatment(s): _____

_____

_____

Therapist signature: _____ Date: ____/____/____

Chapter 9: Discover and Market Your Niche

Direct Contracting Pricing Model Example

You may direct-contract with any type of payment model you like and negotiate with the employer. Simple *reduced fee for service* (rFFS) rates are discounted session rates. *Case rates* would be taking on increased fiscal risk as you would set a fee, say $500, for every referral regardless of the number of sessions you have. The most complicated is quasi-capitation, in which you charge an amount *per employee per annum* (PEPA). For example:

> If $15 PEPA at 100 employees = $1,500 per year, and if client access is 7 to 10 percent, then presume 10 clients for 3 sessions = 30 sessions per year.
>
> If your cost is $25 per session (see Chapter 2 on cost calculations), then the contract will cost $750 to service, yielding a gross profit of $750, or 50 percent gross margin.

The following are examples of services offered and concomitant pricing structures in a flat case rate methodology. These were done with doctoral-level interns and postdoctoral fellows, under supervision, in an integrated behavioral healthcare delivery system. As such, it may not precisely fit nor generalize to your situation.

Services Offered: Plans I, II, and III are case rates charged only for employees utilizing services.

Plan I   Individual, marital, and family therapy: 5 sessions
24-hour-a-day crisis line
Up to 12 on-site workshops per year
Cost for the above: $125
Psychiatric (M.D.) services: 25% discount off of usual, reasonable, and customary charges
Partial hospitalization services: 35% discount off of per diem
Inpatient hospitalization: 45% discount off of per diem

Plan II   Individual, marital, and family therapy: 8 sessions
24-hour-a-day crisis line
Up to 12 on-site workshops per year
Cost for the above: $185
Psychiatric (M.D.) services: 25% discount off of usual, reasonable, and customary charges
Partial hospitalization services: 35% discount off of per diem
Inpatient Hospitalization: 45% discount off of per diem

Plan III   Individual, marital, and family therapy: 10 sessions
24-hour-a-day crisis line
Up to 12 on-site workshops per year
Cost for the above: $225
Psychiatric (M.D.) services: 25% discount off of usual, reasonable, and customary charges
Partial hospitalization services: 35% discount off of per diem
Inpatient hospitalization: 45% discount off of per diem

The following are examples of services offered and related pricing structures in a reduced fee for service (rFFS) methodology. These were done with doctoral-level interns and postdoctoral fellows, under supervision, in an integrated behavioral healthcare delivery system. Your situation may be different.

Services offered: Plans IV, V, and VI are discounted fee-for-service per session rates charged only for employees using services.

Plan IV   Discounted fee-for-service rate of $75 per individual, marital, or family therapy session with a 50% co-pay billed to employer
Psychiatric (M.D.) services: 25% discount off of usual, reasonable and customary charges
Partial hospitalization services: 35% discount off of per diem
Inpatient hospitalization: 45% discount off of per diem

Plan V   Discounted fee-for-service rate of $75 per individual, marital, or family therapy session with a 70% co-pay billed to employer

Psychiatric (M.D.) services: 25% discount off of usual, reasonable, and customary charges

Partial hospitalization services: 35% discount off of per diem

Inpatient hospitalization: 45% discount off of per diem

Plan VI   Discounted fee-for-service rate of $75 per individual, marital, or family therapy session with an 80% co-pay billed to employer

Psychiatric (M.D.) services: 25% discount off of usual, reasonable, and customary charges

Partial hospitalization services: 35% discount off of per diem

Inpatient hospitalization: 45% discount off of per diem

CHAPTER 13: PRESENTATIONS, SPEECHES, AND WORKSHOPS

Professional Speaking Agreement
[Print on your letterhead]

It is my goal to help you have a successful meeting. Please help me contribute to your success by completing this brief questionnaire. Thank you!

General issues

What issues does your industry currently face? _____

_____

What global or internal problems need to be addressed? _____

_____

What type of message do you want me to send? Motivational? Inspirational? Educational? _____

_____

Title of the meeting: _____

Other speakers: _____

Other topics and titles: _____

_____

How would you describe the "personality" of the audience?

_____

Technical Details

Where is the presentation (venue name)? _____

City: _____ State/country: _____

When is the presentation: (day, date, time)? _____

How much time is allotted for my presentation? _____

What is the nature of your meeting? _____

Who will be attending? _____

How many people do you expect to attend? _____

Why are you having this presentation? (What do you wish to occur? What do you want to communicate? What do you want attendees to walk away with?) _____
_____
_____

What is my role: _____ Keynote
                              _____ Reception line
                              _____ Banquet
                              _____ Dinner
                              _____ Chatting/mingling
                              _____ Emcee
                              _____ Awards
                              _____ Other (specify: _____)
Can you duplicate my handouts? _____ Yes _____ No
If yes, who is the person responsible? _____
                                           Name   Telephone   E-mail
Comments: _____
_____

Does my presentation need to be customized in any way? If so, please describe: _____
_____
_____

Expenses covered: _____
_____
_____

Expenses excluded: _____
_____
_____

Who arranges the following:
Air travel: _____ Local transportation: _____
Hotel: _____ Other arrangements: _____
Do you wish to:
Audio-record? ____ No ____ Yes   My fee for this is: _____
Video-record? ____ No ____ Yes   My fee for this is: _____
Whom should I contact to arrange for shipping materials, handouts, etc.?
Name: _____
Address: _____
Phone: _____

Fax: _____

E-mail: _____

Do/can you provide me with evaluation feedback?

_____ No _____ Yes In what format? _____

Details about your organization

Tell me about your work/organization: _____

_____

_____

Tell me about your concerns: _____

_____

_____

Who are the decision makers in your organization? _____

_____

_____

Who did you/they like/dislike at your last meeting and why? _____

_____

_____

My requests

If an overnight stay is required, please secure a nonsmoking room.

My fee is $_____. A deposit of $_____ is due on _____.

Cancellation fee: $_____ if canceled by one month in advance of speaking date. If canceled later than one month in advance, my full fee will be charged.

Please set up the following audiovisual equipment for my presentation:

_____ Overhead projector

_____ 35mm slide projector and carousel

_____ Digital projector

_____ Computer with CD-ROM and Microsoft PowerPoint or
　　　　　　Corel presentation software

_____ Television monitor and VCR

_____ Easel with flip-chart pad

_____ Table at the front of the room

_____ Podium

_____ Lavalier microphone

_____ Cordless microphone

_____ Other: _____

Thank you for your time in attending to this questionnaire. Please return it to [name, address, telephone, e-mail address].

Types of Seating Arrangements

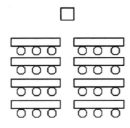

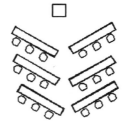

Seminar Arrangement with Tables

Effective seating for a fairly large group who will be taking notes; this is a very comfortable way to seat people for an all-day workshop where they will need to spread out.

V-Shape with Tables

Effective seating for a fairly large group who will be taking notes; the V-shape enables the speaker to step into the audience and establish closer contact than with auditorium-style seating.

Auditorium

An effective arrangement for very large groups; works well for a lecture with minimal interaction.

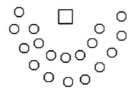

Double Semicircle

Enables the speaker to be closer to the audience members; allows more intimacy.

Semicircle

Provides a more intimate setting for a small group.

Your Presentation Planner

1. What are five topic ideas for presentations you could make within the next six months?

a. _____

b. _____

c. _____

d. _____

e. _____

2. Which of your colleagues could you ask to copresent with you? They don't necessarily have to be therapists. For example, if you present a workshop for people who have been downsized, your copresenter could be a management recruiter. You could focus on maintaining self-esteem, and the recruiter could focus on interviewing skills.

List ideas here: _____

_____

_____

_____

_____

3. List 10 organizations you can approach about making a presentation.

Name of Organization	Contact Person	Deadline

Glossary

Capitation   A set fee paid to a clinician by a payor for providing a range of specified services. The fee is paid regardless of the number of clients seen or the number of visits.

Case rate   A set fee paid to a clinician by a payor for treatment based on the diagnosis and/or presenting problem. The clinician provides all needed services to the client for a specific period of time.

Collateral   Assets pledged by a borrower to obtain a loan or credit. In case of default, these assets may be seized.

Corporate practice of medicine laws   Some states prohibit hospitals from employing physicians to provide outpatient services. In practice, these states permit formation and licensure of business corporations established as professional service corporations (but not nonprofit corporations) to practice medicine, but only if controlled by physicians.

Deregulated markets   Markets that are not government controlled.

Employee assistance program (EAP)   An employer-sponsored program that provides employees with free short-term counseling. Following a limited number of sessions, the EAP may refer the employee to a private clinician for longer-term work at the employee's own expense.

Equity investments   Making investments in companies where one can have an ownership interest, usually by purchasing stock.

Fee for service   An arrangement whereby a client pays a provider for specific services.

Full faith and credit   Agreeing unconditionally to pay interest and principal on a debt.

Gross revenue   Total dollar income before any expenses are subtracted.

Incorporation   A legal process whereby a company files documents (as specified by the state in which it is located) that allow it to operate as a corporation.

323

Limited liability company (LLC)   A type of company where the members are not personally liable for its debts and liabilities and are taxed only once on the profits.

National Practitioner Data Bank (NPDB)   A flagging system that makes it possible to review the professional credentials of healthcare practitioners. For information, visit www.npdb-hipdb.com.

Payee   The person or group who receives a payment for a service.

Payor   A health plan, managed care company, or insurance carrier that pays healthcare providers for services.

Prescriptive authority   The power to prescribe medications for the treatment of mental disorders.

Private corporation   A company whose shares are not traded on the open market.

Pro forma   Financial statements (e.g., balance sheets and income statements) that have assumptions or hypothetical conditions built into the data.

Provider   The person or group (i.e., the clinician) who provides care to the client.

Security interest   A creditor's right to take property that has been offered as security.

Unsecured loan   A loan that is not guaranteed by collateral.

Working capital loan   A short-term loan that provides capital to buy assets that will produce income.

SOURCES FOR GLOSSARY DEFINITIONS

www.duke.edu/~charvey/Classes/wpg/glossary.htm (A financial glossary developed by Campbell R. Harvey, Professor of Finance, Fuqua School of Business at Duke University)

www.investorwords.com (a financial glossary)

www.irs.gov/pub/irs-tege/topicf00.pdf

www.npdb-hipdb.com

www.pohly.com/terms.html (managed care terminology)

References

Ackley, D. (1997). *Breaking free of managed care: A step-by-step guide to regaining control of your practice.* New York: Guilford Press.

Alessandra, Couture, & Baron (1992). *The idea-a-day guide to super selling and customer service.* Chicago: Dartnell.

American Psychiatric Association (1994). *Diagnostic and statistical manual of mental disorders* (4th ed.). Washington, DC: Author.

American Psychological Association (2000). Biennial Survey—Salaries in Psychology, available at http://research.apa.org/99salaries.html.

American Psychological Association Practice Directorate (1994). APA member focus groups on the healthcare environment. Washington, DC: Author.

American Psychological Association Practice Directorate (1996). *Contracting on a capitated basis: managing risk for your practice.* Washington, DC: American Psychological Association.

American Psychological Association Practice Directorate and Coopers and Lybrand, LLP (1996). Financing strategies to meet the challenges of managed care. In C. E. Stout (Ed.), *The complete guide to managed behavioral healthcare.* New York: John Wiley & Sons.

Anderson, D. F., & Berlant, J. L. (1994). Managed Mental Health and Substance Abuse Services. In P. R. Kongstvedt (Ed.), *The managed health-care handbook.* Gaithersburg, MD: Aspen.

APA's Practice Directorate (1996). APA Practitioner's Toolbox Series. APA Books.

Applebaum, P. S. (1993). Legal liability in managed care. *American Psychologist, 48*(3), 251–257.

Association for the Advancement of Psychology (2001, Summer). Psychotherapy finances fee survey reveals decline in practice income, *Advance,* 5.

Bales, J. (1987, April). A few smart habits cut malpractice risks. APA *Monitor,* 48.

Bass, S. (1985). *Successful private practice.* Pasadena, CA: PCG Seminars.

Beals, M. (1990). *Expose yourself: Using the power of public relations to promote your business and yourself.* San Francisco: Chronicle Books.

References

Beckwith, H. (1997). *Selling the invisible: A field guide to modern marketing.* New York: Warner Books.

Bray, J. H., & Rogers, J. C. (1997). The Linkages Project: Training behavioral health professionals for collaborative practice with primary care physicians. *Families, Systems, & Health, 15,* 55–63.

Bray, J. H., & Rogers, J. C. (1995). Linking psychologists and family physicians for collaborative practice. *Professional Psychology: Research and Practice, 26,* 132–138.

Browning, C. H., & Browning, B. J. (1986). *Private practice handbook.* Los Alamitos, CA: Duncliff's International.

Browning, C. H., & Browning, B. J. (1996). *How to partner with managed care.* New York: John Wiley & Sons.

Budman, S., & Steenbarger, B. (1997). *The essential guide to group practice in mental health, clinical, legal and financial fundamentals.* New York: Guilford Publications.

Burns, D. (1999). *Feeling good: The new mood therapy.* New York: Avon Books.

Carrere, R. A. (1996, August 12). In R. A. Carrere (Chair), *Provider-owned HMO: A cutting-edge example of psychologist empowerment.* Symposium conducted at the annual convention of the American Psychological Association, Toronto, Canada.

Chopra, D. (1995). *The seven spiritual laws of success: A practical guide to the fulfillment of your dreams.* San Rafael, CA: Amber-Allen Publishing.

Clark, S. (1994). *Taming the marketing jungle: 104 marketing ideas when your motivation is high and your budget is low.* Seattle, WA: Hara Publishing.

Clayson, D. (1990). Teaching. In E. A. Margenau (Ed.). *The encyclopedic handbook of private practice.* New York: Gardner Press.

Connor, R., & Davidson, J. (1985). *Marketing your consulting and professional services.* New York: John Wiley & Sons.

Council of Behavioral Group Practices (1996). National Register of Behavior Group Practices. Institute for Behavioral Healthcare, 43760 Alpine Road, Suite 209, Portola Valley, CA 94028 (415-851-6465).

Crandall, R. (1996). *Marketing your services: For people who hate to sell.* Chicago: Contemporary Books.

Crick, G. D. (1990, March). When a psychologist is investigated. *Illinois Psychologist, 21,* 4–5.

Cummings, C. A., & Sobel, S. B. (1985). Malpractice insurance: Update on sex claims. *Psychotherapy, 22,*(2), 186–188.

Cummings, N. (1985). The new mental health care delivery system and psychology's new role. Annual Awards address presented at meeting of the American Psychological Association, Los Angeles.

Cummings, N. (1986). For the dismantling of our health system: Strategies for the survival of psychological practice. *American Psychologist, 41,* 426–431.

References

Cummings, N. (1992). The future of psychotherapy: Society's charge to professional psychology. *Independent Practitioner, 12*(3), 126–130.

Cummings, N. (1995). Behavioral health after managed care: The next opportunity to professional psychology. *Register Report, 20*(3), 1, 30–33.

Decker, S. (Ed.). (1997). *301 do-it-yourself marketing ideas*. Boston: Goldhirsh Group.

Drum, D. J. (1995). Changes in mental health service delivery and finance systems and resulting implications for the National Register. *Register Report, 20*(3), 4, 5, 8–10.

Edmunds, M., et al. (1997). *Managing managed care: Quality improvement in behavioral healthcare*. Washington, DC: National Academy Press.

Edwards, P., & Edwards, S. (1999). *Working from home: Everything you need to know about living and working under the same roof*. New York: Jeremy Tarcher.

Edwards, S., & Edwards, P. (1991). *Getting business to come to you: Everything you need to know to do your own advertising, public relations, direct mail, and sales promotion, and attract all the business you can handle*. New York: Jeremy Tarcher.

Edwards, S., & Edwards, P. (1991). *Making it on your own: Surviving and thriving on the ups and downs of being your own boss*. New York: Jeremy Tarcher.

Falkenstein, L. (2000). *Nichecraft: Using your specialness to focus your business, corner your market and make customers seek you out*. Portland, OR: Niche Press.

Fox, R. E. (1997). It's still the economy, stupid. *Independent Practitioner, 10*(2), 16.

Friedman, R., & Altman, P. (1997). *How to design, develop, and market healthcare seminars*. Sarasota, FL: Professionals Resource Press.

Garrity, C. E. (2001, September). Considerations before selecting a vendor. *Advance*, 26–27.

Godin, S. (1995). *e-marketing: Reaping profits on the information highway*. New York: Perigee Books.

Gosney, M., Odam, J., & Benson, J. (1990). *The gray book: Designing in black and white on your computer*. Chapel Hill, NC: Ventana Press.

Graham, A. (1996). Clinical documentation in an outpatient setting. In C. E. Stout (Ed.). *The complete guide to managed behavioral healthcare*. New York: John Wiley & Sons.

Grand, L. C. (2000). *The life skills presentation sourcebook*. New York: John Wiley & Sons.

Grand, L. C. (2000). *The marriage and family presentation sourcebook*. New York: John Wiley & Sons.

Grand, L. C. (2000). *The workplace skills presentation sourcebook*. New York: John Wiley & Sons.

Grand, L. C. (2002). *The therapist's advertising and marketing kit*. New York: John Wiley & Sons.

Grand, L. C. (2002). *The therapist's newsletter kit*. New York: John Wiley & Sons.

Grodzki, L. (2000). *Building your ideal private practice*. New York: W.W. Norton & Co.

Haley, W. E., McDaniel, S. H., Bray, J. H., Frank, R. G., Heldring, M., Johnson, S. B., et al. (1998). Psychological practice in primary care settings: Practical tips for clinicians. *Professional Psychology: Research and Practice, 29,* 237–244.

Heller, K. (1997). *Strategic marketing: How to achieve independence and prosperity in your mental health practice.* Sarasota, FL: Professionals Resource Press.

Holtman, J. A. (1996). *Reengineering the medical practice.* Reston, VA: St. Anthony Publishing, Inc.

Howard, D., & Howard, J. (1990). Group practice. In E. A. Margenau (Ed.). *The encyclopedic handbook of private practice.* New York: Gardner Press.

Irwin. R. D. (1995). Sample Business Plan. *Multimedia MBA* (CD-ROM). Burr Ridge, IL: Compact Publishing.

Kertesz, L. (1996, February). Big employers lean toward local IMOS. *Modern Healthcare, 12,* 100.

Koch, R. (1998). *The 80/20 principle: The secret of achieving more with less.* New York: Currency Books.

Kolt, L. (1996). *The business and marketing training manual for psychotherapists* (4th ed.). Kolt Consulting, 1030 Pearl Street, Suite 3, La Jolla, CA 92037 (858-456-2005; fax 858-481-3662).

Kull, R. K. (1989, February). Risk management. *Carrier Foundation Newsletter,* 140, 1–4.

Lawless, L. (1997). *Therapy, Inc.* New York: John Wiley & Sons.

Leeds, D. (1991). *Marketing yourself.* New York: HarperCollins.

Leslie, R. S. (2002, September/October). Practicing therapy via the Internet—The legal view. *Family Therapy Magazine,* American Association for Marriage and Family Therapy.

Levine, M. (1993). *Guerrilla P.R.: How you can wage an effective publicity campaign . . . without going broke.* New York: HarperCollins.

Levinson, J. (1993). *Guerilla marketing.* Boston: Houghton Mifflin.

Levinson, J., & Godin, S. (1994). *The guerrilla marketing handbook.* New York: Houghton Mifflin.

Levinson, J., & Godin, S. (1997). *Get what you deserve!* New York: Avon Books.

Levinson, J. C. (1993). *Guerrilla marketing excellence: The 50 golden rules for small-business success.* New York: Houghton Mifflin.

Levinson, J. C. (1997). *The way of the guerrilla: Achieving success and balance as an entrepreneur in the 21st century.* New York: Houghton Mifflin.

Levinson, J. C., & Rubin, C. (1995). *Guerrilla marketing online: The entrepreneur's guide to earning profits on the Internet.* New York: Houghton Mifflin.

References

Lowman, R. L., & Resnick, R. J. (Eds.). (1994). *The mental health professional's guide to managed care.* Washington, DC: American Psychological Association.

Maslow, A. H. (1998). *Toward a psychology of being* (3rd ed.). New York: John Wiley & Sons.

Melek, S., & Pyenson, B. (1995). *Capitation handbook: Actuarially determined capitation rates for mental health benefits.* Washington, DC: American Psychiatric Association.

Negley, E. T. (1985). Malpractice and risk management. In P. A. Keller & L. O. Ritt (Eds.), *Innovations in Clinical Practice* (pp. 243–251). Sarasota, FL: PRE.

Parker, R. (1993). *Looking good in print: A guide to basic design for desktop publishing* (3rd ed.). Chapel Hill, NC: Ventana Press.

Perrott, L. A. (1999). *Reinventing your practice as a business psychologist.* San Francisco: Jossey-Bass.

Pope, K., & Vasquez, M. (1991). *Ethics in psychotherapy and counseling.* San Francisco: Jossey-Bass.

Pressman, R. (1979). *Private practice.* New York: Gardner Press.

Pyenson, B. S. (1995). *Calculating risk.* Chicago: American Hospital Publishing, Inc.

Rabasca, L. (February, 2000). Avoiding Contractual Pitfalls. *APA Monitor on Psychology,* 60–63.

Rhode Island Psychological Association (1996). *Peace of mind.* Rhode Island Psychological Association, 500 Prospect Street, Pawtucket, RI 02860 (401-728-5570).

Ries, A. (1996). *Focus: The future of your company depends on it.* New York: HarperCollins.

Roane, S. (1988). *How to work a room: A guide to successfully managing the mingling.* New York: Shapolsky Publishers.

Roane, S. (1993). *The secrets of savvy networking: How to make the best connections for business and personal success.* New York: Warner Books.

Salameh, W. A. (1990). Critical equations in launching a clinical practice. In E. A. Margenau (Ed.), *The encyclopedic handbook of private practice.* New York: Gardner Press.

Schuster, J. M., Lovell, M. R., & Trachta, A. M. (1997). *Training behavioral healthcare professionals.* San Francisco: Jossey-Bass.

Schutt, D., & Lim, Y. (Eds.). (1995). *Pratt's guide to venture capital sources.* New York: Venture Economics Publishing, a division of SDC Publishing, Inc.

Singleton, D., Tate, A., & Randall, G. (2003, January). Salaries in psychology 2001: Report of the 2001 APA Salary Survey. APA Research Office.

Slutsky, Jeff (1989). *Streetsmart marketing.* New York: John Wiley & Sons.

Smith, J., W., & Clurman, A. S. (1998). *Rocking the ages: The Yankelovich Report on Generational Marketing.* New York: HarperBusiness.

Soisson, E. L., VandeCreek, L., & Knapp, S. (1987). Thorough record keeping. *Professional Psychology, 18*(5), 498–502.

Spoelstra, J. (1997). *Ice to the Eskimos: How to market a product nobody wants.* New York: HarperBusiness.

Stout, C. E. (1989). A methodological approach to differential diagnostics. In K. Anchor (Ed.), *The handbook of medical psychotherapy.* Lewiston, NY: Hogrefe & Huber.

Stout, C. E. (1990). Software development for the nonprogrammer: An instructional clinical example. *Behavioral Research Methods, Instruments, and Computers, 22*(2), 200–201.

Stout, C. E. (1994). The Differential diagnosis of psychiatric symptoms. In L. Koziol & C. Stout (Eds.), *The neuropsychology of mental disorders.* Springfield, IL: Charles C. Thomas Publishers.

Stout, C. E. (1995). *Capitation and managed care strategies for mental health.* Nashville: Irwin/Business Network.

Stout, C. E. (1996, Spring). What should psychotherapy cost? *Illinois Psychologist,* 24–26.

Stout, C. E. (1997). *The complete guide to managed behavioral healthcare.* New York: John Wiley & Sons.

Stout, C. E. (1997). *Psychological assessment and managed care.* New York: John Wiley & Sons.

Stout, C. E. (1998). *Technology solutions sourcebook for behavioral healthcare practice.* Providence, RI: Behavioral Health Resource Press/Manisses Communications Group.

Stout, C. E. (2000). *Practice information clearinghouse of knowledge,* APA Division 42, Washington, DC: American Psychological Association.

Todd, M. K. (1996). *The managed care contracting handbook: Planning and negotiating the managed care relationship.* Chicago: Irwin Professional Publishers.

Tuttle, G. M., & Woods, D. R. (1997). *The managed care answer book for mental health professionals.* New York: Brunner-Routledge.

VandeCreek, L., & Stout, C. E. (1993). Risk management in inpatient psychiatric care. In M. B. Squire, C. E. Stout, and D. H. Ruben (Eds.), *Current advances in inpatient psychiatric care* (pp. 53–67). Westport, CT: Greenwood Press.

Walfish, S. (2001, August). *Practice expansion areas.* American Psychological Association's Annual Meeting, San Francisco, CA.

Walther, R. (1994). *Upside down marketing.* New York: McGraw-Hill.

Weissenstein, E. (1995, July). Cut out the middleman. *Modern Healthcare, 3,* 29–30.

Wetzell, S. (1998, July/August). BHCAG: Does eliminating the middleman work? *Behavioral Health Management,* 16–19.

White, S. (1997). *The complete idiot's guide to marketing basics.* New York: Alpha Books.

Wiehl, J. G. (1992). *The direct contracting manual.* Alexandria, VA: Capitol Publishing, Inc.

Yapko, M. (1998). *Breaking the patterns of depression.* Honesdale, PA: Main Street Books.

Yenney, S. L. (1994). *Business strategies for a caring profession.* Washington, DC: American Psychological Association.

Zieman, G. (1995). *The complete capitation handbook: How to design & implement at-risk contracts for behavioral healthcare.* Tiburon, CA: Centralink with Jossey-Bass.

Zieman, G. L. (1998). *Handbook of managed behavioral healthcare.* San Francisco: Jossey-Bass.

WEBSITES

www.aamft.org (American Association for Marriage and Family Therapy)

www.aca.org (American Counseling Association)

www.adaa.org (Anxiety Disorder Association of America)

www.ama-assn.org (American Medical Association; includes information about CPT codes)

www.apa.org (American Psychological Association)

www.apait.org (American Psychological Association Insurance Trust)

www.behavior.net (gathering place for mental health professionals)

www.bplans.com (business planning information)

www.cmhc.com (Mental Health Net information service)

www.coil.com/~grohol (The Insider's Guide to Mental Health Resources Online)

www.drheller.com (Kalman M. Heller, Ph.D., Practice Development Consultant)

www.entrepreneur.com (small business information)

www.fastcompany.com (*Fast Company* magazine)

www.gmarketingcoach.com (Mitch Meyerson and Jay Conrad Levinson offer free marketing articles)

www.grohol.com (Psych Central)

www.healthgate.com (Health Gate)

www.health.org (national clearinghouse for alcohol and drug abuse prevention) www.hp.com/go/printideas (Hewlett-Packard's HP Idea Kit)

www.ibh.com (Institute for Behavioral Health Care)

www.ideacafe.com (information for business owners)

www.ismho.org (International Society for Mental Health Online)

www.kolt.com (Kolt Leadership Group)

www.medicalartspress.com (Medical Arts Press, Mental Health Edition; telephone 800-328-2179)

www.mentalhealth.org/consumer/index.htm (managed care info)

www.naadac.org (Association for Addiction Professionals)

www.naswdc.org (National Association of Social Workers)

www.nsaspeaker.org (National Speakers Association)

www.nimh.nih.gov (National Institutes of Mental Health)

www.onlinepsych.com (Online Psych therapist locator and information)

www.open.americanexpress.com (American Express small business information)

www.palo-alto.com/ (Business Plan Pro software)

www.psychology.com/asksiggy.htm (Ask Siggy)

www.psychotherapyfinances.com (*Psychotherapy Finances* newsletter)

www.psych-web.com (psychology information for students and teachers)

www.psyfin.com (*Psychotherapy Finances* newsletter)

www.sba.gov/starting_business/planning/basic.html (Small Business Association's website offers free business planning information and templates)

PUBLICATIONS

Dynamic Graphics: The Idea Guide to Quick Desktop Success, 6000 N. Forest Park Dr., Peoria, IL 61614. (800-255-8800; www.dgusa.com).

Family Therapy Magazine, published by the American Association for Marriage and Family Therapy, 1133 Fifteenth St. NW, Suite 300, Washington, DC 20005 (www.aamft.org).

Fast Company, P.O. Box 52760, Boulder, CO 80321 (800-688-1545).

Managed Care Contract Negotiator. Monthly newsletter published by Brownstone Publishers, Inc. (800-643-8095; www.brownstone.com).

Practice Builders, 1 MacArthur Place, Suite 200, South Coast Metro, CA 92707-5941 (800-679-1200; www.practicebuilders.com).

Practice Strategies: A Business Guide for Behavioral Healthcare Providers, formerly published by the American Association for Marriage and Family Therapy, 1133 Fifteenth St. NW, Suite 300, Washington, DC 20005 (www.aamft.org).

Psychotherapy Finances, published by Ridgewood Financial Institute, 13901

U.S. Highway 1, Suite 5, Juno Beach, FL 33408 (561-624-1155; www
.psyfin.com or www.psychotherapyfinances.com).

Psychotherapy Networker (formerly *Family Therapy Networker*), 7705 13th St.,
NW, Washington, DC 20012 (202-829-2452; www.psychotherapynet-
worker.com).

ASSOCIATIONS AND ORGANIZATIONS

American Association for Marriage and Family Therapy (AAMFT), 1133
Fifteenth St. NW, Suite 300, Washington, DC 20005 (202-452-0109;
www.AAMFT.org).

American Group Psychotherapy Association (AGPA), 25 East 21st St., 6th
Floor, New York, NY 10010 (212-477-2677; www.GROUPSINC.org).

American Managed Behavioral Healthcare Association (AMBHA), 700
13th St. NW, Suite 950, Washington, DC (202-434-4564; www
.AMBHA.org).

American Mental Health Counselors Association (AMHCA), 801 N. Fairfax
St., Suite 304, Alexandria, VA 22314 (800-326-2642; www.AMHCA.org).

American Psychological Association (APA), 750 First St. NE, Washington,
DC 20002 (202-336-6020; www.APA.org).

American Psychological Association Insurance Trust (APAIT), 750 First
Street NE, Suite 605, Washington, DC 20002-4242 (800-477-1200).
Contacts: Eric Harris, J.D., Ed.D., and Bruce E., Bennett, Ph.D. (www
.APAIT.org).

California Association of Marriage and Family Therapists (CAMFT), 7901
Raytheon Road, San Diego, CA 92111-1606 (858-292-2638; www
.CAMFT.org).

Employee Assistance Program Association (EAPA), 2101 Wilson Blvd.,
Arlington, VA 22201 (703-522-6272; www.EAP-association.org).

Institute for Behavioral Healthcare Tomorrow, 4370 Alpine Road, Suite
2099, Portola Valley, CA 94028 (415-851-6465).

National Academy for Brief Therapists (NABT), 4110 E. Alta Mesa,
Phoenix, AZ 85044 (602-450-4202).

National Association for Social Workers (NASW), 750 First Street NE,
Suite 700, Washington, DC 20002 (800-638-8799; www.NASWDC.org).

National Venture Capital Association, 1655 North Fort Myer Drive, Suite
700, Arlington, VA 22209 (www.NVCA.org).

Technology Capital Network, MIT Enterprise Forum of Cambridge, Inc.,
201 Vassar Street, Building W59-MIT, Cambridge, MA 02139.

Weiner & Eglit, Ltd., Highland Park, IL 60065 (847-266-2040).

Contributors to "Stories from the Real World"

Thanks to the following clinicians who contributed their experiences to this book.

Daniel J. Abrahamson, PhD
Traumatic Stress Institute
South Windsor, CT
dan.abrahamson@tsicaap.com

Susan Back, MSW
Scottsdale, AZ

Sandra Levy Ceren, PhD
Del Mar, CA 92014
858-755-0088

Daniel Kegan, PhD, JD
Kegan & Kegan, Ltd.
Intellectual Property &
    Computer Law
Chicago, IL
312-782-6496 x21
elan@keganlaw.com

John E. Mayer, PhD
Clinical Psychologist
65 East Wacker Place
Suite 1600
Chicago, IL 60601
312-917-1240
JMayer2@AOL.com

Claudette Ozoa, PhD
www.OnePinkRibbon.com

Susan Papalia, MA
Pasadena, CA

Stephanie Pratola, PhD
Licensed Clinical Registered Play
    Therapist-Supervisor
511 Roanoke Boulevard, Suite 1
Salem, VA 24153
540-387-3955
pratola@attglobal.net

Rick Tivers and Associates
633 Skokie Blvd., Suite 260
Northbrook, IL 60062
www.divorce-recovery.com

**Rick Tivers, MSW, and Chet
    Mirman, PhD**
The Center for Divorce Recovery
847-291-0468

Sarah Warren
312-595-1691
DrWarren@multicoach.org
www.multicoach.org

Index